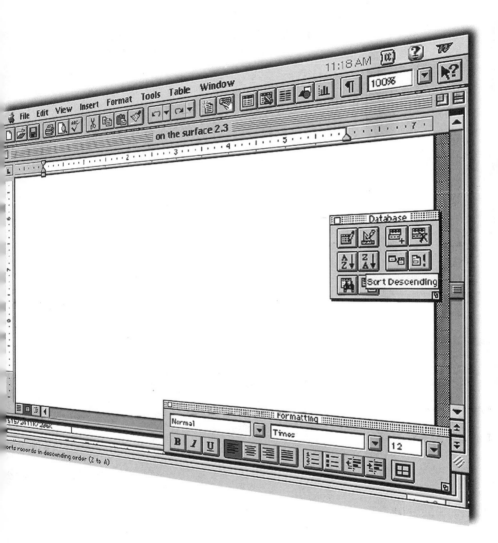

Page to Screen

Page to Screen

Taking literacy into the electronic era

Edited by Ilana Snyder

London and New York

First published 1998 by Routledge
11 New Fetter Lane, London EC4P 4EE

Simultaneously published in the USA and Canada
by Routledge
29 West 35th Street, New York, NY 10001

Set in 11/13pt Sabon by DOCUPRO, Sydney
Printed and bound by KHL Printing Co Pte Limited, Singapore

British Library Cataloguing in Publication Data
A catalogue record for this book is available from the British Library

Library of Congress Cataloging in Publication Data applied for

ISBN 0–415–17465–1 (pbk)
ISBN 0–415–17464–3 (hbk)

For Ray, Gabe and Benj

Contents

Illustrations

Acknowledgements

This book grew out of an invitation to be guest editor for a special issue of *The Australian Journal of Language and Literacy*. Encouraged by a colleague at Monash, Professor Alan Bishop, to seize the opportunity to work up something bigger and more substantial than a journal issue, I did just that.

I thank Professor Fazal Rizvi, Monash University, for including the book in the series 'Studies in Education' which he co-edits with Associate Professor Bob Linguard, University of Queensland. Always enthusiastic about the project, Fazal has also made some very useful and timely suggestions. Elizabeth Weiss, Social Sciences publisher at Allen & Unwin, has provided throughout the enterprise wise and prudent counsel for which I am most appreciative.

Of course, I owe special thanks to the contributors. Editing the book provided me with the chance to engage with new ideas and different ways of thinking about the connections between literacy practices and the new technologies. My own understandings have undoubtedly been enhanced. Together we managed to keep to schedule and work cooperatively along the way. Our use of email certainly made the work much easier than it might have been in former, pre-electronic times. It makes me wonder just how editors of collections such as this managed in the past.

David Yammouni and Sharon Fitzgerald, who operate the Computer Help Desk in the Faculty of Education, Monash, were, as usual, invaluable. With unfailing humour and generosity they solved the technical problems as they arose.

Two chapters in this volume first appeared as articles in the special issue of *The Australian Journal of Language and Literacy* (1996, vol. 19, no. 4). The chapters are Gail Hawisher and Cindy Selfe's 'Reflections on research in computers and composition studies at the century's end' and an earlier version of Jane Douglas's chapter which was then titled 'Abandoning the either/or for the and/and/and: hypertext and the art of argumentative writing'. As editor of the journal issue, and of this book, I thank the National Council of the Australian Literacy Educators' Association, Michele Anstey, the Editor, and the Editorial Board of the *Journal of Language and Literacy* for permission to republish the work.

Finally, I am grateful to my husband Ray and two sons, Gabe and Benj, who have listened to many tales of the making of this book with extraordinary fortitude.

Notes on contributors

Catherine Beavis is a Lecturer in the School of Social and Cultural Studies in the Faculty of Education, Deakin University. Her teaching and research interests include the study of popular culture, textuality and the new technologies in relation to the English/literacy curriculum. She co-edited with Bill Green *Teaching the English Subjects* (1996, Deakin University Press). Email: cathxx@deakin.edu.au

Nicholas C. Burbules is a Professor in the Department of Educational Policy Studies at the University of Illinois, Urbana/Champaign. He has published several essays about hypertext, electronic publishing and the World Wide Web, but has also written dialogue, educational policy and critical social and political theory. He is currently editor of *Educational Theory*. Email: burbules@ux1.uiuc.edu

Jane Crawford lectures in TESOL and LOTE Education at the Queensland University of Technology. Her research interests include the role technology can play in interactive language learning. She is currently researching teachers' response to languages-other-than-English becoming part of the core curriculum. Email: j.crawford@qut.edu.au

Pamela Curtin is a postgraduate student at Griffith University and a primary-school teacher on the Gold Coast. Her main research areas, cultural identity/bias and critical literacy, have informed her work in technology. Currently Pamela is designing and coordinating a number of Internet projects in primary and secondary schools in Australia and overseas. Email: p.curtin@eda.gu.edu.au

Jane Yellowlees Douglas is the Director of the Center for Written and Oral Communication at the University of Florida (Gainesville). Her articles on hypertext and interactive technologies have appeared in journals in the US, UK and Australia. She is also the author of the hypertext narrative *I Have Said Nothing* published by Eastgate Systems. Email: jdouglas@interport.net

Gail E. Hawisher is Professor of English and Director of the Center for Writing Studies at the University of Illinois, Urbana-Champaign. She is co-editor with Cynthia Selfe of *Computers and Composition*. Among her recent projects is *Computers and the Teaching of Writing in American Higher Education, 1979–1994: A History* with Paul LeBlanc, Charles Moran and Cynthia Selfe. Her current research with Patricia Sullivan seeks to explore the many online lives of academic women. Email: hawisher@uiuc.edu

Eileen Honan is writing a thesis on the implementation of the Queensland English Syllabus by upper primary teachers at James Cook University. She is currently a Research Associate in the School of Language and Literacy at Queensland University of Technology, working on a national project investigating the links between technology and literacy education. Email: e.honan@qut.edu.au

Johndan Johnson-Eilola teaches at Purdue University. He has published work on computers and literacy in many journals and edited collections. His cultural study of hypertext genres in technical communication, information brokering, composition and literature, *Nostalgic Angels: Rearticulating Hypertext*

Writing (1996), is published by Ablex. Email: johndan@omni.cc.purdue.edu

Michael Joyce is Visiting Associate Professor of English and the Library at Vassar College. His hyperfictions include *afternoon, a story, WOE, Lucy's Sister, Twilight, A Symphony, Twelve Blue* and *Sister Stories* (with Carolyn Guyer and Rosemary Joyce). His collection of essays *Of Two Minds: Hypertext Pedagogy and Poetics* (1995) is published by The University of Michigan Press. Email: mijoyce@vaxsar.vassar.edu

Michele Knobel is a Lecturer in Language and Literacy Education at the Queensland University of Technology. Her research interests lie chiefly in the area of children's language and literacy practices, and in the field of electronic technologies. She is jointly authoring a book with Ivor Goodson, Colin Lankshear, and Marshall Mangan on the politics and ideology of the computer invasion of classrooms. Email: m.knobel@qut.edu.au

Gunther Kress is Professor of Education (with special reference to the teaching of English) at the Institute of Education, University of London. His publications include *Halliday: System and Function in Language* (1976), *Social Semiotics* (1988), *Language as Ideology* (1993), *Learning to Write* (1994) and *Reading Images: The Grammar of Visual Design* with Theo van Leeuwen (1995). Email: teemggk@ioe.ac.uk

Colin Lankshear is Professor of Education at the Queensland University of Technology. His books include *The New Work Order: Behind the Language of the New Capitalism* (with James Paul Gee and Glynda Hull) (1996); *Counternarratives* (with Henry Giroux, Peter Mclaren, and Michael Peters) (1996), and *Changing Literacies* (1997). He is currently leading a research team investigating the interface between new technologies and language/literacy learning. Email: c.lankshear@qut.edu.au

Charles Moran is Professor of English at the University of

Massachusetts at Amherst. With Gail Hawisher, Paul LeBlanc, and Cynthia Selfe, he has co-authored *Computers and the Teaching of Writing in American Higher Education, 1979–1994: A History.* With Anne J. Herrington, he has co-edited the award-winning *Writing, Teaching, and Learning in the Disciplines* (1992). Email: cmoran@english.umass.edu

Cynthia Selfe is Professor of Composition and Communication and Head of the Humanities Department at Michigan Technological University. With Gail Hawisher, she is the founder and co-editor of *Computers and Composition* and author of many books and journal articles in the area of literacy and technology. She was the Chair for the 1997 Conference on College Composition and Communication. She has also been recognised as EDUCOM Medal award winner for innovative computer use in higher education. Email: cyselfe@mtu.edu

Professor Richard Smith is Head of the School of Education and Dean of the Faculty of Education and Arts at Griffith University, Gold Coast. Since developing the Remote Area Teacher Education Project in North Queensland, the first successful tertiary level multimedia delivery initiative in Australia, his interests lie in educational policy, analysis and technological applications in education and training. Email: richard.smith@eda.gu.edu.au

Ilana Snyder is a Senior Lecturer in Language and Literacy Education, Faculty of Education, Monash University. She has published widely in the area of literacy and technology. *Hypertext: The Electronic Labyrinth* (1996) is published by Melbourne University Press and New York University Press. She is working on a new book, *Silicon Rhetoric*. Email: ilana.snyder@education.monash.edu.au

Page to Screen

ILANA SNYDER

Since electronic technologies first appeared in educational settings, there have been important changes to literacy practices associated with their use. Whether the technology is word processing, electronic mail, hypertext or the Internet, these technologies alter how language, both written and visual, is produced, processed and used. The application of these technologies influences the generation, manipulation, storage, retrieval and revision of texts as well as the products at the end. These products may be anything from a printed paper document to a hypertext web that exists only in electronic form. Further, these technologies offer us new spaces in which to create texts—spaces that are different from those that have preceded them. As a result, we no longer conceive of text as something located exclusively on a page, in a printed book. The new writing spaces include the screen where text is displayed and the electronic memory in which it is stored.

Before I elaborate on the issues and concerns explored in this book, it is important to establish at the outset that the emergence of these new literacy spaces and practices, signified here as the move from page to screen, does not necessarily signal the death of the printed book. The introduction of a new technology of writing does not automatically render older ones obsolete. For example, even though printing completely replaced handwriting in book production, it did not spell the end for handwriting. Rather, the boundaries between the two writing technologies blurred. Today pen and paper serve for notes and personal communications; word processing and typewriting are for texts not ready—or appropriate—for typesetting. The future of writing is not a linear progression in which new technologies usurp earlier ones. A more likely scenario is that a number of technologies will continue to co-exist, interact, even complement each other.

Page to Screen assumes certain understandings we already share as literacy educators and researchers. We know that the use of these electronic technologies affects how we read and write, how we teach reading and writing and how we describe literacy practices. However, moving from this recognition that literacy practices differ when they are used to an understanding of how writing, writers and written forms change, is difficult. Such a move is complicated by the growing realisation that writing and technology are not distinct phenomena. Writing has never been and can never be separate from technology: indeed, writing and technology are 'ineluctably intertwined' (Aronowitz 1992, p. 133) and interdependent.

This book responds to the challenge of accounting for some of the complex connections between literacy practices and the use of these technologies. It also examines the implications of their use for pedagogy and curriculum in literacy settings. Further, it considers their impact beyond the walls of classrooms and the boundaries of educational systems. Implicit in all the chapters is the understanding that, as literacy educators and researchers, we cannot afford to ignore the fact that culture has begun to go through what promises to be a metamorphosis. Electronic communications and information processing technologies have reached a condition of critical mass. Moreover, the escalation of the rate of change is so spectacular that it may be that evolutionary accommodation has been rendered impossible. Although this book focuses specifically on the field of literacy and technology, it is within this broader cultural context of increasingly rapid change that our work and thinking must be located.

Closely connected to the speed and complexity of change in our computer-mediated culture is the widening gulf between students and teachers. If we look at this phenomenon from an historical perspective, it is nothing new. Unlike their students, educators have traditionally greeted new technologies with little interest. The effect of this technology 'reticence' (Turkle 1984) is captured most powerfully by Papert (1993) in the opening chapter of his book *The Children's Machine*. Papert invites the reader to imagine a party of time travellers from an earlier century, among them a group of surgeons and another of school teachers, 'each group eager to see how much things have changed in their profession a hundred years into the future' (p. 1). Papert contends that unlike the surgeons, who would be bewildered by the unfamiliar in the operating room of a modern hospital, the teachers would respond to a modern classroom very differently. They might be puzzled by a few strange objects, but they would see the point of most of what was being attempted and could easily take over the class. Papert's parable is illuminating: the exponential growth of science and technology in recent years has meant that some areas of human activity have changed dramatically. Telecommunications, entertainment and transportation as well as medicine are among them. But, argues Papert, '[s]chool is a notable example of an area that has not' (p. 2).

In Australia, at least, technology has never assumed a significant presence—neither in schools nor in post-school educational institutions. When television arrived fifty years ago, many believed that the new communication medium would transform education. It did not. When the first microcomputers appeared in teaching and learning settings in the late 1970s, similar predictions about how they would transform education were touted. They have yet to do so. Amid the rhetoric of politicians in Australia (and indeed across the globe) who are promising that all schools will soon have Internet connections and that more students will have access to the new electronic technologies, history suggests that we should remain somewhat sceptical about how the wiring of our schools might affect pedagogical practices. But despite an unpromising history, this book argues that as literacy educators we must consider ways in which the new technologies might be employed for useful purposes in literacy education at all levels. Just because we have remained largely impervious to technological change does not mean that this is how we should continue to respond. Even more important, if we are to begin to bridge the growing gulf between ourselves and our students, we cannot afford to remain ignorant of the characteristics of these new technologies and their complex cultural influences.

Of course, it may well be that a restrained approach to the electronic technologies' so-called revolutionary potential may prove to be an entirely appropriate response to their use in educational settings. The technologies might perhaps be used mainly for standard and relatively undemanding activities such as drill and practice. Indeed, perhaps it is wise to step back from the rush to acquire optic-fibre cabling, hardware and software to ask value questions about how we should learn and teach, as well as hard-headed financial questions about cost-effectiveness (Cohen 1988; Moran 1993). But I believe that even while we continue to act prudently, we should also be looking at the many and complex effects of the technologies and how we may use them to our advantage in literacy settings.

So that we are able to use these technologies intelligently, we need theories of electronic literacies that are dynamic, critical and reflexive. These theories must also take into account the linguistic, the psychological and the sociocultural. Each chapter in this book contributes to the development and articulation of such theories. The collection represents authors from Australia, the United States and the United Kingdom, all with different disciplinary backgrounds, all with strong points of view and distinctive contributions to make to the field of literacy and technology. The authors account for what we already know in this field and what we have still to discover. They offer a variety of perspectives on how the new electronic technologies can be used effectively by teachers and their students. They discuss how teachers can participate critically yet productively in computer-mediated literacy practices.

The book is divided into four sections. 'The spaces of electronic literacies' traces the twenty-year history of the field of literacy and technology studies which is complicated by political, social and cultural articulations. The critical overview of research studies, both in first and second-language settings, provides a richly detailed map on which to situate the ideas and debates that comprise the rest of the book. Gail Hawisher and Cynthia Selfe point out that the new technologies have become the focus for hotly contested social struggles in which not only educators but also publishers, commercial hardware and software producers, parents, governments and the tele-communication players of the corporate world vie for position. They suggest that given the importance of the intellectual territory of literacy and technology studies and the challenges educators will face in the coming century, these years at the century's end are an appropriate time for the profession to pause and reflect.

When identifying the claims made about the enormous potential of new technologies to enhance second-language learning, Michele Knobel, Colin Lankshear, Eileen Honan and Jane Crawford remind us somewhat wryly that they are the present-day equivalents of those in earlier decades which championed the use of videos, television, film and a range of audio-visual technologies. The authors compare some of the claims made for the possibilities and effectiveness of computer-mediated communications technologies with the practical experiences of using them for second-language learning in a range of educational settings.

This section of the book sets up some useful parameters for the field of literacy and technology. Both chapters highlight the need to scrutinise the often excessive claims made for the beneficial effects of the technologies. They stimulate further conversations about the challenges of doing research in this field. It seems we should recognise that rather than allow research questions to be dictated by a commitment to a positivist, quantitative tradition or to more subjective, qualitative traditions, those working in the field of literacy and technology should allow research to grow out of the problems and questions of the field (Snyder 1997).

What emerges is a recognition that research in this area has begun the important process of careful and critical borrowing (Flynn 1995). The authors suggest that positivist epistemologies, as theoretical frameworks for research, do not have to be ignored. But on the other hand, the answer is not simply to assume a multidisciplinary approach. To continue to meet the demands of the new settings and sites for research in this expanding and chameleon field, both chapters argue that we must ask appropriate questions, use appropriate methodologies and embrace perspectives that do not leave us vulnerable when challenged. Implicit is the understanding that just as it is problematic to be aligned with the discourses and approaches of the sciences and social sciences, so too is it problematic to be associated with the discourses of resistance—indeed, any uncritical identification can be problematic.

'Emerging literacies' takes as a starting-point the understanding that the use of these technologies produces new literacies which we are only beginning to identify and describe. The three chapters in this section extend the theoretical boundaries of thinking about the new genres, rhetorics and literacies associated with electronic technologies. Gunther Kress focuses on the changes to semiotic practices and how they involve a greater and newer use of visual forms of representation in many domains of public communication—what he characterises as 'a tectonic shift'. Yet despite the growing importance of the non-verbal, he claims that relatively naive notions of visualisation still dominate. Kress examines the ways in which the 'turn to the visual' interacts with electronic texts. He argues that what is happening represents a significant change to how we make meanings.

Also concerned with the rhetorics of the new media, Charles Moran and Gail Hawisher consider electronic mail and other new computer-enabled communication media. They examine the differences between these forms of communication and postal mail, telephony and face-to-face communication and the changes to textual practices associated with their expanding use. With email, Moran and Hawisher argue, we seem to be developing an 'electronic language' that bears an uncertain relationship to the languages of speech and of print. Moreover, the authors note, email is now a 'gated community' (as indeed are all technologies 'gated communities'), with only 2 per cent of the world's population connected to the Internet. They also observe that the code in which email is transmitted exhibits the English-only bias of ASCII (American Standard Code for Information Interchange). Until the online world includes all voices and cultures, they contend, the electronic world will remain exclusive and restricted without the richness of language that might otherwise distinguish these spaces.

Interested in enhancing our ability to 'hyperread' the Web critically, Nicholas Burbules explores the need to reflect on the way that links within hypertext environments, such as the World Wide Web, connote relations, alter the meaning of the points they connect, and govern pathways of association that control and direct movement within a particular information space. As a way of highlighting the significance of links, Burbules reviews a number of literary turns of phrase such as metaphor as providing a way of thinking about how Web links connect ideas and textual sources. Burbules argues that reflecting upon how links work in this manner can enhance our ability to hyperread the Web critically.

'The problems and possibilities of hypertext' is the subject of the third section. Hypertext—a way of connecting text, pictures, film and sound in a nonlinear manner by electronic links—exists only online. Hypertext is fully electronic reading and writing. Hypertext differs from printed text by offering users multiple pathways through a web of information.

In my own chapter, I discuss the hype so often associated with discussions about hypertext. I look at the limitations of polarised responses that either exult or condemn the technology's powers and the need to move beyond them. Hypertext certainly has much potential in educational settings but, I suggest, its influences are best examined with dispassion and more than a modicum of scepticism. Instead of either celebrating or demonising the technology, it seems more productive to try to widen our understanding of developments such as hypertext in order to exploit their educational possibilities. We must continue to look critically at assertions that the technology will either radically transform or diminish the social interactions that are intrinsic to effective teaching and learning (Snyder 1996).

Exploring the potential of hypertext for new forms of argument, Jane Douglas argues that the structure and conventions of print rhetoric do not adapt particularly well to the requirements of many writers and researchers. She is especially interested in sociologists who use traditional print but want to express their ideas in truly reflexive and relativist ways. Douglas examines the difficulties that sociologists, who are social constructivists, face in communicating their research findings when they use the conventions of argumentative writing that have governed print for hundreds of years. In spite of themselves, Douglas contends, the most determinedly reflexive relativists of writers turn into positivists in print. She considers the ways in which a non-linear, computer-mediated technology like hypertext can offer sociologists alternatives for expressing relativistic and reflexive arguments. Her discussion of the conventions governing the writing of argument in print as compared to those governing the creation of argument in hypertext compels us to think hard about our cultural attachment to particular textual forms.

However, despite its possibilities, Michael Joyce argues that much of the promise of hypertext has been subverted within the crass, commercialised, multimedia wastelands of the world wide web, a name he deliberately represents in lower-case letters. It soon becomes apparent that Joyce is not attacking the web because he hankers after some lost cultural practice. Nor is he suggesting we turn the clock backwards as do Sven Birkerts (1994) in *The Gutenberg Elegies*, a nostalgic paean to the book and book culture, and Clifford Stoll (1995) in *Silicon Snake Oil*, a diatribe against computer-mediated communication, in which the author rues the years he wasted on the Internet. Moreover, he is not suggesting that we limit our reading to the new generation of writers who focus on the wired world of computer-mediated communication, such as Bruce Sterling (1992), who wrote *The Hacker Crackdown*, and more books in this genre. Rather, Joyce invokes us to distinguish between 'hypertext' (which has great potential for educators and artists) and 'multimedia', which is merely a variety of television—what Newton Minow dubbed 'the vast wasteland'.

Yet despite his cynical dismissal of the web and all that it has come to represent, Joyce is still optimistic that as teachers of literacy we can find a way, what he calls the 'middle voice', a voice that is neither active nor passive, that will help us and our students to use hypertext to create hyperfictions, texts that continuously rewrite themselves, texts that require and welcome successive readings. Joyce characterises the middle voice as a voice of coherence which may offer us and our students a strategy to attain meaning in the face of the fragmentation and multiplicity of our postmodern times.

'Changing the cultures of teaching and learning' considers the rapidly altering sociocultural settings in which education currently takes place. All three chapters focus on computer games, but from contrasting perspectives. Integral to this final section of the book is a belief that teachers and educators must confront the articulation of these significant cultural shifts or be further marginalised.

Changes to our understanding of space and time—how we must adjust to living on the surface as opposed to experiencing things in depth—are examined by Johndan Johnson-Eilola. In this postmodern space, things happen on the surface in a state of continuous stimulation. We do not pass stories down linearly from generation to generation but experience them multiply and simultaneously, across global communication networks. Johnson-Eilola argues that many adults are terrified of this place; many children live there happily. He refers to the two places respectively as modernism and postmodernism. It is easy for us raised in the first worldview to deride the second as superficial, artificial and dehumanising. But, he believes, we cannot simply reject the cultural shift that is taking place but should, instead, work with it and beyond it by devising new literacies and new ways of living.

Through a sampling of recent communication, education and entertainment technologies, including the Web and the interface designs for computer games, Johnson-Eilola traces the shift toward postmodernism. He concludes with practical ways in which educators can help students and adults alike to live on the surface without succumbing to cultural fragmentation. Tactics include media analysis which allows students to construct critical, ethical positions in response to the global communications media-dominated worlds in which they live.

The social implications for schooling in the age of advanced computer technology are considered by Richard Smith and Pamela Curtin. The authors argue that because students are immersed in a time of ever-increasing technological development, it is possible that their methods of thinking and processing information differ from those of past generations. In their view, the pluralism of identities and perspectives emerging today and the increasing domination of computer technology directly affect the structures of educational systems. They warn that the very institution of education as we know it is challenged by these cultural shifts and that a total reassessment of curriculum and schooling is necessary.

The computer game is just one example of how technology saturates the experiences of young people today as they tune into electronic media of many kinds, argues Catherine Beavis. She asserts that their experience of the world is very different from that offered by schools. Their culture and sense of identity are at odds with many of the assumptions of contemporary curriculum. Beavis examines the implications of new media forms for schools and curriculum and how such forms and young people's engagement with them challenge and redefine the previous generations' notions of narrative, textuality and reading.

A theme taken up by most of the contributors to this volume is the notion of 'newness'. Both directly and indirectly, they ask a number of pertinent questions: How new are computer-mediated literacy practices? Do they signal the dawn of new literacies or do they only re-incarnate old ones? What is 'new' about them? How do we assess them? Does their use enhance literacy practices or diminish them? These questions are raised within the broader context of a culture that valorises, even fetishises, 'newness' at the same time as it extols the traditional and the old. 'Newness' is an extremely powerful tool of consumerism—we know only too well that consumerism has a vested commercial interest in promoting newness. But we also treasure and work hard to preserve our cultural heritage. We build libraries, museums and galleries. Moreover, we are in a flurry to digitise our cultural records to secure our history for future generations. We live, therefore, in somewhat ambiguous times: we are partial, yet also vulnerable, to both 'neophilia' and 'neophobia'.

Questions about 'newness' are integral to examining the research literature in first and second-language applications of the new technologies. It is possible to think about research in this area as an imperative provoked by the desire to understand how the use of the technologies alters things. The research question, put albeit somewhat crudely, becomes: Does their use involve *new* practices or, perhaps, simply an extension of old and familiar ways of doing and seeing things? (McLuhan 1964).

'Emerging literacies' is also directly concerned with newness. Kress confronts a greater and *newer* or, perhaps more accurately, *renewed* use of visual forms of representation. As Kress reminds us, it is not that the visual has never before played a key role, but that the emergence of electronic technologies makes it assume a more prominent role. He discusses 'newness' as intimately connected to the significance of the far-reaching changes we have witnessed in the last two decades. Although in former periods in history the visual had a central place, a major shift is now occurring in the system of media and modes of representation and communication, and in the system of evaluating these. The landscape, in Kress's words, is being 'remade'. The consequence, he argues, is the need for a *new* theory of meaning.

The discussion of the rhetorics of electronic mail begins

with the question: Is email a *new* medium? Moran and Haw-isher argue that while email is new, developing its own rhetorics and languages, it is nevertheless still intimately related to its ancestors. To explain what they mean, the authors suggest that email is new just as we might say that a baby is new. At different times, the baby may remind us of its mother, its father, even its grandparents. But the baby is not simply the product of its genes—she is also shaped by and shapes the sociocultural contexts she inhabits. Similarly, email is related to its antecedents—the letter and the telephone call, for example—but at the same time, it is influenced by and in-fluences the cultural contexts in which it is used.

When considering whether or not reading or 'hyperreading' on the Web is something new, Burbules asks whether the same reading involving the usual skills and strategies is simply being exercised in a new medium. He argues, however, that the question itself is unproductive. New media introduce new contexts, and changes in contexts lead to differences in prac-tices. But at the same time, there is some continuity between these emergent practices and those that are more familiar. Thus, according to Burbules, newness and change are uniquely interconnected.

The exploration of the possibilities and problems associated with the use of hypertext also deals with concerns related to newness. Central to my own argument is the notion that polarised positions seem to be linked directly to the introduc-tion of a *new* technology. Indeed, its very newness seems to provoke extreme responses. Intrinsic to Douglas' discussion of the different groups of sociologists and how they write and make meanings, is the understanding that hypertext offers relativists a *new*, entirely appropriate and liberating medium in which to express their arguments. And Michael Joyce, with more than a touch of irony, as he strings together lists of acronyms and jargon associated with the 'world wide web', tells us that this medium is not really new—it has become just another site for all that we came quickly to despise about television. What was *new* was the promise of hypertext—a medium which makes possible new kinds of stories for new readers, but already Joyce sees this as 'a passing form' in an 'uncertain medium'. 'Passing' since in hypertext the word will probably have to renegotiate its relationship with images and audience, and 'uncertain' because there is no guarantee that any of these works will survive the shift to the web.

The examination of the differences between the worlds students inhabit and those familiar to their parents and teachers can also be seen as a variation on the theme of newness as opposed to traditional ways. Johnson-Eilola distinguishes between modernist and postmodernist times and provides some sort of comfort zone for readers by arguing that even though we cannot retreat nostalgically to a modernist era, we do not necessarily have to adopt all the characteristics of the postmodern—that *new* ways of existing are not totally irreconcilable with the traditional. In fact, they can inform each other. What we should engage in, according to Johnson-Eilola, is a celebration and a remaking rather than a lament.

From the findings of their study, Smith and Curtin believe that schools, teachers and curriculum have to do much more to understand, to take into account and to accommodate the changing worlds of our students. They suggest that teachers will encounter professional dilemmas when dealing with their young students and this *new* era will generate feelings of intellectual incompetence and powerlessness among educators.

Confronted by today's *new* generation of *new* readers and writers, Beavis argues that multimedia and digital technologies are changing what we understand as literacy, so much so that our current understandings will be rendered obsolete. She claims that at least five *new* literacies will be required in the age of the new information technologies: multimedia authoring skills, multimedia critical analysis, cyberspace exploration strategies and cyberspace navigation skills (Lemke 1995), and the capacity to negotiate and deconstruct images, both visual and verbal. Beavis urges literacy educators to find ways to talk about and work with electronic texts alongside those that have traditionally been their concern.

However, whether we characterise what we are witnessing around us as 'new', or an extension of older ways, changes in literacy practices are happening. This book is about those changes. What is certainly occurring is a change in how we *do* literacy. It is more than a paradigm shift or a switch in an epistemological position. As Heim (1987) pointed out a decade ago, 'our access to knowledge changes dramatically as we computerize the arts, sciences and business' (p. xiii). He describes it as an 'ontological shift' (p. xiii), a change in 'the world under our feet' (p. xiii).

The publication of this book is timely. We simply cannot continue with our jobs largely as we always have, as if very little is really changing. We should think carefully before we dismiss the word processor as just a tool, a more efficient way of writing. We cannot continue to see networks, the Internet and the World Wide Web merely as new ways for people to connect. Nor can we argue convincingly that books on disk, encountered on a screen, are not much different to printed books because the words do not change.

Even if slower than in other social settings, the electronic revolution has begun to extend its reach into classrooms across the curriculum, at all levels of education. As educational institutions begin adapting to the integration of electronic technologies, literacy educators and researchers should take the lead in their development and use for literacy purposes. We must incorporate the technologies into our teaching if for no other reason than our students will force us to change. Students are composing with these new technologies, 'using different writing processes, researching in new forums, and connecting critical thoughts in visionary new ways' (Nelson & Wambeam 1995, p. 140).

A more pressing and perhaps even more persuasive reason to incorporate them into our teaching relates to issues of power and how we and our students gain access to it. Just as we know that social, political and economic power is closely associated with access to and knowledge of certain discourse forms (Gee 1990; Lemke 1995), power now is also closely associated with access to and familiarity, affinity and dexterity with the uses of the new technologies for literacy purposes. We simply cannot deny our students opportunities to develop facility with and understanding of the possibilities and influences of these technologies.

The cover of Bill Gates' (1996) best-seller, *The Road Ahead*, features an Annie Leibovitz photograph of the chairman and chief executive officer of Microsoft. In the foreground, on the right-hand side, stands Gates on a highway, hands in pockets, boyish, unassuming, cheerful. The straight road behind him narrows as it disappears into the distance—a somewhat literal image of the unending *Al-Gorian* Information Superhighway. But the highway in the photo is flanked by an orange-brown, seemingly lifeless, desert landscape. Leibovitz has constructed a delightfully ambiguous image, particularly when you consider her subject: yes, the uninterrupted highway appears to go on forever, into the future, but it is carved through a barren, boring terrain.

It seems to me that our responsibility and challenge as educators and researchers is to explore this terrain, whatever its features, to devise the theoretical and practical understandings that will allow ourselves and our students to reconnoitre it wisely. The literacy and textual practices used to traverse the electronic spaces forming the terrain are examined by the contributors to this book from different perspectives. Each chapter adds to our growing knowledge of how these spaces function and influence our semiotic and literacy practices. Each chapter also provokes many questions —there is still much for us to discover and learn. For even if the terrain turns out to be a wasteland, with only a few oases, it does not abrogate the imperative to understand how meanings are made within it. Indeed, it is only with such insights that we can continue to interrogate these spaces and what we and others do within them, so that they do not become naturalised and thereby more difficult for us to appraise. It makes good sense, therefore, to heed the words of the refrain of Michael Joyce's chapter: 'What we are used to, we too often become used by'.

References

Aronowitz, S. 1992 'Looking out: the impact of computers on the lives of professionals', *Literacy Online*, ed. M. Tuman, pp. 119–37

Birkerts, S. 1994 *The Gutenberg Elegies: The Fate of Reading in an Electronic Age*, Fawcett Columbine, New York

Cohen, D.K. 1988 'Educational technology and school organisation', *Technology in Education: Looking Toward 2020*, eds R.S. Nickerson and P.P. Zodhiates, Erlbaum, Hillsdale, NJ, pp. 231–64

Flynn, E.A. 1995 'Feminism and scientism', *College Composition and Communication*, vol. 46, no. 3, pp. 353–68

Gates, B. with Myhrvold, N. and Rinearson, P. 1996 *The Road Ahead*, Penguin, Harmondsworth, England

Gee, J.P. 1990 *Social Linguistics and Literacies*, Falmer Press, London

Heim, M. 1987 *Electric Language: A Philosophical Study of Word Processing*, Yale University Press, New Haven

Lemke, J.L. 1995 *Textual Politics: Discourse and Social Dynamics*, Taylor & Francis, London

McLuhan, M. 1964 *Understanding Media: The Extensions of Man*, Routledge & Kegan Paul, London

Moran, C. 1993 'The winds and the costs of change', *Computers and Composition: An International Journal for Teachers of Writing*, vol. 10, no. 2, pp. 35–44

Nelson, J., Wambean, C.A. 1995 'Moving computers into the Writing Centre: the path to least resistance', *Computers and Composition: An International Journal for Teachers of Writing*, vol. 12, no. 2, pp. 135–44

Papert, S. 1993 *The Children's Machine: Rethinking School in the Age of the Computer*, Basic Books, New York

Snyder, I. 1996 *Hypertext: The Electronic Labyrinth*, Melbourne University Press, Melbourne and New York University Press, New York

—— 1997 'Research methods for studying the use of computers in literacy classrooms', *Encyclopedia of Language and Education, Volume 8*, ed. D. Corson, Kluwer Academic Publishers, Dordrecht, The Netherlands

Sterling, B. 1992 *The Hacker Crackdown: Law and Disorder on the Electronic Frontier*, Penguin, Harmondsworth, Middlesex

Stoll, C. 1995 *Silicon Snake Oil: Second Thoughts on the Information Highway*, Macmillan, London

Turkle, S. 1984 *The Second Self: Computers and the Human Spirit*, Granada, London

Section 1
The spaces of
electronic literacies

1

Reflections on computers and composition studies at the century's end

GAIL E. HAWISHER AND
CYNTHIA L. SELFE[1]

Although computers can be found in great numbers in schools at every academic level, a good deal of controversy continues to accompany their entry into educational settings. On the one hand, they are greeted as revolutionary tools that will cure the ills of outmoded educational approaches and, on the other, they are viewed as expensive instructional delivery systems that have the potential to destroy the human element in education. Clearly both views are extreme. Yet, increasingly, the new technologies have become the focus for hotly contested debates, characterised by complex economic, political, ideological, and historical issues. Vying for position in such disputes are not only educators but also publishers, commercial hardware and software producers, parents, governments, and the telecommunications players of the corporate world. Given the number of contesting forces in the new electronic land-scapes and the range of education and language interests, those of us working in the field of computers and composition are beginning to recognise just how dramatically the values of democratic education and literacy will be played out in the next few years. For these reasons, the history, the present, and the future of technology studies within educational contexts are important intellectual spaces for educators and students of technology to map.

Our chapter focuses on the need to explore the history of research in computers and composition studies in order to understand more fully the present and future of this rapidly changing discipline. Given the importance of this intellectual, cultural, and educational territory—given the challenges educators face in the coming century—these years at the century's end are an appropriate time for the profession to pause and recover its histories of the research in the field. In this chapter we present a synopsis of the research in literacy and technology which has preceded us and then turn to some fruitful points of departure for literacy educators who teach with computers and who hope to contribute to educational change in positive ways. Our chapter attempts to historicise the research literature on the uses of word processing, electronic networks, and hypertext and hypermedia as they relate to writing and writing instruction.[2] Framed by the kinds of questions researchers ask about the study of computers and literacy education, the review also discusses the research methodologies employed in that study. Each section concludes with an overview of the findings that have emerged over the past several years. We then turn to the kinds of studies that we believe could support democratic educational goals and practices.

For over fifteen years literacy educators have tried to assess how the use of computers affects student writers at every level of education. Technological changes since the first fully assembled microcomputers in 1977 sparked a spate of studies that now number well into the hundreds. One of the earliest, Richard Collier's study (1983) of four nursing students, set the stage for the kinds of questions that would drive subsequent research. Collier asked how the use of a computer application (in this case, a mainframe text editor) would influence the student nurses' writing processes (in this case, revision) as well as the quality of the texts they produced. And although he saw no improvement in quality, he found that the writers he studied revised more and produced longer texts with word processing than with conventional tools. Since Collier's early study, educational researchers have continued to probe the relationship among writers and various kinds of computer applications, aiming much of the research at school-based writing and often with an eye toward examining how the teaching of writing might benefit from the use of the new technologies. In recent years, moreover, researchers have extended their study to the newer technologies of electronic communication networks and to hypertext and hypermedia. Yet despite the considerable attention that research in computers and composition studies has received over the years, only a few studies have looked at how the use of computers affects students' interactions with their cultural context or their learning environment.[3] In other words, little systematic attention has been paid to the kinds of research that could inform fundamental changes in education—changes which must be realistically played out within current social, political, economic, and ideological contexts.

Studies in word processing

Studies in word processing, by far the most prolific area of research in computers and composition, continue to abound in the research literature. Since the early 1980s writing researchers and teachers alike have wanted to know whether computers could be used in ways that improve students' writing abilities. Unfortunately, the question has often been framed too simplistically as: 'What is the effect of computers on writing quality?' which attributes far too much power to computers rather than to how writers or literacy teachers might use computers. Today the quality question seems somewhat naive and beside the point; word processing has become the writing technology of choice in school and workplace settings. And, just as English professionals no longer ask whether typewriters improve students' writing, many regard the quality question in relation to word processing as wrongheaded. As word processing becomes increasingly accepted as essential for student and professional writers alike, other research questions must be formulated. Yet a review of dissertation studies reveals that researchers are still asking whether the use of word processing will enhance writing abilities.

Studies in word processing can be divided into two categories: those that employ primarily quantitative methods of inquiry and those that rely on qualitative techniques. Most studies are quantitative or comparative studies, with writers divided into experimental and control groups and the use of word processing established as the primary variable that distinguishes the groups. Questions driving the research include how word processing in combination with process-oriented teaching influences writers' processes—planning, drafting, revising, editing—and products—quality, syntax, length, and number of mechanical errors. Researchers have also been interested in whether students tend to enjoy writing at computers and whether the technology is more appropriate for one group of writers than for another. Among the various groups of writers studied so far are students at all levels, from first grade through graduate school, and professional writers, both technical and creative.

The results of the research are many and varied. Students report positive attitudes toward writing and word processing after working with computers; student writers often exhibit finished products that have fewer mechanical errors than those written with traditional tools; and many writers produce longer texts with word processing than with traditional methods (Hawisher 1988). Conflicting results emerge around the variables of revision and writing quality. As many studies find an increase in revision as those that do not, and only a few studies claim that writing quality improves. In fact, regardless of which group of writers is the focus of the research and whether the research is school-based or otherwise, investigations of writing quality continue to yield conflicting results. (For a meta-analysis of word processing in writing instruction see Bangert-Drowns 1993.)

The qualitative research—case studies and ethnographic research—asks somewhat different questions than the quantitative studies do. It asks how writers adapt their strategies to computer writing, whether their composing habits change with the technology, and how the introduction of computers influences the cultural context into which they are introduced. A general theme drawn from these studies is similar to one from the comparative studies: that is, a writer's or student's particular habits and strategies for composing take precedence over the influence of the computers. Writers bring their routines and patterns of writing with them. If they are not extensive revisers before word processing, they probably will not become so with computers, even when revision strategies are part of the instruction (Bridwell, Sirc & Brooke 1985). (It is interesting to speculate on how this might change with our youngest students, some who are likely to have learned most of their writing processes on computers.)

The few ethnographic studies that have been conducted also contribute new knowledge that the comparative studies cannot reveal. They suggest that while students often do their paper-and-pencil writing silently and privately at their desks, writing at a computer in elementary school settings, for example, may in fact transform school-based writing from a private to public activity as students gather around the computers to read and talk about their writings (Dickinson 1986). In seeking to elucidate the subtle influences of computers in social interactions among students and teachers, the qualitative research (case studies and ethnographies) suggests the importance of the cultural context in shaping writers' work and learning with word processing.

Research on electronic networks

A major difference between research aimed at word processing and the early research on the discourse of the nets, more accurately called electronic networked discourse, is its cross-disciplinary emphasis. Unlike studies of word processing, only a few studies on electronic networks have been conducted in writing classes. For a more complete picture, English professionals must look at studies in distance education, communication research, linguistics, social psychology, and organisational behaviour, to mention a few of the fields studying computer-mediated communication (e.g., Mason & Kaye 1989; Jones 1995; Ferrara, Brunner, & Whittemore 1991; Lea 1992; Sproull & Kiesler 1991).

Since the research is cross-disciplinary, it is somewhat surprising that studies have converged on similar issues, asking similar research questions. The questions focus first on identifying the characteristics of electronic discourse, examining how participants respond to the discourse, and, then, for those working in educational settings, exploring its potential for teaching and learning. Many initial findings are more in the spirit of observations gleaned from experience in working with the medium, not unlike early exploratory studies in word processing. But regardless of whether the research is conducted within or outside educational settings, common questions, findings, and observations emerge.

Researchers agree that networked discourse employs a language that is somewhere on a continuum between spoken and written language. Indeed, researchers often refer to online communication as 'talk' or 'dialogue'. Some participants write profusely on the networks; others seem terse, almost 'telegraphic'. Conventions of language and style are still evolving and will change as the email and conferencing programs become as easy to use as word processing. A number of researchers have noted that a writer's relation to a screen and electronic communication seem different from a writer's relation to a written letter or memorandum. In writing to a screen, writers may at times lose the sense of an audience and, with that, the constraints and inhibitions that the imagined audience provides. At its most dramatic, this difference produces what has been termed 'flaming', or emotionally laden, hurtful language inappropriate for classroom settings. Some researchers contend that the more focused the task, the less likely flaming is to occur. In those studies, with goal-directed electronic activity and participants' roles clearly defined, no flaming was reported (Hartman *et al.* 1991).

Research in various fields, moreover, has suggested that the lack of paralinguistic cues such as one's appearance, tone of voice, and facial expression also invites participation on networks from those who do not normally speak frequently in face-to-face contexts. Sensitivity to the position of individuals in organisations, corporate or academic, tends to silence those who perceive themselves as having lower status. A study by Dubrovsky and his colleagues (1991) looked specifically at electronic discussion in four-person groups with first-year college students and MBA graduate students; the researchers confirmed what they call 'the equalisation phenomenon', that is, those with 'lower status', the first-year college students, asserted themselves more and had greater influence on the group than the first-year college students did in the face-to-face groups. Such studies can have important implications for literacy teachers who hope to encourage all students regardless of their class, race, or gender to participate, but the social science research should be scrutinised carefully before being applied to literacy classes (Eldred & Hawisher 1995).

Basing their claims on similar research in the social sciences, literacy educators often argue that electronic discussion can encourage students who are sometimes silenced because of their status to 'speak up', to participate electronically in ways that they avoid in traditional class settings (e.g., Barker & Kemp 1990; Langston & Batson 1990). However, no empirical research in educational settings has so far supported or contradicted such claims. Note, however, that much of the social science research is conducted with participants who never meet face-to-face. For literacy teachers who use electronic networks mainly to supplement face-to-face class discussion, it is somewhat odd to foreground the network's lack of social cues without acknowledging instructors' and students' many face-to-face interactions. (For a more complete early review of research on electronic networks, see Hawisher 1992.)

Research on hypertext and hypermedia

Researchers in literacy studies have begun to explore the

9

implications of hypertext and hypermedia for writing and writing instruction. One of the problems they encounter, however, is that hypermedia, like networked discourse, is essentially a new medium existing only online, taking many forms; instruction comprises only one of its many applications. And, even when used for instruction, the kinds of applications differ radically. Hypermedia programs can be assembled to mimic old CAI (computer-assisted instruction) programs with their workbook-like structure and dull exercises, or they can take an interactive form where individuals choose their own paths through online text with print, graphics, sound, and sometimes video as part of the text. Moreover, to borrow Michael Joyce's (1988) useful categories, hypertexts can be 'exploratory' or 'constructive', depending upon whether readers 'browse' through a body of information already assembled or 'write' their own texts, transforming prior knowledge by acting upon what they read and write.

For educational settings, the early research on hypermedia environments exists primarily outside literacy studies and often examines readers' and writers' navigational capabilities; that is, researchers look at how users move through large, complex nonlinear bodies of information without losing their sense of connection. Other research questions focus on the design of hypertext systems and ask how material can be presented to optimise learning. Researchers have also begun to ask whether particular kinds of pedagogical problems are more suited for some hypertext environments than for others. Rand Spiro and his colleagues (1990), for example, have designed a system on *Citizen Kane*, which is intended to foster 'advanced knowledge acquisition' or learning beyond introductory material in any discipline. They base their approach, in part, on the notion that learners need not be subjected to the difficulties of navigating nonlinear and multidimensional textual environments to acquire knowledge that could be obtained easily in other ways. Spiro's research suggests that certain hypertextual environments, in allowing instructors to represent knowledge in many different ways, can foster deeper understandings of difficult subject matter than traditional settings can.

Another approach to using hypermedia environments in educational settings is to encourage students to write their own hypertexts and then ask them to describe their experiences in working with the new medium. One exploratory study in a first-year writing class found that most students responded favourably to reading and writing hypertexts (Kaplan & Moulthrop 1991). While they sometimes wondered how they would know when they had finished a reading assignment (there are no pages or specific paths to follow), they devoted much time and energy to reading and writing their own interactive fictions. In these kinds of hypertext environments, it is difficult to know where reading stops and writing begins since both occur in the same space often at the same time.

Researchers and teachers have only begun to explore the exciting opportunities and possible dangers that hypertext and hypermedia pose. For example, we have found no literacy studies research that concentrates on the hypertext environment of the World Wide Web (WWW). We would argue, however, that when hypermedia environments—either on the Web, in CD-ROM format, or in stand-alone applications—do no more than present information in lecture-like formats, they seem less promising than they might be. Yet if they are used to allow readers and writers to make their own connections (with a speed that is unknown in print contexts) and then to create new knowledge from these connections, they suggest a new instructional medium that we have only begun to imagine, much less study.

Cultural theories, critical pedagogy, feminism, and technology

Each of the technologies discussed so far—word processing, electronic networks, hypermedia, and the conflating of the three on the WWW—offer new challenges to literacy educators and researchers. But there are also important issues involved in the incorporation and use of the new technologies in educational contexts, and literacy research must now pay more attention to these issues. For example, we should heed the

11

cultural critics (e.g., Poster 1990; Feenberg 1991; Kramarae 1988; Spender 1995) who remind us that since computers fundamentally shape—and are shaped by—cultural values, they continually magnify and reproduce the complex social conditions connected with those values in fundamental ways—much like educational systems in general. Computers, then, far from encouraging change, can also maintain stasis within existing educational and cultural systems. And, unfortunately, in computer-supported literacy contexts there has been very little research that traces how these cultural processes unfold or finds gaps in this over-determined web of cultural, political, economic, and ideological relations.

Radical pedagogues (e.g., Shor 1987; Freire 1990; hooks 1989, Luke & Gore 1992) can help us see that change in computer-supported literacy environments is often met with a special degree of conservatism—partly a reaction against the fear that computers will dehumanise classrooms and partly a form of scepticism that computers can really support radically democratic, systemic-level changes in the values that shape teaching and learning. Hence, attempting educational reform in computer-supported literacy projects can often prove slower, more temporary, and even more partial than change in non-technological projects. Among the many problems that only a few researchers have studied and that still plague both traditional and computer-supported literacy classrooms are the continued marginalisation of individuals due to race, gender, age, sexual orientation, or handicap; the silencing, intentional or unintentional, of certain segments of our population; and the unequal distribution of power within economic and social groups. These problems persist because they are systemic and politically determined, not only in the framework of our educational systems, but also in that of our cultures and their economies.

The study of implementations of radical pedagogy in computer-supported literacy classrooms can help us see that reform efforts, especially when they are computer-supported, must proceed simultaneously on multiple levels if we hope for success: in local arenas—in the minds of individual teachers and students and in the virtual spaces of computer-supported learning environments—and in broader political arenas where social and educational policy is made. Recent studies of the use of electronic discourse in classrooms (e.g., Faigley 1992; Regan 1993; Romano 1993) begin to show us the complexities that attend it there and the difficulties of bringing about reform even in classrooms led by critical pedagogues. For example, Faigley, Regan, and Romano, in separate studies, suggest that issues of gender, multiculturalism, and sexual orientation cannot be addressed so easily. Even when teachers are able to make students more sensitive to the problems of the marginalised—which Faigley, Regan, and Romano could not always do—translating this new awareness into venues for productive action remains one of the most pressing challenges of the decade.

Some scholars suggest that we cannot hope to understand the roles technology plays in our literacy classrooms until we look critically at the broader relationships between humans and machines in our culture. Mark Poster (1990) and others (cf. Gibson 1984; Zuboff 1988) have pointed out that we are technological and cultural subjects, created in part by the machines we ourselves have created and written in our discursive practices on these machines. We and our students are, in this sense, part technology ourselves—in the way we write, in the way we see the world, in the ways that we think. When this concept of being a cyborg starts to worry us—as it often does—we turn to feminist critics such as Cheris Kramarae (1988), Dale Spender (1995), Donna Haraway (1990), Anne Balsamo (1996), and Claudia Springer (1991) for radical revisions of technology and the roles it can play in our culture and our educational systems.

We have begun to incorporate some of this thinking in conducting our own research. One of the authors, for example, conducted a study (Selfe & Meyer 1991), in which she and her colleague looked at networked discourse on Megabyte University, a listserv aimed at English professionals who teach with computers. One of the aims of the Selfe and Meyer study was to assess the power relationships within the online conference and it used descriptive statistical data from the authors' own analysis of the postings along with an analysis of the patterns of individual participation in the conference. Although this study was not aimed at a literacy classroom *per se*, it revealed that men and those who are perceived as having higher status in the field often get more air-time on the nets than women do. The authors of this chapter were subsequently able to apply some of the same research perspectives to a study we conducted in our own classes at our separate universities (Hawisher & Selfe 1992). Although we were unable to document similar gender inequities in online classroom discourse, we did find an interesting conversational pattern in the role of teachers in online discussions. We had set aside these electronic spaces as discussion areas for students and had refrained from participating, hoping that the students would claim ownership of the e-space. What we found, however, was that Hawisher and Selfe dominated the conversation every bit as much as they might have in offline class discussions—they were hailed and referred to more than any other participants on the list. Rather than being spaces uninhabited by teachers—even when the teachers do not contribute to the discussion—the pattern of participation in some electronic conferences may demonstrate just how much teachers' ideas and attitudes hold sway with students.

More recently, one of the authors collaborated with Patricia Sullivan on a study of the online lives of academic women in composition studies (Hawisher & Sullivan, in press). Research questions concerned how thirty women academics perceive power circulating in electronic contexts and how they negotiate authority within these spaces. The research took place entirely online and focused on two sources of data: email interviews and transcripts from a listserv named 'women@waytoofast'— an electronic discussion group that the women themselves constructed for the study. While the online interviews begin to shed light on how these women in composition studies—graduate students and faculty—understand their participation in electronic discussion groups, the listserv transcripts reveal how the women carve out online identities for themselves. In looking at a particular group of women, whom the 'equalisation phenomenon' is said to benefit, and in tying the research to a study of online gender roles, the inquiry illustrates another approach to research open to literacy researchers. Our tentative conclusion from the study is that online environments are neither egalitarian spaces for women nor spaces devoid of power—some women prevail on the nets despite what feminists have recently regarded as rather hostile environments for women (Kramarae & Taylor 1993). When some of this thinking is applied to studies of other groups of women—adolescent women, for example—we might well find other patterns of participation. Indeed, in a study Nancy Kaplan and her daughter, Eva Farrell, conducted (1994), they found that a group of adolescent girls were very much able to gain influence for themselves in the electronic discussions they participated in for recreation. In looking at a group of adolescent girls outside the school setting, Kaplan and Farrell's study begins to illuminate some of the generational issues that literacy researchers have only begun to explore.

But other kinds of studies are also needed, those that look carefully at face-to-face and online environments in which literacy teachers and students are increasingly asked to participate. For example, we have found little research on the reciprocal relationship between electronic class discussions and teacher–student face-to-face contexts. Little research has attempted to connect the geographical and topological surveys of electronic spaces in classrooms with our culture's existing political, intellectual, and ideological terrain. We hope that this chapter can serve as an impetus for such research, which is vital if we are to understand the relationship between technology and our literate selves more fully. Although it is not possible to predict the degree or magnitude of the changes that will continue on the technological front, we need to make sure that the revolutionary claims made for the use of computers in education—claims that have little to do with how schools, students, and teachers really use computers—are informed by the kinds of research that literacy educators prize.

Notes

1 This chapter first appeared as an article in a special issue on literacy and technology of *The Australian Journal of Language and Literacy* (1996, vol. 19, no. 4).

2 Although we present first the research in word processing, then move on to electronic networks and then hypermedia, we do not mean this to suggest that the field is a fixed entity moving through time—in other words, that first we discovered word processing, electronic networks, and then hypermedia. After all, some hypertexts were available in education before electronic networks became popular. The literacy and technology field and those within it are always changing, with some beginning now what others experienced fifteen years ago. Our chronological organisation is intended as a framework within which we may tell the story of this field's research without sacrificing its complexity.

3 For a sampling of those few noteworthy school-based studies in which the cultural context plays a vital role in the research design, see Dickinson (1986), Herrmann (1987), and Greenleaf (1994).

References

Balsamo, A. 1996 *Technologies of the Gendered Body: Reading Cyborg Women*, Duke University Press, Durham and London

Bangert-Drowns, R.L. 1993 'The word processor as an instructional tool: a meta-analysis of word processing in writing instruction', *Review of Educational Research*, vol. 63, no. 1, pp. 69–93

Barker, T. and Kemp, F.O. 1990 'Network theory: a postmodern pedagogy for the writing classroom', *Computers and Community*, ed. C. Handa, Boynton/Cook, Portsmouth, NH, pp. 1–27

Bridwell, L., Sirc, G. and Brooke, R. 1985 'Revising and computing: case studies of student writers', *The Acquisition of Written Language*, ed. S.W. Freedman, Ablex, Norwood, NJ, pp. 160–71

Collier, R.M. 1983 'The word processor and revision strategies', *College Composition and Communication*, vol. 35, pp. 149–55

Dickinson, D.K. 1986 'Cooperation, collaboration, and a computer: integrating a computer into a first-second grade writing program', *Research in the Teaching of English*, vol. 20, pp. 141–59

Dubrovsky, V.J., Kiesler, S., and Sethna, B.N. 1991 'The equalization phenomenon: status effects in computer-mediated and face-to-face decision-making groups', *Human-Computer Interaction*, vol. 6, pp. 119–46

Eldred, J.C. and Hawisher, G.E. 1995 'Researching electronic networks', *Written Communication*, vol. 12, pp. 330–59

Faigley, L. 1992 *Fragments of Rationality: Postmodernity and the Subject of Composition*, University of Pittsburgh, Pittsburgh

Feenberg, A. 1991 *Critical Theory of Technology*, Oxford University Press, New York

Ferrara, K., Brunner, H., and Whittemore, G. 1991 'Interactive written discourse as an emergent register', *Written Communication*, vol. 8, no. 1, pp. 8–34

Freire, P. 1990 *Pedagogy of the Oppressed*, trans. M. Bergman Ramos, The Continuum Publishing Company, New York

Gibson, W. 1984 *Neuromancer*, Ace Books, New York

Greenleaf, C. 1994 'Technological indeterminacy: the role of classroom writing practices and pedagogy in shaping student use of the computer', *Written Communication*, vol. 11, pp. 85–130

Haraway, D. 1990 'A manifesto for cyborgs: science, technology, and socialist feminism', *Feminism/postmodernism*, ed. L.J. Nicholson, Routledge, Chapman & Hall, London, pp. 190–233

Hartman, K., Neuwirth, C., Kiesler, S., Sproull, L., Cochran, C., Palmquist, M. and Zubrow, D. 1991 'Patterns of social interaction and learning to write', *Written Communication*, vol. 8, pp. 57–78

Hawisher, G.E. 1988 'Research update: writing and word processing', *Computers and Composition*, vol. 5, pp. 7–27

——1992 'Electronic meetings of the minds: research, electronic conferences, and composition studies', *Re-Imagining Computers and Composition: Research and Teaching in the Virtual Age*, eds G.E. Hawisher and P. LeBlanc, Boynton/Cook, Portsmouth, NH, pp. 81–101

Hawisher, G.E. and Selfe, C.L. 1992 'Voices in college classrooms: the dynamics of electronic discussion', *The Quarterly of the National Writing Project & the Center for the Study of Writing and Literacy*, vol. 14, Summer, pp. 24–8, 32

Hawisher, G.E. and Sullivan, P.A. (in press) 'Women on the networks: searching for e-spaces of their own', *In Other Words: Feminism and Composition*, eds S. Jarratt and L. Worsham, Modern Language Association, New York

Herrmann, A. 1987 'An ethnographic study of a high school writing class using computers: marginal, technically proficient and productive learners', *Writing at Century's End: Essays on Computer-Assisted Composition*, ed. L. Gerrard, Random House, New York, pp. 79–91

hooks, b. 1989 *Talking Back: Thinking Feminist, Thinking Black,* South End Press, Boston, MA

Jones, S.G. 1995 *Cybersociety: Computer-Mediated Communication and Community*, Sage, London

Joyce, M. 1988 'Siren shapes: exploratory and constructive hypertexts', *Academic Computing*, pp. 10–14, 37–42

Kaplan, N. and Farrell, E. 1994 'Weavers of webs: a portrait of young women on the net', *Arachnet Electronic Journal of Virtual Culture*, vol. 2, no. 3

Kaplan, N. and Moulthrop, S. 1991 'Something to imagine: literature, composition, and interactive fiction', *Computers and Composition*, vol. 9, pp. 7–23

Kramarae, C. 1988 ed. *Technology and Women's Voices: Keeping in Touch,* Routledge & Kegan Paul, New York

Kramarae, C. and Taylor, H.J. 1993 'Women and men on electronic networks: a conversation or a monologue?', *Women, Information Technology, and Scholarship*, eds J.H. Taylor, C. Kramarae and M. Ebben, University of Illinois Center for Advanced Study, Urbana, IL, pp. 52–61

Langston, M.D. and Batson, T.W. 1990 'The social shifts invited by working collaboratively on computer networks: the ENFI project', *Computers and Community*, ed. C. Handa, Boynton/Cook, Portsmouth, NH, pp. 160–84

Lea, M. 1992 ed. *Contexts of Computer-mediated Communication*, Harvester/Wheatsheaf, New York

Luke, C. and Gore, J. 1992 *Feminisms and Critical Pedagogy*, Routledge, New York

Mason, R. and Kaye, R. 1989 eds *Mindweave: Communications, Computers and Distance Education*, Praeger, New York

Poster, M. 1990 *The Mode of Information: Poststructuralism and Social Context*, University of Chicago Press, Chicago, IL

Regan, A. 1993 ' "Type normal like the rest of us": writing, power, and homophobia in the networked composition classroom', *Computers and Composition*, vol. 10, no. 4, pp. 11–24

Romano, S. 1993 'The egalitarianism narrative: Whose story? Which yardstick?', *Computers and Composition*, vol. 10, pp. 5–28

Selfe, C.L. and Meyer, P.R. 1991 'Testing claims for on-line conferences', *Written Communication*, vol. 8, no. 2, pp. 163–92

Shor, I. 1987 *Critical Teaching and Everyday Life*, University of Chicago Press, Chicago

Spender, D. 1995 *Nattering on the Net: Women, Power, and Cyberspace*, Spinifex, North Melbourne, Victoria

Spiro, R.J. and Jehng, J. 1990 'Cognitive flexibility theory and hypertext: theory and technology for the nonlinear and multidimensional traversal of complex subject matter', *Cognition, Education, and Multimedia: Exploring Ideas in High Technology*, eds D. Nix and R. Spiro, Lawrence Erlbaum, Hillsdale, NJ

Springer, C. 1991 'The pleasure of the interface', *Screen*, vol. 32, no. 2, pp. 303–23

Sproull, L. and Kiesler, S. 1991 *Connections: New Ways of Working in the Networked Organization*, MIT Press, Cambridge, MA

Zuboff, S. 1988 *In the Age of the Smart Machine: The Future of Work and Power*, Basic Books, New York, NY

2

The wired world of second-language education

MICHELE KNOBEL, COLIN LANKSHEAR, EILEEN HONAN AND JANE CRAWFORD

Introduction

Over the past ten to fifteen years many claims have been made about the enormous potential of new electronic technologies for enhancing second-language education in diverse ways and on a range of levels. What may now be seen as 'first generation' claims championed basic skill-and-drill computer software, spelling and grammar checks, thesauruses, and the like, for their capacity to improve fluency and accuracy in target languages. The potential of simulations software for promoting talk in the target language 'around the computer' was also much vaunted. More recently, a 'second generation' of claims has emerged, focusing on innovative possibilities for using communications and information technologies (CITs) to promote confidence and fluency in target languages, and to offer access to rich stores of resources and ideas relevant to language learning and language education.

No longer regarded as merely a quirky or faddish 'add-on' to second-language education, CITs are now becoming an organic part of everyday classroom life for many second-language teachers and learners. CITs encompass information technologies (ITs) and computer-mediated communications technologies (CMCs). By ITs we mean electronic hardware and software used to produce, distribute, access, and exchange information goods and services. From a language-education standpoint, using ITs covers such things as accessing relevant databases, using professional development CD-ROMs, and accessing Internet resources such as Web sites, file archives, electronic journals, and online foreign language newspapers and magazines. CMCs include electronic mail, interactive spaces on Web sites, news and discussion groups, MOOs and MUDs, and online conference facilities.

The situation in second-language education mirrors the larger educational scene so far as the hard and soft sell of electronic technologies for pedagogical purposes is concerned. Frankly, the claims made still outstrip the evidence (and the quality of the evidence) available to support them. The higher profile of electronic technologies generally, and of CMCs specifically, doubtless encourages educators keen to do lead-ing-edge work in relating technological and social innovations and changes to second-language education contexts in princi-pled and informed ways. At the same time, however, there is a danger that the use of CITs in second-language education will assume 'magic bullet' and 'cure all' status in the eyes of many language educators caught in the thrall of media hype (Green & Bigum 1996): with the result that whatever genuine potential CITs have for revolutionising second-language edu-cation may pass us by. Educators and learners alike face massive hype and pressure from commercial and political sources to 'technologise' teaching and learning. It is important that our research and scholarly literature does not become yet more hype and pressure 'in drag'. Current and future second-language educators must be encouraged to scrutinise the claims made about the ability of new technologies—indeed, any and all technologies—to enhance teaching and learning: including claims they make themselves, based on their own experiences of incorporating CITs into second-language work.

It is beyond the scope of this chapter to examine the potential value and use of anything like a full range of CITs for second-language education. Instead, the chapter will identify, categorise, and assess some typical claims made about the potential of asynchronous communications—and, especially, electronic mail (email)—to enhance second-language education. These claims cover uses of CMCs applied directly to teaching and learning target languages, as well as wider applications to second-language education which do not necessarily involve communication in the target language. Clear evidence of the rapidly growing acceptance and appropriation in second-language classrooms of CMCs in particular is apparent in the burgeoning literature concerned with the use of email in second-language education (Warschauer 1994, 1995a). It is this literature that provides the major backdrop to the discussion that follows.

Computer-learning networks and computer-mediated communications activities

Warschauer (1995a, p. 8) defines a computer network as 'a group of computers that are electronically linked together', whether 'by special cable, ordinary telephone lines, or by satellite'. Computer networks are either Local Area Networks (LANs) or Wide Area Networks (WANs). LANs comprise a number of computers joined up in one place, such as in a language lab, a well-stocked classroom or office, or across multiple classrooms or offices within the same organisational unit. WANs comprise two or more LANs connected to each other. At their most local, WANs can exist within a single organisation. At their widest, however, WANs are truly global (e.g., BITNET—a computer-mediated network involving hundreds of academic and research organisations in dozens of countries across the globe). Ultimately, vast numbers of LANs and WANs are connected together by the Internet, the global 'network of networks'.

Computer-*learning* networks are LANs or WANs which have been established or are used expressly for learning purposes. They may be more or less permanent and 'material', such as purpose-built LANs, or more or less ephemeral, as in the case of negotiated links for the duration of a course or semester, between learners and teachers in one place and those in another (or others). It is important to recognise that learning networks are much more than mere *infrastructures*: they are also *relationships*. What makes for a computer-learning network is both the existence of hardware and software wired together, and the 'coming together' of people in learning relationships *mediated* by the network as infrastructure.

Computer-learning networks permit different types of communication activities between participants. On the dimension of time, synchronous communications require participants to be online at the same time. Asynchronous communications, by contrast, do not. Participating in a MOO is synchronous. Email, however, is asynchronous. Email is basically a means of sending messages between computers asynchronously, on any scale: from posting messages to the next-door computer in a lab or classroom, to contacting computers on the other side of the world.

Within asynchronous communications a further distinction can be drawn between the kinds of communicative relationships involved. We may distinguish between direct person-to-person exchanges (whether one-to-one, one-to-some, or one-to-many) and list-mediated exchanges. In the former, participants post messages to personal email addresses they have obtained by one means or another (e.g., verbally, face-to-face; from an email discussion or mailing list, or a conference program; or, perhaps, by guesswork based on knowledge of institutional protocols). These participants may know each other well or, at the other extreme, may never have been in contact before. In list-mediated exchanges, participants subscribe to an email list, post messages to the list, and receive messages posted to the list via their respective 'mailboxes', with notification of messages showing up on their 'in box' or 'in screen/window'. (News groups are another facet of asynchronous communications, but are beyond our scope here.) Email mailing and discussion lists range in size and scope from international 'giants', like TESL-L, all the way to purpose-built class discussion lists created by a teacher (see below).

In a purpose-built classroom LAN we may find email being used for teacher-student/student-teacher communication, teacher-student dialogue journals, teacher-student writing conferencing, and student-student exchanges (see Warschauer 1995a). Variations include class mailing and discussion lists, class news groups, collective journals, pre- and post-discussion of classroom topics, collaborative writing activities, and so on. Activity aimed to enhance language learning can, of course, include interactions in both the target language and the first language, according to purposes and circumstances (e.g., at early stages feedback on work and explanations of grammatical rules might best be provided in the first language). At the other end of the spectrum from activities on a LAN operating in a single classroom, learners may engage in a range of cross-cultural and long-distance email exchanges with native speakers of the target language, as an integral facet of classroom-based language learning assisted by access to a WAN. These may include key pal exchanges (Cononelos & Oliva 1993; Warschauer 1995a), communication via international email student discussion lists (Warschauer 1995a), and participation in email team-teaching initiatives across regions and countries—such as those found in the International Education and Resource Network (I*EARN) (Cummins & Sayers 1995; Warschauer 1995a).

Looking beyond applications of CMCs in classroom practices, teachers themselves may use computer networks to access and discuss new ideas for second-language pedagogy via person-to-person interactions, or through participation in news and discussion groups. More generally, teachers may use a range of CITs to locate and transfer files containing information, to access articles in electronic journals, and to visit sites dedicated to language theory and pedagogy on the World Wide Web, in order to inform their classroom practice or to do practice-enhancing research. Of course, it is their use of asynchronous communications that is of most direct relevance here, so far as informing their practice by recourse to CITs is concerned.

The potential of asynchronous communications: a classification of common claims

For the purposes of our inquiry we have grouped, under three broad headings, a number of claims frequently made about integrating email into second-language education. These are:

1. *Asynchronous communications activities enhance target language mastery in preferred or mandated approaches to second-language learning*

Somewhat against the swing of moves during the past decade to reassert 'basics' in many areas of curricular learning, with frequent pleas to return to drill-and-skill approaches in such areas as numeracy and early literacy instruction, second-language learning has witnessed a growing trend toward so-called 'communicative competence' and 'authentic communication' paradigms. In Australia, for example, the national curriculum profile for LOTE (Languages Other Than English) explicitly endorses the communicative competence paradigm. The conceptual basis of *Languages other than English: A Curriculum Profile for Australian Schools* (Curriculum Corporation 1994), framed to guide syllabus and curriculum development in the various Australian states and territories, is derived directly and explicitly from the communicative approach. The goal of LOTE is that school-based instruction should develop the ability to convey meaning in a variety of contexts for a variety of purposes with a variety of interlocutors in their other language. The statement asserts further that fundamental to the concept of communicative language use is the recognition that effective communication involves a dynamic interaction between the context, the language user and the interlocutors. Within this conception, the need to learn explicit knowledge and skills about the structure of the language is subsumed under the expectation that teachers will emphasise

25

communicative competence. Interestingly, so far as the application of new electronic technologies to second-language learning is concerned, this emphasis is at least in part a reaction to trends in CALL (Computer Assisted Language Learning) which often reduced computer-assisted learning to a tool for drilling and skilling students in the grammar and syntax of their target language.

A number of proponents of computer-learning networks describe using asynchronic communications, particularly email and news groups, to realise more authentic communication in the classroom. Cononelos and Oliva (1993), for example, claim that CMCs have a distinctive part to play in promoting language learning whereby students become capable of producing, transmitting, and receiving *authentic meanings and content* in the second language, via processes which focus on content produced and conveyed through the target language, rather than prioritising instruction in the *structure* of the language. They endorse a conception of language as being much more a *facility* to be used by people in meeting authentic social purposes and engaging in real-life practices than an all-important *form or structural 'essence'*. According to this conception, pursuing communicative competence for authentic language purposes and uses requires, among other things, meeting four key conditions: first, building into the learning the eventual uses learners will make of the target language; second, considering use as well as usage; third, exposing learners to meaningful language in use; fourth, emphasising the needs and interests of learners.

This is where Cononelos and Oliva (1993), among many others, see computer-learning networks coming into their own. They claim that 'in contrast to language software programs, computer networks can be used to increase authentic communication in the language classroom and to foster content-based and learner-centred education' (p. 528).

2. *Asynchronous communications activities actualise generic learning values and pedagogical principles seen as particularly important in second-language learning*

Many proponents of computer-learning networks advocate using CMCs to enhance student autonomy and control over the language learning process (Cononelos & Oliva 1993; Armstrong & Yetter-Vassot 1994; Hoffman 1994; Warschauer 1995a). In 'Computer Learning Networks and Student Empowerment', Warschauer, Turbee and Roberts (1994) review literature pertaining to the potential of email and other networked computer communications activities to enhance student empowerment, by promoting learner autonomy and greater equality among students in the learning process.

Among the typical generic claims advanced here for the potential of asynchronous communications activities we find the view that 'computers joined in a network can be a means of liberation, particularly for those students who are often marginalised' (Faigley 1990, p. 291). We are told, moreover, that 'networks create an unusual opportunity to shift away from the traditional because they create entirely new pedagogic dynamics' (Batson 1988, p. 32), and that 'the electronic mail system . . . permits a new type of relationship between students and teachers' (Barson, Frommer & Schwartz 1993, p. 576).

There are more specific and empirically testable claims about outcomes, processes, and second-language learning principles. With respect to outcomes, there are numerous claims that asynchronous communications activities enhance student autonomy in the second-language learning process. Drawing on the review of literature undertaken by Warschauer, Turbee, and Roberts (1994), we have distilled four main claims about student empowerment outcomes believed to accrue from second-language learners engaging in networked communications. It is claimed that learners initiate more discussion with teachers and peers and exert greater control over this discussion. Moreover, learners' expression of ideas allegedly becomes more natural and communicative, rather than aiming merely to please the teacher or meet required tasks. Higher levels of student-centred discussion are claimed to result. Finally, networked activities are said to generate greater student control over course content.

In addition, enhanced *equality* is alleged to result from

asynchronous communications activities. Specifically, it is claimed that higher levels/rates of communicative participation are found among student groups that are often excluded or marginalised in conventional classroom interchange: for example, shy students, female students, reticent students and speech-impaired students (Warschauer, Turbee & Roberts 1994).

Beyond claims about outcomes, various specific claims have been made about *processes* inherent in asynchronous communications activities thought to enhance student autonomy in second-language learning. Here it is claimed that asynchronous communication frees students from constraints of time and direct access when they initiate communicative exchanges. They can make 'communicative contact' any time they have access to email, not only in face-to-face situations. Networks are said to free students from the constraint of teacher voice in matters of topics to raise, sequences to follow, and the like, so that students have more opportunities to suggest topics, control sequences, and manage 'turns'. The very nature of networked communication activities, it is claimed, tends to frame the teacher more as a facilitator than as a director. Moreover, it is assumed that networks instigate a 'logic' which allows groups to produce knowledge through collaboration. Finally, so far as empowerment processes are concerned, the potential to engage via email in long distance/global communications, experienced as *authentic,* is believed to energise and commit learners, translating into self-directed and efficacious language learning via communication (Cononelos & Oliva 1993; Warschauer, Turbee & Roberts 1994).

Likewise, of the claims made about processes thought to enhance equality among learners, four claims in particular stand out. First, being neither face-to-face nor immediate, asynchronous networked communications reduce 'static social context clues', such as gender, disability and perceived status, which in more conventional settings inhibit the bearers of these 'clues' from participation. Next, 'dynamic social context clues' which may impede participation, such as hesitation, body language, gestures—one's own, or others'—are similarly reduced. Third, asynchronous activities provide 'space' and anonymity for crafting exchanges and responses, thereby reducing traditional classroom dynamics that tend to favour the quick, the 'pushy', and the confident. Fourth, advocates of networked communications activities claim that asynchronous activities also afford time for considering and framing responses and initiating exchanges, so that those who are tentative have time to *compose*, and to *be composed* when communicating (Warschauer, Turbee & Roberts 1994, pp. 5–6).

We also find claims that network-based communications actualise important learning principles. Cononelos and Oliva identify five principles of content-based and learner-centred language learning, and claim that each of these principles (identified by italics) is at work in network-based communication. Their case is made with particular reference to activities involving Usenet (NEWS). According to Cononelos and Oliva (1993):

> . . . by guaranteeing opportunities for authentic communication with native speakers, the use of NEWS *incorporates the eventual uses the learner will make of the target language* . . . allows *a focus on use as well as usage* . . . and provides the necessary conditions for *meaningful language in use* . . . To the extent that students introduce and discuss topics of their own choosing, NEWS gives them the opportunity to *build on previous learning experiences* . . . and to *pursue their own interests* . . . thus introducing a learner centred element into the course. (pp. 529–30; our italics)

3. *Asynchronous communication activities assist the acquisition of sophisticated learning skills and can help second-language educators enhance their classroom practice and extend their knowledge of language learning theory*

Warschauer, Turbee and Roberts (1994) suggest that the inherent nature of online asynchronous communications enhances the development of a range of sophisticated learning skills. They advance three tentative claims, recognising the lack of compelling empirical evidence to date. First, they suggest that getting students to *write* encourages them to *think* and, hence, to *develop ideas*. This shifts students' conceptions of learning away from notions of reproducing teacher (or other authoritative) words and, instead, toward producing their own ideas. Second, where wide-area computer networks are *global*, the very act of participating in them inevitably promotes familiarity and ease with 'the global scale'. Third, since computer networks are grounded in 'the mode of information' (Poster 1990), participants are inevitably involved in handling information.

Communications and information technologies are rapidly usurping face-to-face courses and conventional print resources as media for accessing ideas, examples, and materials believed to be valuable for language education, research, and professional development. Practising teachers and 'student teachers' are being urged to exploit Internet sites and lists on the grounds that these contribute greatly to improving teaching practices and professional knowledge bases. How far these trends will be vindicated remains to be seen.

Assessing the case for asynchronous communication activities

Any or all of the claims sampled above may be true. In most cases, however, they are not self-evident. Certainly, they are empirical claims and must be checked out against experience. Furthermore, their verification in particular cases may have a lot to do with local circumstances (e.g., resourcing, teachers' knowledge and experience). Given the failed promises made about earlier technological 'fixes' for challenges presented by classroom learning, we should not take these claims on face value. What, then, is the evidence? And how does it fall?

We will draw on evidence from two sources in an attempt to indicate the current state of the art. First, we will draw on evidence reported in a selection of second-language education studies. We will then report some preliminary findings from a local study of the claims identified above, in the light of our own evaluation of the research literature. We believe that the most reasonable interpretation of the empirical evidence we have sampled so far is that 'the jury is still out'. The evidence is mixed, and probably raises as many questions as it suggests answers.

Some evidence from the literature

We present this evidence in two parts: first, we refer to some relevant research studies reported in scholarly journals; second, we report some projects from the field. These have been drawn from Warschauer's (1995b) compilation, *Virtual Connections: On-line Activities and Projects for Networking Language Teachers*, augmented where possible by our own email conversations with the project authors and by information from the World Wide Web.

1. Evidence from research reports

The research literature on the use of asynchronous communications in second-language learning is not extensive. We have surveyed eight studies from a broad range of journals and books in the second-language field (Barson 1991; Soh & Soon 1991; Mathieson 1992; Cononelos & Oliva 1993; Armstrong & Yetter-Vassot 1994; Chun 1994; Hoffman 1994; Markee 1994). Most of these studies are either direct sources of the claims under investigation here, or else are referred to as bases for such claims.

Beginning with evidence bearing on empowerment outcomes in terms of enhanced student autonomy, the unfortunate fact is that most reporting of evidence alleged to support claims that asynchronous communications enable students to make more 'natural' and communicative expression of ideas and purposes in their target languages is incidental, impressionistic and anecdotal. Furthermore, most classes involved in the studies are small—for example, the class study reported by

31

Cononelos and Oliva (1993) contained only six students. It is, therefore, impossible to generalise on the basis of such numbers.

In addition, some of the studies surveyed have not accounted adequately for variables outside the email network. For example, Hoffman (1994) appears to decontextualise his experiences of working with English as a foreign language (EFL) students. He characterises email as a warm, personal network without considering how other factors, such as his own pedagogical approach and classroom atmosphere or learners' familiarity with new technologies, may have influenced his students' perceptions. As we have found in an Australian study (Crawford & Knobel 1996), many learners—including students who are new to CMCs—find email an impersonal, detached, cold, functional medium. Such simple discrepancies should make us wary of attributing essences and 'essential effects' to asynchronous communications. In Hoffman's case, the effects he attributes to email appear much more likely to derive from his pedagogical approach.

Despite conceding that the small numbers in their study prevent generalisation to larger populations, Cononelos and Oliva (1993) nonetheless proceed in effect to do so. They draw on other reported descriptions of email language-learning outcomes to flesh out their claims, without indicating the reliability of these other studies, or even the kinds of study populations and designs employed. Indeed, none of the authors of the studies we reviewed has questioned whether the alleged empowerment and increased student-centred discussion attributed to email applications might in fact result from small class sizes and/or from the educators' teaching styles (e.g., student-centred, interpersonal, and so on).

With respect to alleged equality outcomes, Chun's (1994) detailed analysis of student participation in online class discussions seems to counter the claims that computer networking (including email applications) 'allows more equal participation by those who are often excluded or discriminated against, including women, minorities, disabled, shy students, students with unusual learning styles, and students who are apprehensive about writing' (Warschauer, Turbee & Roberts 1994, p. 5). Chun's data indicate that females in the group generally wrote less than the males (i.e., f=386 messages, m=519 messages), although females wrote more complex sentences (189) than did males (156). Moreover, while Chun *did* find that several of the more quiet and/or shy students participated more in the online class discussions, these students tended to be male, while some of the less extroverted female students tended to make fewer contributions to discussions than others in the group. Although her study focused on synchronous computer-mediated communication, and her research population was small, Chun's findings nonetheless pose a challenge to taken-as-given claims associating CMCs with more equitable student participation. Chun's study suggests that such claims need further empirical tests.

The picture is barely any rosier when it comes to evidence supporting claims that network-based communications activities are conducive to *processes* which enhance student empowerment. Beginning with processes thought to promote autonomy, we found very little empirical evidence of the quality of interactions in the articles we have surveyed. Barson (1991) makes a touch-and-run reference to email as an ideal medium for realising Krashen's[1] notions of $i+1$, but does not support this claim with empirical research data. Where student email texts are included in study data they tend to be discussed anecdotally, rather than in terms of applying a theoretical framework for analysing and interpreting what was happening, or for testing in systematic ways hunches about what was happening.

Once again, Chun's study is probably the most carefully framed study on offer here, although its concern with synchronous communication invites caution in applying it to claims about the efficacy of asynchronous communications in second-language learning. Chun's research purpose was to analyse the range of discourses generated by fifteen students (who were learning German as a foreign language) participating in an online classroom discussion. Focusing on turn-taking, Chun found that students initiated and expanded upon more topics than the teacher did. Unfortunately, Chun's examples of interactions suggest that most of these exchanges were light conversations and ends in themselves, as opposed to exercises in autonomous learning based upon sophisticated text production and exchange. Not only is it difficult to see how such experiences reflect learner autonomy in any significant sense, it appears also that notions of autonomy vary from study to study. Tighter conceptual work is required if 'autonomy' claims are to do significant work in second-language learning research and practice.

Claims that egalitarian processes are enhanced by asynchronous communications fare similarly. Equality claims tend to focus on physical attributes as markers of marginalisation, rather than on learning styles, or first and second-language competence levels. Specific levels of individual students' literacy competence are not explicitly reported in the studies we surveyed, apart from references to levels of schooling. Hence, students' levels of language knowledge and proficiency are largely homogenised, thereby discounting what may in fact be significant differences affecting claims made about email and equality.

For example, Chun (1994) found that the most 'target-language literate' student in her class participated least in class online discussions. Chun did not comment further on this finding, and it was not mentioned in Warschauer, Turbee and Roberts' (1994) summary of Chun's findings. Once again, Chun's findings challenge conventional claims, inviting further investigation.

Evidence from research reports is likewise thin when it comes to the enhancement of sophisticated learning skills via network communications activities. Although several studies mention the *possibilities* for email to enhance thinking skills, little empirical evidence is offered in support. Soh and Soon (1991) report an increase in students' willingness to use critical thinking skills in a cross-cultural exchange; however, their collaborative project was organised around complementary units of work, and email applications were supplemented by published texts, fax machines, telephones and word processing programs. This suggests that claims about email and enhanced thinking skills may need to be re-examined in light of what else is happening in class over a period of time.

Most articles surveyed comment on students' enhanced computer skills (e.g., keyboarding is addressed by Warschauer, Turbee & Roberts 1994; computer and Internet use by Warschauer 1995a; technological literacy by Armstrong & Yetter-Vassot 1994; grasp of technology by Soh & Soon 1991), but only in quite general and instrumental terms, *and only in relation to the immediate context*. Cononelos and Oliva (1993, p. 531) make a useful point when they ask: 'Do students continue to use the network to maintain contact with target-language speakers after classes have ended?' To substantiate claims that learning skills are relevant to contemporary life, replicable and more longitudinal studies are needed.

Our survey of typical studies reported in the area appear to draw on informally surveyed—even *surmised*—student attitudes toward using email applications and their willingness to use their target language in email exchanges, rather than on carefully designed empirical studies of thinking processes and/or skill development. In our assessment, claims that sending email messages enhances students' thinking and stimulates ideas remain largely speculative. Soh and Soon (1991, p. 5) claim that 'computers and communication are closely inter-related, and . . . a marriage of the two can allow students to organise and process their knowledge at the touch of a keyboard button'. Such claims, however, are potentially mis-leading for second-language educators. Students in Soh and Soon's classes were, of course, doing much more than merely 'touching keyboard buttons', or 'operating computers'. They were engaging in a wide range of online and offline language learning and cultural awareness activities, hence their learning skills cannot be attributed to computers and communi-cation alone. This, and other examples (e.g., Hoffman 1994, Cononelos & Oliva 1993) suggest that more rigorous research into email applications and thinking skills is needed to support the claims in question.

2. Projects from the field

Four projects described in Warschauer (1995b) were examined in the light of typical claims about the efficacy of CMCs in second-language education.

Project A: Individual electronic mail with native speakers, by Cindy Kendall

In this activity, US secondary students learning Spanish used email to correspond with native speakers of Spanish about a set list of topics, including US culture and the culture of the Spanish speaker, the school system, and problems confronting youth (Kendall 1995, pp. 109–15). The project aim was to familiarise students 'with electronic mail and the Internet as well as providing real-life interaction with Spanish speakers' (p. 109). In an email follow-up, Kendall said: 'Of course I was only looking for something neat for the kids to do with the Internet and e-mail at the time' (Kendall 1996, in personal communication).

To help evaluate the activity, students were asked eighteen questions under five headings: General Information, Culture, School System, Problems Confronting Youth, and Conclusion. Four questions referred specifically to language learning: What are the appropriate phrases for greeting and leave-taking in a letter?; What information does the first paragraph of your letter contain?; What are the differences between letters sent electronically and through regular mail?; Did you encounter slang? Write some examples and [state] what they mean (Kendall 1995).

Kendall offers a range of evaluative comments, particularly on technological aspects of the project such as access to computers, time allocated to solving technological problems, and use of a word processing program. While specific data are not formally reported, general evaluative comments are. For example:

> On the negative side, the limitation of having only two computers at school meant students could not access computers outside of class. So an agreement was reached that students

could work at the computer during class, still being responsible for the material covered during the time they worked on
the computer . . . Using Word Perfect, they wrote their letters
in advance and uploaded them in class. (Kendall 1995, p. 110)

On the positive side:

> . . . students who previously had little interest in computers,
> now enjoyed working at one . . . They wrote drafts, edited,
> proofed, and re-wrote, before sending their letter off to their
> native speaker. They wanted their letter to be understood.
> They also wanted to understand the native speakers' letters.
> They actually wanted to read Spanish! This was an exciting
> moment for me as a teacher, because naturally the volunteers
> wrote at a higher level than my students, and my students
> enjoyed the challenge of understanding the personal responses
> they received. (Kendall 1995, p. 110)

While 'the beginning ten minutes of each class day was
[designed to be] spent in training and discussion of the Internet
and electronic mail . . . on some days, the initial ten minutes
of discussion turned into twenty minutes'. Kendall comments:
'Was this time well spent? Definitely. Did it take away from
the subject matter usually covered in class? Yes, I did not cover
the amount of material I normally would. Would I do this
project again? Yes' (Kendall 1995, pp. 109–110).

At a non-formal level the project deals with some of the claims
surveyed above. Kendall affirms that the students were 'very
excited' about the project, and that they 'definitely enjoyed the
insight they gained into the Spanish-speaking world' (Kendall
1995, pp. 109, 110). On the other hand, her only specific
claim about language learning itself was that 'the writing level
of the students increased exponentially with every letter'
(p. 110), but no formal data were presented to support this.

Project B: Mirandonos: looking at us—email/snail-mail project, by Marilyn Hannan

A second project involving email interchanges with native
speakers of Spanish is reported by Hannan (1995). Part of 'a
multi-national mail exchange project between classes from all

over the world' (p. 199), this project involved email and (by conventional post) artefact exchanges between secondary students, native speakers and language learners. The project is described as having presented 'a wonderful incentive to learn Spanish' (p. 200), although no formal data are reported. In personal email communication which we initiated to obtain more details, Hannan described the project aims as being: 'to introduce students to other cultures'; 'to realise that people really do write and communicate in Spanish'; 'to improve their ability to communicate in Spanish'; 'to get them to be excited about Spanish'; 'to show them how SMALL the world is today and that technology can help bring us together'; and 'to introduce them to the use of computers and the Internet'. Although formal data are not available to indicate how far these aims were achieved, we were informed that 'language learning was improved by the students being more careful that they spelled and said things correctly', and students 'looked up words they didn't know'.

Project C: L'histoire, mon histoire: comparing family histories via email, by Rick Kern

This project, still running, involves exchanges of email and (by conventional post) artefacts between a class of secondary students in France (i.e., native speakers of French) and a group of US university students learning French (Kern 1995). The students in France had published a book which aimed to 'approach the study of history from a personal perspective, to illuminate the diversity of the students' cultural and historical backgrounds and to give voice to a traditionally disenfranchised class of young people' (p. 132). Kern's goal was to set up an exchange of information between his university students and the secondary students in France to investigate similarities and differences between their family experiences of immigration and acculturation. Exchanges were organised 'by mode of expression (description, narration, and argumentation)' (p. 132).

Since this project was still in progress at the time of

publication, its description and evaluation are tentative and cast largely in terms of what Kern anticipated. Specific reference was made to student enthusiasm: 'student response has been overwhelmingly favorable'; 'students have expressed great satisfaction'; 'students have been pleasantly surprised'. Kern commented also on the link between second-language learning and cross-cultural learning: 'While ostensibly an exercise in communicative language use, this e-mail exchange has been at least as significant in enhancing students' cultural and historical awareness as well as their overall motivation in learning French' (p. 132).

In email correspondence which we initiated to obtain further information, Kern confirmed his belief that communicative-language use and cross-cultural learning 'are both essential and in a way inseparable'. With respect to language use, the kind of email interchanges employed in Kern's project give second-language learners the chance 'to use the language with native speakers who are interested in what they are saying', and 'to ask "real" questions and to get more or less immediate feedback'. Early experiences in the project suggest that students 'are highly motivated because the message is addressed to them'; 'students pick up words and expressions from their correspondents and often incorporate them into their subsequent messages'; 'it makes language learning exciting not only for students but also for teachers (it includes them in the learning process and insures that every semester will offer something new)'.

In many ways, the evidence available from the three projects described so far help to bulk out in more specific and testable ways the content of some of the claims identified in earlier sections. It is clear, however, that 'hard data' remain in relatively short supply at the level of second-language teachers researching their own practice (or having their practice researched for them). This is hardly surprising, given the constant pressures many second-language teachers confront, particularly when trying to integrate new technologies with pedagogy in under-resourced contexts. At the same time, however, it is important that we endeavour to obtain and report plausible, empirical data as far as possible, in the interests of monitoring our own practice and seeking to enhance the practice of colleagues.

The final project reported in this section goes some way toward these ends, as—we hope—will our preliminary account of a special research study in the next section. Note, however, that both studies deal more directly with claims about student interest and motivation, technical considerations, and administrative considerations, than with the efficacy of asynchronous communications in learning a second language.

Project D: The HUT projects, by Ruth Vilmi

Vilmi's work is among the most systematic attempts to describe email second-language activities and report their evaluations. Her approach to the use of CMCs is evident in a signature theme accompanying her email messages: 'Tell me and I'll forget, Teach me and I'll remember, Involve me and I'll learn'.

Vilmi (1993, 1994) has established several Web sites for providing information about her work. The sites contain papers about the projects, evaluations of the projects by participants including teachers and students, and links to other sites that promote CMC use in second-language learning. Project evaluations deal most specifically with technological and administrative issues such as mailing lists, managing the mail, selecting the topics, email experience and technical problems (Vilmi 1993). In a paper published on the Web, Vilmi outlines her aims for the collective projects. She wants her students to have:

> . . . meaningful intercultural and ethnocultural communication. This should provide an environment which will inspire the students to enjoy writing and to give of their best, as well as fostering global awareness . . . [The] students should learn about different styles and realise that the language used in e-mail is very different from that used in an academic paper. (Vilmi 1993)

The International Environment Activity used a specific task to set up dialogue among students at the Chinese University of Hong Kong, Finnish university students learning English, and US university students. Task aims were: 'to find a solution to a real-world environmental problem; to present the solution orally, both to peers and outside visitors; to publish the final documents on the WWW; to enjoy cross-cultural communication with students from other countries through team work; and to practice writing in English via email' (Vilmi 1995, p. 205).

The evaluation of this project specifies technical and administrative difficulties, whilst mentioning that 'all the students and teachers found this team activity rewarding but extremely demanding' (p. 207). Student evaluations likewise focused on technical and administrative difficulties; notably, the age of students, and their degree of experience with email. In an interesting highlight, all three sets of student evaluations reported on the Web emphasise the massive amount of work involved in the activity and the fact that this work was not reflected in the credit points allocated to the subject. Their appraisals of global learning were somewhat less than enthusiastic. As one student laments:

> . . . it is unbelievably time-consuming to put together a decent report describing a totally new problem field for the team— especially when the other half of the team speaks another language, lives on the other side of the world, comes from another culture and has another way of approaching and handling a problem situation. (Vilmi 1994)

Another student says: 'It has to be taken into consideration that team work between different cultures takes much more time and discretion than working with people from one culture' (Vilmi 1994).

Two Hong Kong teachers involved in the HUT projects have assembled an informative evaluation called 'International Email Projects in ESL Curriculum—What Works, What Doesn't?' They conclude, first, that email by itself, though powerful as a means of communication, does not necessarily improve writing skills. Second, they conclude that email must be built into a carefully designed, well-structured, task-based curriculum. Finally, they maintain that improvement in language skills and thinking skills are yet to be proved (Vilmi 1994).

A local study: Email in LOTE teacher education

While we are sympathetic to the informed use of asynchronous communications in second-language classrooms, we certainly do not accept at face value claims about their benefits, and we are less than convinced by available reports of empirical evidence. At the same time, if critique is to be positive and constructive, it is necessary to draw on extant studies as a basis for further exploration. With this in mind, in 1996 a focused study was made with the cooperation of a LOTE class enrolled in a graduate diploma teacher education program in an Australian university Faculty of Education (Crawford & Knobel 1996).

Twenty-eight students from a class of thirty-two participated in the study. All students had completed at least one degree, most in a second language. As prospective second-language teachers, these students were expected to be fluent, or to become fluent in their target language, which in this case ranged over European and Asian languages: nine of the twenty-eight students were from non-English speaking backgrounds. The class met once a week for three hours to develop a repertoire of pedagogical approaches to LOTE teaching. They were required to present seminars to the class on ways of teaching aspects of their target language, and to reflect on their peers' seminars and the set readings for the week by making weekly journal entries which they submitted to the lecturer via email on a LAN.

At the beginning of the semester class members were shown how to log-on to the university computers, access their email account, build mailing lists, and send and read email messages. They were also strongly encouraged to use email for discussion and for learning purposes other than their weekly logs entries.

The lecturer had decided to use email because she thought it would greatly benefit individual students' learning purposes, experiences and needs, and offer an ideal medium for reflecting critically on the interface between language-learning theory and classroom practice. The researchers were especially interested in four questions.

The first concerned the extent to which the students would use class-based email networks to explore relevant ideas and concepts, and among whom the interactions would occur. Second, the researchers wanted to discover the relationship, if any, between the frequency and distribution of the students' individual email communications and the kinds of communication each individual engaged in during face-to-face class discussions. The third question asked whether students believed that participating in email networks would increase opportunities for learning, and for participating in class discussions—whether face-to-face, electronic, or otherwise. The final question concerned students' purposes for using email.

The fact that one third of the participants had English as their second language gave at least some indication of how to compare second-language students' willingness to use their target language (i.e., English) in email with their reaction to face-to-face, immediate response settings. In addition, of course, it would not be unreasonable to expect that LOTE teacher-education students would at least occasionally use email to communicate ideas in their target language with peers who shared the same target language.

Over the fourteen weeks of the first semester, data about students' interactions with each other and their lecturer were collected by means of specially designed schedules, during in-class observation, and by archiving the email messages. These interactions were recorded and coded under five main headings concerned with the sources and probable purposes of each interaction. The five main categories were defined by sociocultural theories of interactions and language use (Halliday 1985), and comprised:

- interactions that referred to sources outside the immediate context;
- transactions of one kind or another involving explanations, reports, sharing information and/or knowledge;
- procedural interactions;
- questions and requests; and
- discourse management.

The twenty-eight students sent a total of 279 messages during the semester. Of these, 194 (69.5 per cent) comprised their mandatory weekly learning logs. The remaining 85 messages (30.5 per cent of the total) broke down into four main groups.

In group one, 31 messages were directly related to clarifying assessment requirements, and most were sent to the lecturer. Of these, 21 contained draft seminar outlines (5 went to the whole class); 3 contained questions or comments on seminar grades; and the rest concerned matters such as additional and wrongly attributed references, requests for special consideration, and responses to lecturer feedback.

In the second group, 17 messages concerned using email: 5 of these were test messages, 4 notified new email addresses (2 to the whole class), 7 dealt with problems with using email, and 1 offered hints for converting file attachments.

In group three, 28 messages dealt with administrative or procedural concerns: 6 were about practicum timetables, 3 about teaching portfolios, and the rest addressed sundry matters like professional development requirements, reports on practicum experiences, and so on.

In group four, the 9 remaining messages covered questions about LOTE teaching or the curriculum (5); resource information (1); and responses to the lecturer's 'welcome back' message after their mid-semester break (2). Only one message in the email data corpus was sent in a student's target language (with apologies for the romanised script enforced by the email software).

Plainly, the data are not good news for the claims made on

behalf of email. Contrary to claims that email networks enhance student autonomy, the great bulk of messages sent to the lecturer sought either to clarify or check procedures, or asked about assessment requirements for the subject (the learning log). In fact, compared with previous classes which did not use email networks, email appeared to increase student dependence on the lecturer. None of the students introduced topics for discussion on this network, despite being encouraged and shown how to do so.

Contrary to claims that email networks facilitate higher levels and quality of discussions online, only 2.5 per cent of messages sent by the students were directed to the entire class. Two likely contributing factors have been identified. One is the lecturer's own personal interest in the potential of email to assist with individualising instruction, although this was offset by her encouragement to use the LAN for purposes much wider than this. The second concerns difficulties accessing and operating email accounts on an overworked university network. Technical support was in scarce supply and students often found they had to 'go it alone' in more demanding uses such as sending and decoding attachments—although some constructive networks were gained by the students' collaborative efforts to master the medium.

With respect to enhancing equality, the data are sketchy. Female students seem to have used email slightly more frequently than the males, whereas male and female participation in whole class face-to-face discussions was more or less equal. On the other hand, students whose first language was not English responded more fully and more often to seminar content and set readings via email exchanges to the lecturer than they did during face-to-face tutorials. Hence, claims that email networks enhance the opportunities for *some* students to voice their opinions and share understandings are consistent with the study data.

Claims that using email networks to supplement classroom discussions can enhance learning skills are difficult to substantiate. The current data suggest that despite a paucity of inter-student discussion on the network, the weekly learning logs did provide a forum for students to engage with content, including theories of second-language learning and pedagogy and effective classroom practices. Data recording and analysis included a specific focus on the student interactions that contained references to language-learning theories (as a central component of their subject content). Some interesting patterns emerged. While most students referred to subject content in their weekly learning logs, only six appeared to *increase* their references to explicit content as the semester went on, whereas fourteen students showed little change, and seven actually *decreased* their references to language-learning theories during the last four weeks of the semester (during which time messages about procedural and administrative matters increased). This 'finding' begs the question of whether more frequent discussion of theory and pedagogical issues indicates sophisticated learning skills, although this does seem likely. Certainly, further investigation is merited here, and nothing in the study data helps substantiate the original claim that email enhances sophisticated learning skills.

In short, students tended to use email primarily for 'functional' purposes. Incidental evidence (such as log entries) indicates strongly that only three or four of the students used email for any purposes besides meeting the assessment requirements of the unit. Limited access to email facilities undoubtedly accounts for at least some of this outcome, indicating that general claims about the efficacy of email are indeed risky—its benefits vary from case to case.

Present findings suggest strongly that the particular purposes to which email networks are put can significantly influence learning outcomes. For example, without the weekly learning logs, would students have reflected spontaneously on theory and pedagogy? If email discussions had become an assessment item (not that we are suggesting that it should), would this have made a difference to the interactional patterns we observed? If students were expected to send messages in at least two languages, or keep a log of target language interactions, would this have also changed interactional patterns? Although the findings are provisional, they will be used to inform future use of email in this particular subject, and the study cohort of students will be followed into their teaching jobs to see whether—and if so, how—they use email and other electronic networks with their own students.

Conclusion

Bold claims are made about the enormous potential of new electronic technologies for enhancing second-language education. These claims are more complex than they may appear to be at first blush. For example, they span matters of learning outcomes as well as learning processes; of what learners can *do* with a target language as well as how they *feel* about engaging with a language via email. The sketchy 'evidence' available from studies and projects we have investigated suggests that proponents of email are longer on 'process' than they are on 'outcomes', and tend to emphasise attitudes and feelings over downright competence in language use. Even here, however, the reported evidence seems rarely to have grown out of systematic and tightly designed investigations. There is a real danger here that enthusiasm for a medium may be adding to current commercial and policy 'hype' aimed at technologising learning in our classrooms. Here, as elsewhere, enthusiasm and corporate interests may be spawning wishful thinking.

At the same time, we are convinced that CITs, like any technologies in the hands of competent teachers and motivated and reflective learners, *can* enhance learning: in any field, including second language. Blind enthusiasm, wishful thinking, and romantic adoption of fads and trends will not, however, contribute to this cause. What we need are sober and systematic assessments of actual practices, and the careful elucidation of exemplar cases across as wide a range of approaches, contexts, resource bases and experiences as possible. We hope this chapter contributes something to taking up and meeting this challenge.

Notes

1 Stephen Krashen (1980) proposes that language *acquisition* as distinct from language *learning* occurs 'naturally' where learners encounter language features (especially grammatical features) slightly ahead of where they currently are (i.e. = 1). According to Krashen, where input (i) is comprehensible—because of support provided by the context—and marginally in advance of where the language learner is at (i + 1), acquisition of language structures occurs naturally. Barson (1991) suggests that email can be used to shape a conversation in such a way that new structures and vocabulary are learnt, rather than the teacher imposing a textbook or a construct to demonstrate something about the language.

References

Armstrong, K. and Yetter-Vassot, C. 1994 'Transforming teaching through technology', *Foreign Language Annals*, vol. 27, no. 4, pp. 475–86

Barson, J. 1991 'The virtual classroom is born: what now?', *Foreign Language Acquisition Research in the Classroom*, ed. B. Freed, D.C. Heath, Lexington, pp. 365–83

Barson, J., Frommer, J. and Schwartz, M. 1993 'Foreign language learning using e-mail in a task-oriented perspective: inter-university experiments in communication and collaboration', *Journal of Science Education and Technology*, vol. 4, no. 2, pp. 565–84

Batson, T. 1988 'The ENFI project: a networked classroom approach to writing instruction', *Academic Computing*, vol. 2, no. 5, pp. 32–3

Chun, D. 1994 'Using computer networking to facilitate the acquisition of interactive competence', *System*, vol. 22, no. 1, pp. 17–31

Cononelos, T. and Oliva, M. 1993 'Using computer networks to enhance foreign language/culture education', *Foreign Language Annals*, vol. 26, no. 4, pp. 527–34

Crawford, J. and Knobel, M. 1996 'Computer learning networks and LOTE teacher education: an empirical analysis of claims, learning processes and student outcomes', Project in progress, Faculty of Education, Queensland University of Technology

Cummins, J. and Sayers, D. 1995 *Brave New Schools*, St Martins Press, New York

Curriculum Corporation 1994 *Languages Other Than English: A Curriculum Profile for Australian Schools*, Curriculum Corporation, Carlton, Victoria

Faigley, L. 1990 'Subverting the electronic workbook: teaching writing using networked computers', *The Writing Teacher as Researcher: Essays in the Theory and Practice of Class-Based Research*, eds D.A. Daiker and M. Morenberg, Heinemann, Portsmouth, NH, pp. 288–94

Green, B. and Bigum, C. 1996 'Hypermedia or media hype?: new technologies and the future of literacy education', *The Literacy Lexicon*, eds M. Anstey and G. Bull, Prentice Hall, Sydney, pp. 193–206

Halliday, M.A.K. 1985 *An Introduction to Functional Grammar*, Edward Arnold, London

Hannan, M. 1995 'Mirandonos: looking at us e-mail/snail-mail project', *Virtual Connections: On-line Activities and Projects for Networking Language Learners*, ed. M. Warschauer, University of Hawai'i Press, Honolulu, pp. 199–201

Hoffman, R. 1994 'The warm network: electronic mail, ESL learners, and the personal touch', *ON-CALL*, vol. 8, no. 2, pp. 10–3

Kendall, C. 1995 'Individual electronic mail with native speakers', *Virtual Connections: On-line Activities and Projects for Networking Language Learners*, ed. M. Warschauer, University of Hawai'i Press, Honolulu, pp. 109–15

Kern, R. (1995) 'L'histoire, mon histoire: comparing family histoires via e-mail', *Virtual Connections: On-line Activities and Projects for Networking Language Learners*, ed. M. Warschauer, University of Hawai'i Press, Honolulu, pp. 131–3

Krashen, S. 1980 'The theoretical and practical relevance of simple codes in second-language acquisition', *Research in Second Language Acquisition*, Selected Papers of the Los Angeles Second Language Research Forum, Newbury House, Rowley, MA, pp. 11–2

Markee, N. 1994 'Using electronic mail to manage the implementation of educational innovations', *System*, vol. 22, pp. 379–89

Mathieson, A. 1992 'Electronic communication media and second language learning', *ON-CALL*, vol. 7, no. 3, pp. 1–8

Poster, M. 1990 *The Mode of Information*, Polity Press, Cambridge

Soh, B-L. and Soon, Y-P. 1991 'English by e-mail: creating a global

49

classroom via the medium of computer technology', *TESL-L File Archive*, May

Vilmi, R. 1993 'Global communication through e-mail: an ongoing experiment at Helsinki University of Technology', <http://www.hut.fi/~rvilmi/autumn93/global.html>

——1994 See <http://www.hut.fi/~rvilmi/autumn94/env/105eval1.html>

——1995 'International environment activity', *Virtual Connections: On-line Activities and Projects for Networking Language Learners*, ed. M. Warschauer, University of Hawai'i Press, Honolulu, pp. 205–7

Warschauer, M. 1994 E-mail projects, *TESL-L File Archive*, March

——1995a *Email for English Teaching: Bringing the Internet and Computer Learning Networks into the Language Classroom*, TESOL Inc, Alexandria, VA

——ed. 1995b *Virtual Connections: On-line Activities and Projects for Networking Language Learners*, University of Hawai'i at Manoa, Second Language Teaching and Curriculum Center, Honolulu

Warschauer, M., Turbee, L. and Roberts, B. 1994 'Computer learning networks and student empowerment', *NFLRC Research Notes no. 10*, University of Hawai'i at Manoa, Second Language Teaching and Curriculum Center, Honolulu

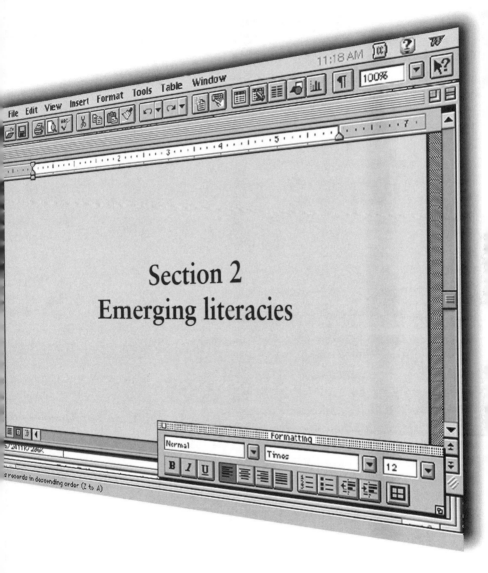

Section 2
Emerging literacies

3

Visual and verbal modes of representation in electronically mediated communication: the potentials of new forms of text

GUNTHER KRESS

Technology, communication and society

We know that it is both a common and a serious error to treat technology as a causal phenomenon in human, social and cultural affairs. So when we look at the far-reaching and deep changes in forms of communication which characterise the present—email and its changing forms of language, for instance—it is tempting to attribute these changes to some technological innovation but erroneous to do so. It is erroneous because even now we can see social forms of control emerging which can counteract those changes. Technologies flourish only in part because something has become known and possible: witness the invention of gunpowder by the Chinese, some thousand years before its 'discovery' in the West. The fact that the stuff started the art of fireworks in China, but was immediately turned to violent use in the West, had something to do with the social and political state both of Imperial China and of Medieval Europe.

Many of the changes in communication happening at the moment give the deceptive impression that they have their provenance in technological know-how. Technology is socially applied knowledge, and it is social conditions which make the crucial difference in how it is applied. The changes in language noted in uses of email—greater informality in all sorts of ways, greater proximity to speech than to formal writing-like forms of language—can be interpreted in a number of ways. Making technology prior for instance, we could say that this form of communication is so quick, so speedy, but also so democratic that it is the technology itself which enables and therefore encourages informality. Making the social prior, we could say that the informality of language in general and of speech in particular is a factor of social proximity. If I am in a relation of solidarity and/or intimacy with certain people, and especially if I can see them and their reactions, then of course I will shape my language use in a particular direction. From such a position email produces new social relations—it effectively puts me in the temporal even if not geographical co-presence of my interlocutor, somewhat like a situation typical of the use of speech. And it is this remaking of the social situation which then reshapes language in the direction of speech-like form.

What is most important about the present is that it is characterised by a conjunction of several deeply significant trends: a conjunction of social, political, economic and cultural as much as of representational/communicational and technological developments. Changes in social and political configurations have brought new arrangements and distributions of power. These have had positive effects for groups previously excluded, marginalised or oppressed, so that social and communicational changes tending to greater informality cannot be said to have just a technological origin: social, political and technological elements coincide.

This chapter focuses on the change that involves a greater and newer use of visual forms of representation in many domains of public communication. This is frequently, and I believe misleadingly, discussed under the heading of 'visualisation', a term which tends to imply that information is 'translated', relatively unproblematically, usually from the written mode into the visual mode. Despite my earlier words of caution, I believe that while the rapidly increasing use of visual modes of communication has a complex set of causes, the simultaneous development and the exponential expansion of the potentials of electronic technologies will entrench visual modes of communication as a rival to language in many domains of public life.

This may be further assisted by a complexity of factors: the visual may be more useful for transmitting large amounts of certain kinds of information. It also may be the case that the information-based economies of the post-industrial era (in which information is at the same time raw material, tool, and product) will need visual forms of representation and communication as more effective means of processing. The exponential growth in the availability of bandwidth will nurture this development: those who provide this commodity of 'bandwidth' will wish, and increasingly will need, to find means of using it productively.

However, at the moment, relatively naive notions of visualisation dominate. Visualisation is seen as an unproblematic kind of 'translation' from one semiotic mode into another—as a simplistic kind of translation from one language to another. But just as English makes available certain forms of expression which are not available in the very closely related language of German, and vice versa, so also with 'translations' from the verbal (written or spoken) to the visual. The sequentially, temporally organised medium of sound is vastly different in its potentials of representation and communication to the simultaneously, spatially organised medium of graphic substance, as expressed in 'lettered representation' in 'literacy'. Each makes possible certain kinds of things, in its particular way, and each prohibits certain things.

One possible explanation may be this reliance on the medium of writing for communication and representation which has produced the present situation of information overload—quantities of information beyond what can be productively handled by humans, even with the aid of machines. Yet it seems that the visual is a vastly more efficient mode for carrying and 'processing' great amounts of information:

it is not an accident that the flight decks of airliners use visual and not verbal means for nearly all the information displayed. Nor is it an accident that dealers on the forex markets have information visually and not verbally displayed on their screens. In both cases, vast amounts of information often have to be processed in microseconds. It may be that a newer reliance on the visual is the solution: a problem caused by over-reliance on one medium may be soluble by a shift to a new medium, better able to handle large amounts of data.

In this chapter I explore, in a preliminary way, some issues in this area which must be addressed at this point in our move toward taking literacy into the electronic era. The 'turn to the visual' interacts with electronic technologies in a number of ways. While that is not the focus of this chapter, I will make just four comments. One is obvious to anyone who looks at a computer screen: the visual is there, and the possibilities even of producing written text focus on visual aspects—font-types and size, layout, visuals to accompany the linguistic text— much more so than did the former technology of typewriters and typesetting. Even when the major element, quantitatively speaking, is writing, its visual aspects are more in the foreground, and are much more easily controlled. The 'look of the page' is now not a matter only for a specialised group of producers of texts; it is a general concern and the means for page design are readily there.

The second is equally obvious: contemporary technologies of page or text production make it easy to combine different modes of representation—image can be combined with language, sound can be added to image, movement of image is possible. In the production of the traditional film, distinct crafts were involved in producing elements of the film's soundtrack, photography and the lighting, whereas these can now be produced with a single technology and with the skills of one person. But this one person now has to understand the semiotic potentials of each mode—sound, visual, speech—and orchestrate them to accord with his or her *design*. Multimedia production requires high levels of multi-modal competence based on knowledge of the operation of different modes, and highly developed design abilities to produce complex semiotic 'texts'.

Third, all this is taking place in the context of technological developments which are likely to produce convergence rather than divergence in the technologies, and in presently distinct 'appliances'. But with convergence of technologies (telephone, television, radio, computer), competence in all modes of representation and communication will simply be assumed—even though what is assumed may not in fact be available.

And finally, a fourth comment. The wider, and ultimately telling context is that of the processes of globalisation and of internationalisation. On one level, these processes are insensitive to deep cultural diversity but, on another level, cannot avoid them. We know from debates over English as a global language that there are deeply problematic issues involved, for instance those of witting and unwitting cultural imperialism (see Phillipson 1992). Global communication which relies on the visual may seem to offer a means of avoiding these problems; paradoxically, they are at least as significant, though neither understood nor acknowledged—the visual apparently offering neutral means of communication. The visual is, however, as much formed by differences of culture as the verbal is. It is essential, therefore, to develop a clear sense of these issues, even if at the moment knowledge is still relatively scant.

The change in the landscape of communication

The last two decades have seen a far-reaching change in media and in modes of communication. On the one hand, this change has attracted widespread comment and yet, on the other, it has not really been fully acknowledged or understood. A comparison of texts from any of the major media across the last thirty years or so clearly reveals the differences. In newspapers, the pages of the 1960s are black and white, and covered in print; in the 1990s, by contrast, there is colour, there are images; and in many contemporary Western newspapers print has very nearly been pushed off the page. If we look at television of the 1960s, at a news program let us say, the screen is dominated by the figure of the newsreader: usually in a medium shot, showing the person from about chest up. Note that then, and to some extent even now, the term in use was 'newsreader': the news was a *linguistic* event, by and large, even on television. Now, of course, the term 'presenter' is more commonly used: the news still has verbal elements, but the task of the 'mediator' has shifted from 'reading' more to that of 'presentation'.

What *is* presented in the TV news is information in the form of images, though the film and video footage which make up so much of the television news does have sound as another important element; and speech is used to do the 'presenting'. The landscape of communication of the 1990s is very different; it is irrefutably a multi-semiotic one; and the visual mode in particular has already taken on a central position in this landscape. Other modes are also becoming more significant as forms of representation and of communication than they have been in the more recent past. Sound, as I mentioned, whether in the form of 'soundtrack', 'music', or 'background noise', is one of these; and as the body is coming to be used as a medium of communication, so aspects of bodily motion are increasingly used as modes of representation and communication. Even a brief look at a contemporary rock video will illustrate this clearly enough.

It is important to remind ourselves at the start that these changes are not in themselves new: the body has been used in many cultures and in many periods as a medium of communication; the visual has had a central place in communication in other periods, even in 'the West'. The point is rather this: that after a period of some two to three hundred years of the dominance of writing as *the* means of communication and representation, there is now, yet again, a deep shift taking place in the system of media and modes of representation and communication, and in the system of evaluating these. The change is of great significance in its social and political ramifications. To call it a 'tectonic shift' may not be an exaggeration, because the landscape of communication and representation, the semiotic landscape, is indeed being remade. Where before there was the single, central mountain range of written language, now another alpine system is being thrust up by forces of a complex kind: in part, social, political, technological, and, as yet less recognised, by economic forces as well.

In this chapter I focus on three related aspects of this change: the newer relations of language and image; changes to *writing* which may be a consequence of this; and a new theory of meaning, which is, I believe, essential to consider in the light of these developments. I say very little about causes, though it is essential to comment about the interrelation of technological change and the possibilities it affords. I conclude with some programmatic statements about curriculum; not just the curriculum of institutionalised education, but a wider concept—a broad, social, economic, cultural curriculum of representation and communication.

Language and image

My cautionary words about the novelty of these changes should be matched by a similar assessment of the general characteristics of the communicational landscape at *all* times. Even though writing has been the most valued means of communication over the last few centuries—the one that has regulated access to social power in Western societies—other means have of course always existed together with writing. Even the densely printed page of novels, or of older textbooks, as of governmental reports, had aspects of layout, used typefaces of a certain kind, had paragraphing, all of them *visual* elements. The fact that the layout of the book adhered strictly to the observance of regular margins around the text, therefore displaying writing as a *block of print*, both obscured this fact of layout by making it invisible through its 'naturalness', and at the same time intensified the meaning of *regulation*, much as did the stiff collar worn by the military and white-collar worker alike. Of course, speech has always been there—except

Figure 3.1 **Extract from front page of the *Frankfurter Allgemeine*, 19 December 1996**

Frankfurter Allgemeine

ZEITUNG FÜR DEUTSCHLAND

2,00 DM   D 2954 A

Donnerstag, 19. Dezember 1996, Nr. 296/51 D   Herausgegeben von Jürgen Jeske, Hugo Müller-Vogg, Günther Nonnenmacher, Johann Georg Reißmüller, Frank Schirrmacher

Solidaritätszuschlag soll um zwei Punkte gesenkt werden

200 Menschen in Peru als Geiseln in der Hand von Guerrilleros

Überfall auf die japanische Botschaft / Vermittlungsversuche des Roten Kreuzes / Kinkel bietet Hilfe an

Jum Schnuppern

„Netanjahu verhindert Klärung des Schicksals von Ron Arad"

Schmidbauer: Ich gebe die Hoffnung nicht auf / Vorwürfe aus Teheran / Der Schlüssel bei den Syrern?

Parteienlandschaft Ost

Von Friedrich Karl Fromme

---

for the members of speech-impaired communities—and it has always accompanied all other modes.

Communication has always been multi-semiotic. What is happening at the moment is therefore not in itself new; and yet it is a significant change. Over the last few centuries, writing has assumed cultural and political dominance and this dominance made the ever-present facts of multi-modality invisible. The recent re-emergence of the visual has to be understood in that context: not as new in itself, but as new in the light of the recent history of representation, and of the nearly unshakeable commonsense that developed along with writing's preeminence.

My focus from here on will not be language-as-such (a theoretical fiction in any case), but language in its written form (see Halliday 1989; Kress 1994). A simple means of illustrating the shift from the previous situation to the present one is to

Figure 3.2   Front page of the *Sun*, 26 February 1997

compare the front pages of newspapers—either of one contemporary newspaper with a copy from, say, thirty years ago; or, to compare one of the few papers still adhering to the older mode with one exemplifying the contemporary situation. Figures 3.1 and 3.2 demonstrate the second.

Figure 3.2 illustrates, literally, the metaphor of 'writing being pushed to the margin'. That is characteristic of many forms of public communication—publicity materials, brochures, advertising texts, and so on. Here I will explore a different instance of this changed relation, which I want to characterise, among other things, as 'specialisation'. My example consists of two science textbook pages: one from 1936, and one from 1988. Both are aimed at students aged about fourteen years.

In Figure 3.3 language as writing is dominant. In terms of space on the page, the image here takes a little more than one third of the page; this is, however, not characteristic of the pages in this book, since most consist wholly of print, or use smaller illustrations. Writing is used as the vehicle for providing *all* the information judged to be relevant, important. Language (in the written form) is considered as a *full* medium of representation and communication: everything that needs to be said is said in language; the implicit assumption is that everything that can be said can only be said in language.

When language has the role, as here, of expressing all the essential information, images are assumed to have the function of 'illustration'. That is, something is assumed to be conveyed fully by written language, with the image merely repeating that information. Nothing new is added or provided, nothing which is independent or not subordinate to the written part of the message. There is one direct link here between written text and visual illustration—in the clause 'in the direction indicated in the figure'. Language is used to point. The question arises: what is the actual function of images in this context? In other words, is this really an illustration; or, just what is illustration? This textbook was praised by reviewers for the author's 'enlivening use' of images. This may point in one direction, namely pleasure; and through pleasure perhaps to an enhancement of learning and remembering. But beyond that lies an implicit assumption that, in any case, certain forms of

Figure 3.3 **'Magnetism and Electricity', 1936 Science textbook**

76   MAGNETISM AND ELECTRICITY

the magnetic poles. Fig. 62(c) shows the combined field of (a) and (b) when the wire is placed between the poles.

Note that, in Fig. 62(a) and (b), the lines of force on the left of the wire are in the same direction as those of the external field, while those on the right of the wire are in the opposite direction. Consequently in the combined field of Fig. 62(c) the field to the left of the wire is strong—there are a large number of lines, while the field to the right is weak.

If we assume, with Faraday, that the lines of force are in tension and trying to shorten (see p. 18), we should expect the wire to be urged to the right. This is precisely what we find by experiment.

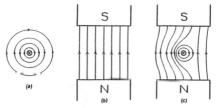

Fig. 62. (a) Magnetic field due to current in straight wire. (b) Field due to magnetic poles. (c) Combined field of (a) and (b).

The principle of the electric motor.

The simple electric motor consists of a coil pivoted between the poles of a permanent magnet (see Fig. 63). When a current is passed through the coil in the direction indicated in the figure we can show, by applying Fleming's left-hand rule, that the left-hand side of the coil will tend to move down and the right-hand side to move up. (Remember that the direction of the field due to the permanent magnet is from the N. to the S. pole.) Thus the coil will rotate in a counter-clockwise direction to a vertical position.

information may be better represented and communicated by visual rather than by verbal means.

The page from the textbook of the 1980s functions very differently (see Figure 3.4).

Here writing is not dominant. The proportions of space taken up by language and image on the page are now reversed—about one third is writing, two thirds are given over to image—though that alone is not as significant as the implicit assumption that writing is *no longer* the vehicle for conveying all the information, and that language here is a medium that can only *in part* express and represent what requires representation. In this sample, everything that has to be communicated is not deemed communicable in the written mode alone; the assumption is that some things are best done by using writing, and others are best done by using images.

Figure 3.4 'Circuits', 1988 Science textbook

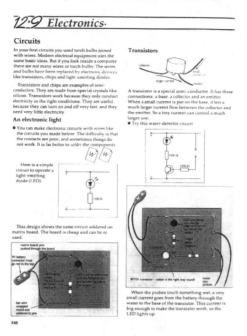

In the Figure 3.3 text, the major meaning was carried by language alone (or that at least was the ostensible assumption); in the Figure 3.4 text, it might be said that the main meaning is carried by the images. Take as an example the relation between the verbal text and the image under the heading 'An electronic light'. The text says: 'Here is a simple circuit . . .' and the image then shows what a circuit is like. It is the image which carries the information.

This is *not* the relation of *illustration*, where the written text fully carries all the information, and the image 'repeats' that information, for whatever reason. Here, both writing and image are informative. However, they are not informative in the same way or about the same things. A certain degree of specialisation has occurred. Language has—here at least— the functions of *narrating* ('you did this, then you did that . . .'); of *pointing* ('Here is a simple circuit'); and still, of

describing/explaining/classifying ('Transistors *are* examples
. . . ', 'they *are* made from . . . ', 'they *are* useful . . . '). But
central, perhaps *the* central, aspects of information—what a
circuit is like, how it works, what its components are—are
now communicated by an image.

In this example we seem to have an instance of a new code
of writing *and* image, in which information is carried differ-
entially by the two modes. Information that *displays* what the
world is like is carried by the image; information that orients
the reader to that information is carried by language. The
simpler syntax does not mean that the text—the verbal and
visual elements together—is less complex than the 1936 example. The diagrams have taken over some of the functions that
language carried in the earlier text. The diagram just discussed
is a highly abstract representation of a circuit; as a topological
representation it focuses on relations abstractly rather than
'realistically'. In other words, abstraction and generalisation
are not absent from this page, and the cognitive demand made
of the reader/viewer is as great (though different in character)
as that of abstractions made in verbal language.

In the age of print, in the period of the high valuation of
writing, the book may be regarded as the defining medium of
dissemination. The book, with its densely printed pages, is the
particular achievement of the era of print literacy and the
indissoluble link with conceptions of knowledge. Whether as
novel or as scientific treatise, the book presents an integral,
coherent account of a world. It does not matter whether that
world is factive or fictive. In the book, authority and knowledge are inextricably intertwined: it presents a coherent,
cohesive account of a part of the world. The book was, in the
last resort—other than, beyond and above the author's name—
the guarantor of knowledge. The contemporary science
textbook is no longer a book in that sense at all; it functions
as a packaged resource kit. The relevant element is no longer
the book itself, nor its chapters. The relevant element now is
something else; in the newer science textbook, the relevant
element is the 'unit of work'. Whereas the old-fashioned book
was read from beginning to end, this new book is not *read* at

all, it is *used*. The shift here has been from an older organisation of *text* to a newer organisation of *resource*; from an older concern with knowledge, to a newer concern with gathering information to manage a task demanded by, or set, in a unit of work. The book now makes *resources* available. The *work* in 'unit of work' has to be taken seriously; it signals the shift from the inwardly focused, contemplative activity of 'reading', to outwardly focused, physical and cognitive action.

As such, the newer book is in line with other organisations of semiotic materials. The hypertext is, similarly, a *resource to be used* for making texts for particular purposes. The hypertext and its non-linear, rhizomic organisation supersedes older textual organisations such as that of narrative, for instance. And that demise of textual organisation is evident in other semiotic forms, such as the music video. Here a rhythmic beat provides an integrating base on top of which various elements are assembled. These videos are not narratives in any sense at all.

Is language changing?

One of the new buzzwords in information technology circles is *visualisation* (see Tufte 1990; Lanham 1994; Brown *et al.* 1995). This names the trend towards the visual representation of information which was formerly solely coded in language. With the increasing availability of 'bandwidth', visualisation is now a possibility, and will become more so in the near future. 'Visualisation' in this sense proposes one answer to the question whether language and image are 'doing the same thing': it says, yes, they are; it is merely a matter of translating between the two modes. Just as it is possible, so the argument goes, to translate from one language to the next, so it is possible to translate from one semiotic mode to another. Of course this bald formulation leaves out of account *why* anyone would want to engage in this translation if both modes convey 'the same' information, in the same way, with the same effects. As I have already suggested, the visual and the verbal offer fundamentally distinct possibilities for engagement with the world they provide, so that my own view is that the translation from one mode to another has to be seen in the more radical sense—as 'transformation'. In such transformations the translator, as a socially formed and located person with his or her own interest, must (as always) be taken into account. But that apart, the 'affordances'—what any language or other semiotic system makes possible or rules out—make the starting-point for any serious attempt to understand this process of translation/transformation. We should begin by asking: Are language and image doing the same? Can they ever do the same?

A second set of questions concerns the interaction/interrelation of the two languages or semiotic modes between which translation takes place. Do they merely co-exist? Or do they interact? To what degree do they interact? If language and image do not merely co-exist, but interact, what are the consequences? If they have different potentials, will they serve different functions, and then inevitably become specialised, both representationally and communicationally? There is a third set of questions which I will not engage with here: Is the visual as a mode of representation systematic, rule-governed, an effect of the values of the culture in which it is used? I will simply assert that it is, and that the patently obvious cultural differences in visual forms and in their modes of use point precisely in that direction (see Kress & van Leeuwen 1996).

To answer the first set of questions requires a departure from usual ways of thinking about and theorising language, that is, it requires a focus on the material and formal aspects of language in ways which are not part of the theoretical mainstream. Within the latter, language has been treated in a quite abstracted way, as an 'immaterial' phenomenon—in conceptions such as Saussure's 'langue', Chomsky's 'competence', and the many transmogrifications of that term; and indeed in much discussion whether in linguistics or in psychology. But to understand the semiotic potentials of language we need to engage with its material manifestations: either as speech—in its physicality and materiality as *sound*, as well as in its more abstract grammatical/syntactic/textual organisation; or as writing—in its physicality and materiality as *graphic substance*, as well as in its more abstract grammatical/syntactic/textual organisation.

Of course, in certain approaches to language such aspects have always been included: the study of poetry has dealt in detail with aspects such as pace, rhythm, sound-shapes, whether used in rhyme, assonance, alliteration, or in phono-aesthetic considerations. And indeed in linguistics—in phonetics as well as in some grammatical theories—certain suprasegmental features have been at the centre of attention (e.g., Firth 1957; Crystal & Quirk 1964; Halliday 1989). Nevertheless, these concerns have not entered the mainstream of linguistic theorising, but have always appeared on the margin, in stylistics, perhaps, or in certain forms of applied linguistics; though usually more marginally as paralinguistic, or extralinguistic, concerns.

However, from a more radically material point of view, language has to be thought about as either speech or writing, and each of these must then be described further in terms of its multiple material aspects. Writing, for instance, is not only distinct through its characteristic syntax—though that is one crucial distinguishing factor—but also in material terms such as its multiple forms of visual display, on multiple forms of surface.

From this perspective, speech and writing differ greatly. Speech is necessarily a temporally, sequentially organised mode, using the medium of air and the mode of sound, depending on sets of physiological characteristics of the so-called speech organs, and the organs of hearing. Its temporality and sequentiality lead to an underlying logic, namely that of sequence in time: the logic of the iteration of one thing after another. This logic lends itself readily to the representation of sequentially conceived events in the world—sequences of actions, sequences of events, and then their arrangement. Sequences of actions and events in their turn can readily be changed into the textual form of narrative. Speech is oriented to action and event. The implicit and foundational questions posed by the organisation of speech are: What are the salient events?; in what sequence do they occur?

The visual, by contrast, is a spatially and simultaneously organised mode, using the medium of light, and the materiality of certain kinds of surfaces, in the mode of graphic substance. It too relies on physiological, bodily characteristics. Its spatiality and simultaneity also lead to an underlying logic, namely that of the co-presence of elements and their relation: the logic of the simultaneous expression of a number of related elements. This logic can, of course, be turned into a sequence of one image following another, but its inherent characteristics are those of *display*: showing the salient elements in the world and the spatial relations between them. *Arrangement* and *display* are the essential features of the logic of the visual. The implicit fundamental questions posed by visual representation are: What are the salient elements? In what spatial relation to each other do they stand?

Of course, aspects of sequentiality—such as anteriority and posteriority, before and after, can be used metaphorically to signal other meanings: 'before' can become 'cause', and 'after' can become 'result'; or, 'first in the sequence' can become 'most important'. Similarly, spatial relations can be used in metaphors of various kinds. The technology of film and video sequentialises and temporalises visual images. But the initial logic remains, and the metaphoric developments are just that: developments of a particular orientation towards and engagement with the world. Here, as an illustration, is a child's recollection through the visual mode of an event, a school outing to a toy-museum.

By asking the child to 'draw a story', the teacher mixed the categories of 'narrative' and 'display'. The child's drawing is indeed a recollection: a reordering and a reconstitution of a complex event (taking place during a visit of about one and a half hours): a representation of salient elements in a particular order. It is *not* a drawing of a particular shelf or display case in the museum: it is a mental *remaking*, and a visual representation of that internal remaking. It shows salient elements; in a particular arrangement—in a line, ordered by size; and in a particular relation to the maker of this representation. Note that this is a cognitive act of reshaping an event from

69

Figure 3.5   'My visit to the toy museum'

the point of view of this maker of the representation. Images are ideological constructs, just as are verbal textual objects.

Had the teacher requested a written story, or a spoken account of the visit, the resulting semiotic object would have been entirely different: not the classification of elements as here, but the recounting of events in sequence: 'first we did this, then we did that, then Lucy lost her bag, then we saw the dolls' house'. In other words, the inherently distinct possibilities of speech and of the visual would have led to different cognitive action, and to different representations. As we face the new era of the world mediated everywhere on the visual space of the screen, this is a fact of fundamental importance. Speech-based cultures, oriented to the world through the deep logic of speech, are thus likely to differ distinctly from image-based cultures: their engagement with the world is different, their habitual modes of representing the order of that world are different; and these differences become, over time, normal and then 'natural'.

The logic of *writing* participates in the logic of the visual (writing *is* a visual mode) and in the logic of speech (writing, even in highly literate societies, still has a complex, dynamic and close relationship with speech). Hierarchy—a metaphoric spatiality with 'higher' and 'lower' expressed via the syntactic means of embedding as well as by other forms of subordination is a feature of many forms of writing in the public domain. In addition, there is the actual spatiality of the graphic material on the surface that displays the writing. Not only does this permit a going back over written text, a visual reassembly, it also affords other possibilities of the visual through the multiplicity of means of layout: paragraphing; spacing of lines and letters; indenting; the use of bullet points; size and shape of letters; and so on. The syntactic hierarchy of clauses can in this way be amplified, underscored, or counteracted through directly visual means. Writing is thus doubly spatial: once metaphorical, through the order of syntactic hierarchy, and once actual, through the visual display on a surface.

In pages such as those discussed earlier (Figure 3.4), blocks of writing come close to becoming one element in the set of elements of the visual unit of the page. In contemporary usages pages differ in the extent to which they are either 'written text' as such, or a 'block of text', a visual unit. In any case, as I mentioned earlier, language in its written form is becoming specialised, as in Figure 3.4, which is not at all an unusual example. In this new specialisation written language tends syntactically in the direction of speech, and tends semantically in the direction of the inherent logic of speech—the reporting/recording of actions and events, and of the use of language in issuing commands: look at this, copy this drawing, follow this line. In this new specialisation written language is getting closer to speech-like forms than to what are still considered (formal) writing-like forms.

As illustrated in Figure 3.4, images are taking on certain functions formerly carried out by language. Again, these functions tend in the direction of the inherent logic of spatial display: showing the salient elements, and their relations. Whereas in the former situation all these tasks were performed by writing, now a separation is evident: the functional load of the two modes is becoming distinct. And so the answers to my earlier questions are: No, the two modes are not doing the same thing; and, No, they are not merely coexisting; and, Yes, there is, it seems, strong interaction between the two which could, over time, have real effects on language in the written mode.

Both modes produce semiotic objects—messages, textual forms. If texts are metaphors of the organisation of the world, then the two modes produce quite distinctly different takes on the world, different images of that world, and different dispositions by their users—whether as text-producers or as text-consumers—towards the world. The shift I have described here could be characterised, in perhaps oversimplified form, as a move *from narrative to display* (to use two basic categories to name the essence of that shift). Narrative and display as ways of organising representations of the world each have the most fundamental consequences for an individual's or a culture's orientation in the world, so that this shift is bound to have equally fundamental repercussions in social, cultural and economic practices, and in the subjectivities of individuals. This is a story still in the process of being told, and a display still in the process of being sketched.

The issue I have been discussing connects directly with the focus of this book: the 'screen' is the new space of representation. How it will be organised—as a largely visual entity or as a largely linguistic entity—will have far-reaching repercussions. It is too early to know, though my money is on the visual.

New theories of representation

The semiotic changes which characterise the present and are likely to characterise the near future cannot be adequately described and understood with current linguistic theories. Most obviously, if language is no longer the central semiotic mode, then theories of language can at best explain only a part of the communicational landscape. Moreover, theories of language will not explain the other semiotic modes, unless one assumes that in every significant way they resemble language; nor will theories of language explain and describe the *interrelations* between the different modes, language included, which are characteristically used in the multimodal semiotic objects— 'texts'—of the contemporary period.

In other words, and as a first requirement, multimodal texts/messages need a theory which deals adequately with the integration/composition of the various modes in these texts: both in production/making, and in consumption/reading. This in turn presupposes adequate understandings of the semiotic characteristics of the various modes which are brought together in multimodal compositions. At this level, a semiotic theory which is too much tied to and derived from one particular mode—for instance, our conventional language-based theories of communication and meaning—will permit neither an adequate nor an integrated description of multimodal textual objects, nor of multimedia production.

A second issue is that contemporary, and in particular mainstream, theories of semiosis are theories of *use* rather than of remaking and transformation. That is, individuals are seen as more or less competent users of a stable, static system of elements and rules. This view has historic as well as contemporary social and political-ideological causes. One of these has, as an unacknowledged consequence, the widely entrenched commonsense about the arbitrary relation in the sign between signifier and signified. That relation is seen to be established and sustained by convention. Yet all the examples discussed here speak of change: changes in forms of text, in uses of language, in communication and representational potentials. Indeed, change is the whole point of this chapter. But change and conventionality are not easy bedfellows: the common understanding is that convention impedes change and reinforces stability. If change and convention are not to be treated as mutually exclusive terms, then the vital question still remains: How are we to account for change?

My argument is that the semiotic landscape is changing in fundamental ways, and that this change relates to other changes in social, cultural, economic and technological domains. While a semiotic theory which could not easily account for change was never adequate for the facts of semiosis, it may have been sustainable in periods where change was less intense than it is at the moment. A semiotic theory which does not have an account of change at its core is simply inadequate and implausible in the present period.

Dominant theories of semiosis—in linguistics by and large—are *theories of use* that regard language as a stable (and largely autonomous) system of elements, categories, and rules of combination. All the examples in this chapter demonstrate changes in the use, extension, and function of both the categories *and* the rules. In other words, they show a situation quite different to that portrayed—largely implied—in current theory. The other point demonstrated by the examples is equally important: the changes in use, form and system arise as a result of individuals' *interested* actions. The needs of individual makers of texts prompt them to stretch, change, adapt, modify the elements, and thereby change the whole set of representational resources with its internal relations.

An adequate theory of semiosis must be founded on a recognition of the 'interested action' of socially located, culturally and historically formed individuals, as the remakers, the transformers, and the reshapers of the representational resources available to them. Notions of language *use*—that is, use of existing resources without changing them—will have to be replaced by notions of the constant remaking of the resources in the process of their use, in action and in interaction. Remaking the resources is an effect both of the demands of particular occasions of interaction, and of the social and cultural characteristics of the individual maker of signs. Both together account for the sign-maker's *interest* in representing a phenomenon in a particular way, and in communicating it in certain media. This interest is personal, affective and social and it shapes the remaking of the resources. On the one hand the remaking reflects individual interest, and on the other, due to the social formation and location of the individual, also reflects broad sociocultural trends. Semiotic change is thus shaped and guided by the characteristics of broad social factors, which are subsequently individually inflected and shaped.

The focus on language alone has meant neglect, even repression, of the potentials of representational and communicational modes in particular cultures; a repressive and systematic neglect of human potentials in many of these areas; and a neglect, as a consequence, of the development of theoretical understandings of such modes. Semiotic modes have different potentials, so that they afford different kinds of possibilities of human expression and engagement with the world, and through this differential engagement with the world, differential possibilities of development: bodily, cognitively, affectively. Or, to put it provocatively: the single, exclusive, intensive focus on written language has dampened the full development of all kinds of human potentials, in all kinds of respects, cognitively and affectively, in two- and three-dimensional representation.

Just at the point where 'literacy'—socially made forms of representing and communicating—is changing radically due to the revolutionary effects of the 'Electronic Age', it is essential to question the adequacy of present theories of semiosis and their effects. If we do not, we deny ourselves the possibility of actively participating in the shaping of this 'age'.

Synaesthesia

This newer theory of representation must account for the changes in the semiotic landscape—changes in forms of text, in uses of language and in modes of communication. It must permit an integrated description of multimodal texts and their production. This newer theory may prove adequate to the demands of several urgent tasks posed by the electronic technologies: the need for dealing with constant change and the need to treat individuals as agents, *not only* in relation to the production of their textual objects, but also in relation to their constant remaking of their community's representational resources. The theory must also take into account the *interaction* of many semiotic modes in a text and do so from both the maker's and the reader's point of view. The interaction of different modes and of different possibilities of expression in multimodal texts and multimedia production poses questions not only at the level of text, but also at the level of cognitive processing: new demands are made cognitively (and no doubt affectively) by the new technologies and by their textual forms. A new theory of semiosis will have to acknowledge and account for the processes of synaesthesia, the transduction of meaning from one semiotic mode in meaning to another semiotic mode, an activity constantly performed by the brain.

In the most immediate past, as in our present, synaesthetic activity has been suppressed in institutional education, due to the social and cultural dominance of language in the written mode in the public domain. Culture affects and even structures, through privileged and thereby habituated usages, which semiotic modes are available or not, which are made focal and valued, and made useable or not, and which are ruled out of or into the public domain of communication. Social and cultural forces thus determine which modes are 'there' for humans to use in particular domains; they affect how they are used. The school, in Western societies, says that writing is serious and most highly valued; music is for the aesthetic development of the individual, as is visual art. These structures, pressures, and actions have shaped not only the representational landscape, but also the cognitive and affective potentials of individuals. A more developed understanding of these processes is essential to open up full and productive access to the multiplicity of representational and communicational potentials, which will be essential for competent practice in the electronic age, in the socialities and economies of the near future.

Design

In a *theory of use* the task of the individual is to understand and have competent control of the representational system and its capacities. Although the system potentially offers a vast—even infinite—range of textual forms, its scope is still limited by convention: hence the valuation of 'creativity' as 'rare' in such a theory. In that theory, change (apart from creativity) is produced via *critique*: that is, existing forms, and the social relations they arise from, are subjected to analytical scrutiny to reveal the rules of their constitution. It is now essential to offer a critique of critique, by showing it to be a response to particular circumstances in a particular period, showing it as an historical phenomenon and not as something that exists naturally (see Kress 1995, 1996).

In periods of relative social stability, critique has the function of introducing a dynamic into the system. In a situation of intense social change, the rules of constitution of texts and of social arrangements are in crisis. In the new theory of representation, in the present technological context of electronic, multimodal, multimedia textual production, the task of text-makers is that of complex orchestration. Further, individuals are now seen as the remakers, transformers, of sets of representational resources—rather than users of stable systems, in a situation where multiple representational modes are brought into textual compositions. All these circumstances call for a new goal in textual (and perhaps other) practice: not of critique, but of *design* (see Buchanan & Margolin 1995). Design takes for granted competence in the use of resources, but beyond that it requires the orchestration and remaking of these resources in the service of frameworks and models that express the maker's intentions in shaping the social and cultural environment. While critique looks at the present through the means of past production, design shapes the future through deliberate deployment of representational resources in the designer's interest. Design is the textual principle for periods characterised by intense and far-reaching change.

Design rests on a chain of processes of which critique—as

distanced analytic understanding—is one: however, it can no longer be the focal one, nor be the major goal of textual practices. Critique leaves the initial definition of analysis to the past, to the past production by those whose processes are subjected to critique. It leaves the definition of the agenda of those whose purposes are not mine. The task of the critic is to perform analysis on an agenda that someone else has made. The idea of the intellectual as critic corresponds to certain kinds of social arrangements and distributions of power, rights and responsibilities; that is, arrangements in which some individuals set the agenda and others either follow or object. Design takes the results of past production as the resource for new shaping, and for remaking. Design is the action of setting an agenda of future aims, and of finding means and resources for carrying it out. The social and political task of the designer is fundamentally different to that of the critic.

It is here I wish to make two brief points about curriculum. Curriculum is a design for the future. The contents and processes put forward in curriculum and in its associated pedagogy are the design for future human dispositions. They provide one set of important means, one important set of resources, for the individual's transformative, shaping action in making him or herself as social humans. That is one point. The other is that the sites of education are now also changing as are their aims. The state's withdrawal from institutional education, with its aim of producing *citizens*, in favour of the market with its aim of producing *consumers* is one strand of that change. New (and very ancient) sites of education are coming into the foreground: the workplace (as in the ancient guild system) and now the multiplicity of mediated communication modes, which represent not only the 'mass media', but quite new media—still barely knowable—and their educational aims and effects. All these pose entirely new questions for 'curriculum', in which the category of design is basic.

Critique and design imply widely different positions and possibilities for human social action; and widely different positions for human subjectivities and their places in social and economic life. The shape of the near future indicates that the facilities of design rather than those of critique will be essential for equitable participation in social, economic and cultural life. It would be an unforgivable dereliction of the responsibilities of intellectuals if the potentials offered by current developments were not fully explored, and a concerted attempt made to shape their direction to bring about at least some of the much talked about utopian visions of communication in the electronic age.

References

Brown, J.R., Earnshaw, R., Jern, M. and Vince, J. 1995 *Visualisation—Using Computer Graphics to Explore Data and Present Information*, Wiley, New York

Buchanan, R. and Margolin, V. eds 1995 *Discovering Design—Explorations in Design Studies*, University of Chicago Press, Chicago

Crystal, D. and Quirk, R. 1964 *Systems of Prosodic and Paralinguistic Features in English*, Mouton, The Hague

Firth, J.R. 1957 *Studies in Linguistic Analysis*, Blackwell, Oxford

Halliday, M.A.K. 1989 *Spoken and Written English*, Oxford University Press, Oxford

Kress, G.R. 1994 *Learning to Write*, Routledge, London

——1995 *Writing the Future: English and the Production of a Culture of Innovation*, National Association of Teachers of English, Sheffield

——1996 *Before Writing: Rethinking the Paths to Literacy*, Routledge, London

Kress, G.R. and van Leeuwen, T. 1996 *Reading Images: the Grammar of Visual Design*, Routledge, London

Lanham, R.A. 1994 'The implications of electronic information for the sociology of knowledge', *Leonardo*, vol. 27, no. 2, pp. 155–63

Phillipson, R. 1992 *Linguistic Imperialism*, Open University Press, Milton Keynes

Tufte, E.R. 1990 *Envisioning Information*, Graphics Press, Cheshire, Connecticut

4

The rhetorics and languages of electronic mail

CHARLES MORAN AND GAIL E. HAWISHER

E-mail—a new medium?

In the field of composition theory, and in related fields such as communications, management, distance education and linguistics, there has been a great deal of excitement about the emergence of computer-mediated communication (CMC) as a new space for writing. Because this is a new space, many have argued, it contains new possibilities: a place where gender roles can be redefined and hierarchies flattened, and where voices previously marginalised can be made to be heard. We share in this excitement, believing that CMC and its subset, electronic mail, are new, but we want to be clear about what we mean by *new*. In this chapter we argue that e-mail is new in the sense that one might say a child is new. The child, in some lights and at some moments, looks very much like her mother; in other lights and at other moments, she resembles her father; and sometimes she even reminds you of a grandparent.

So when we argue that e-mail is a new medium, developing its own rhetorics and languages, we mean that although new, it is intimately related to its ancestors. In its gene pool are all former and current modes and styles of human communication, written and spoken. Some, such as the letter and telephone call, seem now to dominate its make-up. Yet the e-child is still young, and other genes and influences are still waiting for the proper conditions for their expression. The e-child has been, and will be, shaped by her cultural contexts, and as an agent she will shape the culture that she joins.

Further, this new mode—consider it, for a moment, the e-child of print and an unnamed other—alters its parents. This is a reverse-heritage model, one invoked by Margaret Mead in *Culture and Commitment* (1970) where she argues that in rapidly changing societies the child teaches the parents, and classroom teachers speak of learning from their students. Print is thus altered by the existence of e-mail. This chapter, as an example, is more collage like than the conventional book chapter, perhaps because of our subject. And as we read the literature of composition studies, we find that the collage, the dialogue and the interchange are becoming academically respectable forms, found not only in new and 'hip' journals such as *Wired* but in mainstream professional journals such as *College Composition and Communication*. Not that print has been itself a monolithic medium—many of the characteristics of e-text are shared by extraordinary print texts like Lawrence Sterne's eighteenth-century novel *Tristram Shandy*, which still, as an exception, tests the rule.

A note on access

The literature on technology and writing seldom deals with the question of access. Olson (1987) asked a decade ago, 'Who computes?' and found the answer: a small, moneyed and technologically privileged elite. Olson's essay is occasionally cited in the literature of composition studies, but often only as a quick aside. As Herring notes, in research on e-mail in particular, 'the question of "access" in the broader sociopolitical sense has barely begun to be addressed' (1996, p. 5).

The most optimistic estimates of Internet use top out at 100 million users worldwide (Collot & Belmore 1996). This is a huge and growing number, yet it is a tiny fraction—less than 2 per cent—of the world's population. Anderson *et al.* (1995) have analysed data from the US Census Bureau's Current Population Survey, and find that in the US in 1993 only 3 per cent of the households in the lowest income quartile used network services at home or at work, compared to 23 per cent from the top quartile (Anderson *et al.* pp. 19–24). A recent Nielsen Media Research report (Nielsen 1996) polled 2,800 Americans and Canadians aged over sixteen in August 1995 and April 1996. In August 1995, 10 per cent of those polled had used the Internet at least once in the past six months; in April 1996 the percentage had risen to 17 per cent ('More log onto Net,' *Daily Hampshire Gazette* 1996, p. 1). The headline, of course, reads, 'Internet use surges', but the growth, however exponential, begins from a small base. Even in the world of the American university, Internet access is 'free' only to most academics, and the professors' universities pay handsomely for their privilege. Someone on the 'outside' will pay at least $9.50 per month for access, not a trivial sum to many citizens of the Western world and to people who live outside a cash economy in the 'undeveloped' portions of the globe. As Crew has written, 'Billions of exclusions have been effected long before one of us applies for [an electronic] mail address' (quoted in Kaplan 1991, p. 24). We think access to technology is an over-riding issue, which is why we place it at the head of our chapter.

We do see e-mail as a relatively inexpensive technology that could easily be made available to large numbers of people. Anderson *et al.* (1995) have argued that the United States should push for what they term 'universal access'—by which they mean access comparable to the access we now have to the telephone: 93 per cent, though in Camden, New Jersey, only 80.6 per cent of households have telephones, and families on food stamps 'lag 20.4 percentage points behind households not on food stamps' (Anderson *et al.*, pp. 7–8). We share Anderson and colleagues' optimism and advocacy of the policy changes that would bring 'universal access' to the citizens of the world. We know that e-mail, by itself, does not require a powerful computer. One of us (Charlie) co-edited a book in 1988, using e-mail to Bitnet chapters back and forth to and from his co-editor in New Orleans, using a then powerful Leading Edge 286 with a black and white monitor, 640K of RAM, a 40MB hard drive, and a 1200 baud modem—a computer that it is difficult to give away in 1997. The other (Gail) still has her 1983 IBM PC with no hard drive, still operable in her study's closet and on which she experimented with the profession's first electronic discussion list, PARTI, in 1984. Inexpensive computers that include e-mail capacities are now selling for $250 in sets of 20 or more for K–12 school use, though the marketing of these computers has not spread beyond the world of K–12 education. With Gail's ancient IBM PC, or Charlie's Leading Edge 286, or with one of today's inexpensive computers, one could make full use of e-mail. The Web would be off-limits, but listservs, MOOs, MUDs, discussion groups, Usenet—any of the other e-mail-enabled modes of communication—would be available to the user. We proceed with our topic, therefore, knowing that e-mail is not available to all, but knowing, too, that of all the computer uses current now among us as writers, scholars, and teachers of writing— Web surfing, desktop publishing, high-end word processing, hypertext, hypermedia—e-mail is the least expensive to use. E-mail is therefore potentially accessible to large numbers of people.

The rhetorics of e-mail

Public/private audience: who's been reading my mail?

E-mail, like writing and speech, can be used for practically any imaginable human purpose. The e-mail writer can send a request for information to a discussion group; a notice of an upcoming meeting to a workgroup; or, from a Web Page, can request book-ordering information from a publisher. The e-mail writer can also engage in intimate, personal communication between family members, friends, and would-be sexual partners.

So it is not easy to tease out the ways in which e-mail is different from its ancestors, partly because we are using e-mail in the way we used earlier kinds of communications media. To the new medium we bring the voices and purposes we brought to the old, and in the new medium we address the audiences we have always addressed. Yet there are differences. The crucial difference between e-mail and postal mail (p-mail)—and, indeed, all earlier forms of communication—is the ease with which e-mail can be stored, retrieved, and copied. E-mail exists in digital form. P-mail can be scanned and digitised, to be sure, and so can voice, but there are intermediate, expensive, and not yet 100 per cent accurate procedures for translation. A second difference between e-mail and p-mail is e-mail's speed of transport and resultant rhythms of response. E-mail differs markedly from face-to-face communication in its absence of paralinguistic cues and the potential geographical distance between correspondents. Crucial differences between e-mail and telephony are that on e-mail the speaker and correspondent are not, except on the fastest chat relays, in real-time conversation; and that e-mail, once again, lacks the paralinguistic cues that can be conveyed by voice.

One rhetorical problem that the e-mail writer has to solve, or simply deny, is that e-mail is not as secure as p-mail. E-mail draws on its ancestor for its last name, yet it differs by having no envelope. In p-mail, we trust that our letter, sealed in an envelope, will not be read by others. Opening other people's p-mail incurs penalties that have a long history and have built themselves into the conventions of the p-mail letter. Not so long ago, p-mail was sealed by wax that was stamped with the sender's seal, often by a seal ring. Today we glue the flap on the paper envelope and trust, reasonably enough, that the contents will not be read by persons other than the intended recipient(s). We may be asked, in special situations, to sign over the envelope seal, to assure the recipient that the envelope has not been opened and resealed.

But e-mail is not at all like the envelope-wrapped letter. It is even more open to others' scrutiny than the p-mail postcard. The postcard can be read by anyone in the send-and-deliver process, and by anyone in the recipient's household, but that is still a relatively small potential audience. The audience for e-mail is, potentially, the world. A fine example of private communication gone public is the recently published *White House e-mail* (Blanton 1995), in which the reader is given print and ASCII (American Standard Code for Information Interchange) copies of inter-office e-mail from the Reagan and Bush White House: some 200 pages of paper text, and 475K of ASCII text available to any of us willing to take the book and its disk out of a library and copy the disk onto our own hard drive. Further, this commercially available e-text is but a tiny fraction of the thousands of White House system back-up tapes that will be open to public inspection through the efforts of the National Security Archive. Clearly the authors of this e-mail never thought it might become public. They assumed that they could destroy the tapes when they left the White House, arguing in the courts that the e-mail was not an historical record but like old office furniture—clutter which should be removed for the convenience of the new occupants. And thumbing through this book, one can understand why the White House staffs of the Reagan, Bush, and Clinton administrations fought against archiving and preserving this e-text. As the editor notes, 'Publication of this e-mail will, no doubt, cause acute embarrassment for some. The authors were not writing for a public audience or even "for the file", the way so many government documents are created. As a result, there's an urgency, an immediacy, and a level of candor very rarely displayed in public records' (Blanton 1995, p. 3).

Here is Jock Covey, then Special Assistant to the President and the Senior Director of the NSC office of Near East and South Asian Affairs, writing to Admiral John Poindexter on 11/10/85 at 16:46:31:

> Agree we should quietly press on with business as usual in the Arab world. It is right that counter terror prep should be meticulous and imaginative. At the same time, we should expect some weaseling and snubs from our 'friends,' who will not yet have figured out how to cope with complex pressures generated by Mubarak's wacky behavior, the PLO's 'big lie'

approach to the Klinghoffer murder, and our own resolute, mostly successful, pursuit. These terrorists have slimed everything they have touched in the last few days. (Blanton 1995, p. 106)

This is not at all the language of diplomacy and was clearly not intended to be part of what it now is, the public record.

Even our own e-mail, unlike p-mail, is systematically monitored. When we send a single message to a single recipient through our own e-mail connection, at some level we know that our system operator (sysop) has access to every message that travels through the system. Indeed, the sysop may have a legal obligation to maintain discipline on a system. Though it is practically impossible for a sysop to read all the e-mail that flows through a system, it is theoretically possible, and that theoretical possibility can, and should, influence the writer as she composes the e-mail message.

We know, too, that our correspondent may forward our e-message to another reader. E-mail, unlike p-mail, is in digital form and can therefore be copied infinitely at practically no cost and with little effort. Correspondents routinely forward what they may judge to be interesting or humorous messages to friends, family, or even to discussion lists. Some e-mail programs make it possible to send a 'blind copy' to others without the ostensible receiver knowing that others are reading the message. Blind responses, in turn, can contain messages that the original correspondent did not intend to be forwarded to anyone. A number of groups, and some correspondents, have conventions that control such forwarding, but still, it is possible that what you have written for one person will be read by others in that person's circle of correspondents.

Further, e-mail boxes are not themselves as secure as p-mail boxes. In the world of the American academy, the spouse is likely to have access to the mailbox, usually for correspondence with children and friends. In our experience these arrangements have been 'secure' in that the person sharing the e-box reads only mail from the children. But still, when you write to a mailbox shared with a spouse or partner, the possibility of a second reader is present.

Finally, if you belong to lists, it becomes possible to send your message not to the intended correspondent but to another correspondent, or to hundreds, or thousands, of list members. Again here, the ease and convenience of e-mail is its own enemy. Newcomers to a list may send what they think is a reply to a single correspondent, but if they simply 'reply' to the list message, their reply goes out to all members. Further, the 'alias' function that accompanies most mailers saves time by permitting you to address your message rapidly, but you also risk mis-addressing your message with the notorious single keystroke. Suppose that your alias list has PH for Patricia Hunter, and PL for Paul LeBlanc, or PaulL for LeBlanc and PaulP for Paul Prior: you might, as both authors of this chapter, send more mail to Paul LeBlanc than you intend.

This lack of privacy is part of the e-mail 'situation' that shapes the message. Like p-mail, e-mail is written, and therefore leaves a 'paper trail'. But unlike p-mail, e-mail is digital, exists in already copied and further copiable form, and is part of a system that is monitored. This lack of privacy, or security, can shape the message that is being written: it can force gaps and omissions, make the writer hold back, obfuscate, withdraw. The writer's situation can become like that of someone writing a paper memo to the 'file', or to one person but with cc:s to several others. The writer needs to hold in mind a complex audience situation: 'She will read this; so will he, and she, and she, too; and the letter will go into three filing systems and perhaps be reread, at some future time, by people I've not met or known'. The e-mail writer's situation is like that of a person leaving a voice-mail message: one does not know, really, who will listen to the voice message. Perhaps several people, before it is erased.

Yet paradoxically, the ease with which e-mail can be composed, transmitted, copied, and stored may provide its own measure of security, because in this case ease of use begets tremendous volume. No sysop is really able to read all the e-mail that passes through a system. And no investigator or historian is going to read all the White House e-mail posted and saved during the Reagan and Bush administrations, when it all finally becomes available. The White House e-mail lawsuit saved these materials from destruction: 1,055 computer tapes from the Reagan White House, 800 of which were open-reel magnetic tapes; 4,852 computer tapes from the Bush White House, of which 4,409 were cartridge tapes; and 135 hard disks from the Bush National Security staff. Blanton (1995) notes that 'printing out just the first 163 tapes from the Reagan White House would produce as much as five million pages of e-mail' (p. 12). Yes, this enormous body of information, because it is digitised, can be searched. But the likelihood of finding a 'smoking gun' in such an enormous archive is small indeed. Perhaps our secrets are safe, after all!

The illusion of intimacy

Despite what we have written above—that e-mail is often actually, and always theoretically, public—e-mail as a medium can create the illusion of intimate, private communication. The e-mail correspondent often feels that what is being 'said' on e-mail is being said on a secure channel appropriate for intensely personal communication. Many researchers have noted what is often called the 'warmth' of e-mail communication. Deuel (1996) has described the range of virtual sex that occurs on MOOs and MUDs. And Korenmann and Wyatt (1996) have noted that to participants, 'Interaction on WMST-L feels like interaction within a group' (p. 239). Even in large listserv discussion groups, participants note the intimacy they feel with other participants. Selfe and Meyer (1991), for example, have documented electronic exchanges which suggest that members of Megabyte University, a listserv for writing teachers, think of themselves as a close-knit group who 'chat away like old friends' (p. 173). Similarly, Chesebro and Bonsall (1989) found that messages in such conferences are often more 'socially oriented' than 'task related' and that they seem to foster among participants a sense of belonging (p. 5). And Harriet Wilkins (1991) notes that during three months on

Presbynet, participants came to think of one another as friends. One participant, for example, stated: 'I am still constantly amazed at the "companionship" and warmth one can find on a computer terminal' (p. 71).

In this virtual intimacy, lacking the physical presence, all the correspondents have to go on is electronic 'print', and here as elsewhere the skilful rhetor can deceive. One of the most poignant stories of deception is the narrative Lindsy Van Gelder (1991) relates that appeared in *Ms. Magazine*: 'The strange case of the electronic lover'. In this report, a fifty-something male psychiatrist poses on-line as Joan, or 'Talkin' Lady', a woman supposedly crippled and mute after an accident involving a drunk driver. 'Talkin' Lady' became a CompuServe celebrity, giving much advice and support to disabled women. Many on-line participants came to love 'her' and were surprised when Joan never showed up at face-to-face meetings they sometimes arranged. When participants discovered the deception, their trust in the particular on-line community was shattered, but that is not to say they became more cautious about future on-line attractions. E-mail entices participants to play along and in most instances performs as a powerful and seductive technology.

This sense of immediacy is almost certainly a function of the speed of e-mail transmission and the potentially rapid rhythm of response. As Feenberg (1989) has noted, the author of an e-mail message seems to require a quick response. 'Communicating on-line', Feenberg writes, 'involves a minor but real personal risk, and a response—any response—is generally interpreted as a success while silence means failure . . . As a result when we leave a message in computer memory we feel an intense need for response' (pp. 23–4). Perhaps because of the difficulty of screen reading as well as the speed of transmission, the medium does not encourage rereading and careful reflection. Particularly on a list, if you postpone responding you may miss a full cycle in the 'conversation' because the first question, superseded by a second, has become the electronic equivalent of the 'dead letter'.

Yet in the absence of the body, the on-line persona is not necessarily rooted in the material and can therefore float free of the grit and hum of physical life and assume a virtual, non-material existence. The sense of immediacy that is part of the e-mail writer's situation can create an intimacy that is different from the kinds of intimacy we have grown to expect. In studying the e-mail correspondence between his American students and East-Asian students, Ma noted what he termed 'self-disclosure without serious commitment' (1996, p. 184). Our guess is that in this case the geographic distance contributed to the lack of 'serious commitment', and we argue that the quick response rhythms of e-mail, and its voice-like written language, prompted what Ma regarded as an unusual degree of 'self-disclosure'. Perhaps e-mail fosters a new kind of relationship here, with overtones of the postmodern—uncommitted intimacy.

The social role of the e-mail writer

It seems that e-mail, and CMC in general, is a medium in which social cues become radically reduced. Compared to face-to-face communication, there is no body language; compared to voice communication, there is no intonation, timbre, all the nuances that make it possible to voice-print an individual. Compared even to written correspondence, there is no handwriting: each letter appears on the screen in uniform ASCII style, bearing no trace of the writer's personality. Nor is there paper to reflect the writer's individuality or bear wine and coffee stains hinting of a material life beyond the text. E-mail writers have gone to great lengths to personalise their correspondence, with emoticons, signature files, and conventions intended to carry the body into the e-type, as in <LOL> for 'I Laugh Out Loud'. Yet these attempts to add, through print, hints of face-to-face or voice communication demonstrate that the e-mail user feels restricted by the conventional written language.

The issue is not whether e-mail lacks many of the paralinguistic cues we are accustomed to in other kinds of communication, but how to determine what effects this narrow-band communication might have on the social roles adopted by on-line writers. Here there are two camps: those who suggest that the reduction of social cues permits anti-social and convention-breaking behaviour; and those who argue that the reduction of social cues forces us back on our own store of more or less stock social roles. Both hypotheses might account for 'flaming', or outrageous and often hurtful language transmitted as a part of the e-mail message, an on-line phenomenon that has been recognised and discussed frequently and thoroughly (e.g., Shapiro & Anderson 1985).

The 'reduced social cues' hypothesis has become accepted as an explanation for what has been termed 'anti-social on-line behavior' (e.g., Sproull & Kiesler 1991). More recent research has argued powerfully against the 'reduced social cues' position, making the case that without powerful social cues we become *more* social: that is, we do not become anti-social, but become hyper-social (Spears & Lea 1992; Hall 1996; Herring 1996; Kollock & Smith 1996). Because our correspondent is not cueing us into the role(s) we might appropriately take in a particular discourse situation, we are forced to fall back on our stock of available roles, those given us by our culture. According to Spears and Lea, 'paradoxically CMC may represent a more intrinsically "social" medium of communication than the apparently "richer" context of face-to-face interaction, and one that gives fuller rein to fundamentally social psychological factors' (p. 31). They note, further, that e-mail itself occurs in a social context which can powerfully affect the social roles adopted by the correspondents: 'In most organisational contexts in which CMC is used . . . (e.g., managers communicating with other managers or their staff) these social categories, roles and relationships are likely to be well defined quite independently of the presence of interpersonal cues or mystificatory notions of "social presence" or "psychological distance" ' (p. 46). Following the same line of reasoning, Hall has argued that 'rather than neutralising gender, the electronic medium encourages its intensification. In the absence of the physical, network users exaggerate societal notions of femininity and masculinity in an attempt to gender

91

themselves' (p. 167). Matheson (1992) too has observed a stereotypical response to gender in her study of on-line participants' reaction to a computer program, which was sometimes represented as a male persona, at other times as female, although it was programmed to give the same response regardless of the persona attributed to it. Invariably, participants interpreted the female persona as a kinder, more personable negotiator and regarded the male persona as a fair, but tough negotiator. In this case, you had the same written electronic words but different interpretations, each driven by a social stereotype.

What is clear from both strands of research is that e-mail offers a space within which one can construct any number of many possible selves—to role-play on a virtual stage, to an audience, without the risks of a live performance. In *Life on the Screen* (1995) Turkle takes this stance, although as a psychologist she is sometimes uneasy with the notion of multiple selves. She notes that in virtual communities, 'people either explicitly play roles (as in MUDs) or more subtly shape their on-line selves', often becoming 'multiple and fluid' (p. 256). Turkle sees this as an opportunity, for some, to try on masks—to play with other roles—and to reflect more closely on the daily masks we don in real life. What effect this notion of multiple selves has on the e-mail reader and writer can only be conjectured at this point. We suggest, however, that e-mail as a 'writing space' invites writers to create identities and to move freely among their roles as students, colleagues, friends, lovers, advisers, and parents. The first time one of us wrote to her daughter on-line she had a difficult time signing the most common of signatures, 'Mom'. She had not assumed the parental role in e-space before, and the electronic 'Mom' felt odd, especially wrapped in hugs as ((((Mom)))), a notation new to her.

For teachers, on-line space offers a new space in which to construct an identity, one that may differ substantially, though not pathologically, from the identity they assume in their face-to-face interactions with their students. Those who have taught in computer-equipped classrooms have found themselves constructing on-line personae that complement those they present elsewhere. In Carbone *et al.* (1993) 'Writing ourselves on-line', first-year writing teachers document their construction of on-line personae that are radically different from their off-line personae. One of the teachers, McComas, found himself, and was observed by others, to be warm and almost physical in his off-line relationships with his students, and strict and business-like in his on-line correspondence with them. Ostermiller, on the other hand, was warm and playful in her on-line correspondence with her students, and firm and somewhat distant in her face-to-face communication with them. Unlike the situation in Fletcher's (1996) novel, *E-mail: a love story*, in which the heroine has to choose between her on-line and off-line lovers, these teachers were able to use their e-mail teaching space to express different and complementary aspects of themselves, thereby enhancing their effectiveness as teachers.

The languages of e-mail

To the extent that e-mail, the medium, is part of the situation—what Burke would call the 'scene' of writing—it drives the language we use: we make linguistic, syntactic, and graphic choices that we would not make in a p-mail letter or in face-to-face conversation. We know that speech is different from writing; sometimes we refer to the 'written language' as a dialect of English. With the invention of the telegraph came a telegraphic style. And, as Haas (1996, pp. 3–6) and others have argued, the difference between speech and the written language is a function of technology: the stylus and tablet, the pencil and paper, and the typewriter have made language material and thus changed it. Perhaps the technology of e-mail, moving language from the page to the screen and making it digital, has changed the language that it bears and conveys.

Since early in its history, users and researchers have felt that the language of e-mail was a hybrid, a mixture of elements from the written and spoken languages (Spitzer 1986). Some

93

linguists have argued that when new situations for language use arise we borrow from existing resources. For Ferrara, Brunner and Whittemore (1991), the language of e-mail is 'forged out of elements of postcardese, headlinese, and telegraphese . . .' (p. 12). They and others argue that e-mail has the spontaneity and informality of speech, though it is 'written' and thus carries with it the written language. The extent to which e-mail is the spoken language has been seen as a problem for writing teachers, who are charged with teaching the written language, and perhaps even a formal version of this written language, academic discourse. In writing-across-the-curriculum workshops, faculty from other disciplines often comment on how their students' writing is becoming 'contaminated' or 'corrupted' by the informal on-line discourse they use. Although we see the language of e-mail as working to change academic discourse, often in positive ways, not all colleagues welcome such alterations in the language of their discipline.

Some recent research has attempted to prove that e-mail as 'scene' has produced its own electronic language. Collot and Belmore (1996) have analysed a substantial corpus of the language people use on bulletin board systems (BBSs). They argue that writing to a BBS carries with it a unique set of constraints: the language is neither spoken nor written; the messages appear chronologically but can be retrieved by 'thread'; the messages are public; participants may come from all backgrounds and be any age; the status markers are limited; and the topics and purposes are varied (pp. 14–15). Collot and Belmore create a corpus of 'Electronic language' by sampling nine different conferences ranging from 'Science' to 'Photo' to 'Cooking'. They compare these samples with pre-existing samples of the written and spoken language, basing their comparison on six 'dimensions' of the written and spoken languages defined by Biber in 1988. These are their findings:

- Along Dimension 1, Informational vs. involved production: Despite the heavily informational nature of the correspondence, 'the language in which this is couched is more similar to that of spontaneous genres such as interviews, spontaneous speeches, and personal letters, than it is to that of informative genres such as official documents, academic prose, or press reportage' (p. 22).

- Along Dimension 2, Non-narrative vs. narrative: Electronic language was closest to 'professional letters, conversations, press reviews, and interviews' (p. 23).

- Along Dimension 3, Situation-dependent vs. explicit: Electronic language was close to 'humor, press reportage, and interviews' (p. 23).

- Along Dimension 4, Overt expression of persuasion: It was 'near the high end of the scale . . . between personal letters and editorials' (p. 24).

- Along Dimension 6, Degree of informational elaboration ('that' clauses): It scored high, 'between spontaneous speeches and editorials' (p. 26). (The comparison along Dimension 5, Non-abstract vs. abstract, produced confusing results.)

Though this study does not convince us that there is a discrete 'electronic language', we accept Collot and Belmore's (1996) assumption that the situation of the BBS correspondent shapes the language chosen by the correspondent, and that this accounts for the similarity between BBS language and public forms of discourse, such as the spontaneous speech, the interview, and the editorial. One finding that surprised the researchers as well as us: there appears to be no difference, along Biber's (1988) six dimensions, between e-language composed on-line and e-language composed off-line (p. 26). We would have expected on-line composing to produce language closer to the genres of speech, but this apparently is not the case.

In a second study, Yates (1996) compared samples of spoken and written languages with CMC samples drawn from open conferences on the British conferencing network CoSy. Three samples are compared along four continua: the type/token ratio or (the relationship between the number of different words (type) to the total number of words (token)); lexical density (the ratio of lexical to grammatical items); the degree of personal reference; and the degree of modal auxiliary use (may, might). In 'type/token ratio' the CMC samples scored 0.590, compared to writing (0.624) and speech (0.395). It is no surprise that Yates found CMC 'more akin to writing than speech in terms of range of vocabulary used' (p. 35). In 'lexical density', CMC scored 49.28, writing 50.32, and speech 42.29. Yates concludes that in terms of lexical density, 'CMC users package information in text in ways that are more written than speech-like' (p. 39). In modal auxiliary use CMC scored 18.3, writing 13.7, and speech 14.5. This seems to set CMC apart from both writing and speech, as Yates concludes: 'The use of modals in CMC is significantly higher than that of either speech or writing, with writing having the lowest usage of all three' (p. 43). 'Personal reference' is a more complex category, because the study looked at numbers of first, second, and third-person pronouns. CMC was much lower in third-person reference than either speech or writing; but in its use of first and second-person pronouns, it scored closer to speech than to writing. Yates concludes that 'CMC makes greater proportional use of first and second-person pronouns than either speech or writing' (p. 42). From the full study, he concludes that CMC is neither simply speech-like nor simply written-like' (p. 46) but is its own language.

In a third study, Werry (1996) investigates the language of Internet Relay Chat (IRC), a form distinct from the CoSy conferences and the BBSs studied by Yates and Collot and Belmore in that it is exclusively synchronous. Werry defines IRC as 'social spaces made available on bulletin boards, servers, and in sites across much of the Internet in which people converse and interact' (p. 48). Unlike the Yates and Collot and Belmore studies, Werry's is descriptive, not comparative. He finds in IRC language features that seem unique to the medium: a 'high degree of addressivity' (p. 52), a 'strong drive towards brevity and abbreviation' (p. 54), 'paralinguistic and prosodic cues' (p. 56)—e.g., 'ba-a-a-a-ad', and 'an almost manic tendency to produce auditory and visual effects in writing' (p. 58). Further, Werry finds text representations of virtual actions and gestures—e.g., 'Marcia hugs Eric'. He also finds formulaic language, phrases apparently generated by macro-functions at the writer's computer (p. 58). He concludes that what he has been describing, IRC, has 'distinctive linguistic and interactional features' (p. 61). He senses that in IRC the language has been 'shaped at many different levels by the drive to reproduce or simulate the discursive style of face-to-face spoken language' (p. 61). From our own experience, we consider IRC the most rapidly interactive form of on-line discourse, practically indistinguishable from LAN-chat programs such as 'InterChange', and really more like a MOO or MUD, although it seems even faster. Because college-age students become so involved with IRC (some might argue that it is addictive) and tend to monopolise available computers, many universities do not permit IRC at their various public computer sites.

We do not want to leave this section, however, without noting that since the many languages of e-mail are now and for the foreseeable future all English or English-ed, they put the native speaker of English in the position of a late 1990s cultural colonist. ASCII, the American Standard Code for Information Interchange, is American. As Selfe and Selfe (1994) remind us, ASCII is based on a seven-bit code and can therefore handle only 95 'characters': upper and lower-case letters, numbers, and punctuation marks. Therefore, to e-mail our friends Martín or Björn, we are obliged to 'english' their names, omitting the accents on the 'i' of Martín and the 'o' of Björn, leaving both somewhat Ellis-Islanded, Americanised. What is true of ASCII, the language of e-mail, is also true of computer interfaces, and of most word processing programs, where adding an accent to a letter is a complex, four- or five-move process. This neo-colonial move plays inevitably and silently in the rhetorics of e-mail, so long as ASCII defines the character sets available to us.

An inconclusion

We return to our original hypothesis: e-mail is 'new,' in the way that a child is 'new': the child is an individual with agency, but shaped by its history, its genetic heritage, and the cultures into which it is born. We may be at a watershed, a time when language goes digital. We are reminded of another watershed, the development of writing, and of Socrates' unfavourable comparison of this new medium speech, in the *Phaedrus*: 'Once a thing is put in writing, it rolls about all over the place, falling into the hands of those who have no concern with it just as easily as under the notice of those who comprehend; it has no notion of whom to address or whom to avoid' (*Phaedrus* 275, Plato 1956). Just as the technology of writing made language material and, in a sense, took it away from its author, so the technology of e-mail has made writing digital, easily copied and broadcast to anyone with the technology and time to read it. We are still adjusting to the change and, given the rapid rate of technological change, we are likely to continue in a state of adjustment for some time to come.

So what we present here is a snapshot, really, a record of a moment in time. This snapshot shows us as writers and readers beginning to come to terms with e-mail's apparent intimacy and its ability to be broadcast, copied, and re-broadcast to audiences the author could not imagine. The snapshot includes the evolution of what may or may not be distinct on-line languages but certainly are on-line conventions new to the world of the written language. The snapshot includes our new tendency to use on-line space as a space for creating alternative selves, experimenting with roles we might not have assumed in face-to-face, 'live' communication.

What lies ahead? Rapid change, new rhetorical situations, and new forms of language. There seems to be general agreement that communications technologies will converge—that fax, voice-mail, e-mail, and telephony will come together, all digital and therefore 'readable' in the same way. In these times, we are always already in transition. What will happen to the written language when we can easily voice-access our computer screens? Will we then need to re-learn the ability to give dictation to a silent other? We welcome a world of truly universal e-mail, and beyond, but only if these worlds are truly universal. The world of e-mail is now a gated community. Until it includes all voices and cultures, its discourse will not be as diverse, rich, and democratic as it should be and will not therefore be a world that we willingly inhabit.

References

Anderson, R.H., Bikson, T.K., Law, S.A. and Mitchell, B.M. 1995 *Universal Access to E-mail: Feasibility and Societal Implications*, The Rand Corporation, Santa Monica CA

Biber, D. 1988 *Variations across Speech and Writing*, Cambridge University Press, Cambridge

Blanton, T. ed. 1995 *White House E-mail: The Top Secret Computer Messages the Reagan/Bush White House Tried to Destroy*, The New Press, New York NY

Carbone, N., Daisley, M., Federenko, E., McComas, D., Moran, C., Ostermiller, D. and Vanden Akker, S. 1993 'Writing ourselves on-line', *Computers and Composition*, vol. 10, no. 3, pp. 29–48

Chesebro, J.W. and D.G. Bonsall 1989 *Computer-Mediated Communication: Human Relationships in a Computerized World*, University of Alabama Press, Tuscaloosa AL

Collot, M. and Belmore, N. 1996 'Electronic language: a new variety of English', *Computer-Mediated Communication: Linguistic, Social and Cross-Cultural Perspectives*, ed. S.C. Herring, Benjamins, Amsterdam, pp. 13–28

Daily Hampshire Gazette 1996 'More log onto Net', 14 Aug 1996, p. 1

Deuel, N.R. 1996 'Our passionate response to virtual reality', *Computer-Mediated Communication: Linguistic, Social and Cross-Cultural Perspectives*, ed. S.C. Herring, Benjamins, Amsterdam, pp. 129–46

Feenberg, A. 1989 'The written world', *Mindweave: Communication, Computers, and Distance Education*, eds R. Mason and A. Kaye, Pergamon Press, New York, pp. 22–39

Ferrara, K., Brunner, H. and Whittemore, G. 1991 'Interactive written discourse as an emergent register', *Written Communication*, vol. 8, pp. 8–34

Fletcher, S.D. 1996 *E-mail: a love story*, Donald Fine, New York

Haas, C. 1996 *Writing Technology: Studies on the Materiality of Literacy*, Lawrence Erlbaum, Mahwah NJ

Hall, K. 1996 'Cyberfeminism', *Computer-Mediated Communication: Linguistic, Social and Cross-Cultural Perspectives*, ed. S.C. Herring, Benjamins, Amsterdam, pp. 147–70

Herring, S.C. 1996 *Computer-Mediated Communication: Linguistic, Social and Cross-Cultural Perspectives*, J. Benjamins, Amsterdam

Kaplan, N. 1991 'Ideology, technology, and the future of writing instruction', *Evolving Perspectives on Computers and Composition Studies: Questions for the 1990s*, eds G.E. Hawisher and C.L. Selfe, NCTE, Urbana IL, pp. 11–42

Kaplan, N. and Moulthrop, S. 1991 'Something to imagine: literature, composition and interacting fiction', *Computers and Composition*, vol. 9, no. 1, pp. 7–23

Kollock, P. and Smith, M. 1996 'Managing the virtual commons: cooperation and conflict in computer communities', *Computer-Mediated Communication: Linguistic, Social and Cross-Cultural Perspectives*, ed. S.C. Herring, Benjamins, Amsterdam, pp. 109–28

Korenmann, J. and Wyatt, N. 1996 'Group dynamics in an e-mail forum', *Computer-Mediated Communication: Linguistic, Social and Cross-Cultural Perspectives*, ed. S.C. Herring, Benjamins, Amsterdam, pp. 225–42

Landow, G.P. 1992 *Hypertext: The Convergence of Contemporary Critical Theory and Technology*, Johns Hopkins University Press, Baltimore

Ma, R. 1996 'Computer-mediated conversations as a new dimension of intercultural communication between East Asian and North American college students', *Computer-Mediated Communication: Linguistic, Social and Cross-Cultural Perspectives*, ed. S.C. Herring, Benjamins, Amsterdam, pp. 173–85

Matheson, K. 1992 'Women and computer technology: communicating for herself', *Contexts of Computer-Mediated Communication*, ed. M. Lea, Harvester/Wheatsheaf, New York, pp. 66–88

Mead, M. 1970 *Culture and Commitment*, Anchor Press, Garden City NJ

Nielsen 1996 <http://www.commerce.net/work/pilot/nielsen_96/exec.html>

Olson, C. P. 1987 'Who computes?', *Critical Pedagogy and Cultural Power*, eds D. Livingstone, Bergin and Garvey, South Hadley MA, pp. 179–204

Plato 1956 *Phaedrus*, trans. W.C. Helmbold and W.G. Rabinowitz, MacMillan, New York

Selfe, C.L. and Meyer, P.R. 1991 'Testing claims for on-line conferences', *Written Communication*, vol. 8, pp. 163–98

Selfe, C.L. and R.J. Selfe, Jr. 1994 'The politics of the interface: power and its exercise in electronic contact zones', *College Composition and Communication*, vol. 45, no. 4, pp. 480–504

Shapiro, N.Z. and Anderson, R.H. 1985 *Toward an Ethics and Etiquette for Electronic Mail*, The Rand Corporation, Santa Monica CA

Spears, R. and Lea, M. 1992 'Social influence and the influence of the social in computer-mediated communication', *Contexts of Computer-Mediated Communication*, Harvester/Wheatsheaf, New York, pp. 30–65

Spitzer, M. 1986 'Writing style in computer conferences', *IEEE Transactions on Professional Communications*, vol. 29, no. 1, pp. 19–22

Sproull, L. and Kiesler, S. 1991 *Connections: New Ways of Working in the Networked Organization*, MIT Press, Cambridge MA

Turkle, S. 1995 *Life on the Screen: Identity in the Age of the Internet*, Simon and Schuster, New York

Van Gelder, L. 1991 'The strange case of the electronic lover', *Computerization and Controversy: Value Conflicts and Social Choices*, eds C. Dunlap and R. Kling, Academic Press, New York, pp. 364–75

Werry, C.C. 1996 'Linguistic and interactional features of Internet Relay Chat', *Computer-Mediated Communication: Linguistic, Social and Cross-Cultural Perspectives*, ed. S.C. Herring, Benjamins, Amsterdam, pp. 47–63

Wilkins, H. 1991 'Computer-talk: long distance conversations by computer', *Written Communication*, vol. 8, pp. 56–78

Yates, S.J. 1996 'Oral and written linguistic aspects of computer conferencing: a corpus-based study', *Computer-Mediated Communication: Linguistic, Social and Cross-Cultural Perspectives*, ed. S.C. Herring, Benjamins, Amsterdam, pp. 29–46

5

Rhetorics of the Web: hyperreading and critical literacy

NICHOLAS C. BURBULES

One of the perennial questions about reading on the Internet, particularly in reading hypertexts (Burbules & Callister 1996a; Snyder 1996), is whether this mode of reading is something new, or whether it is the same reading, involving the usual skills and strategies, simply being exercised in a new medium—whether, indeed, hypertext itself is even something new, or simply another attempt, this time in the digital domain, to deconstruct linear narrative.

This way of framing the question, as a choice between 'new' reading or 'the same' reading, is unhelpful from the start. Reading is a practice, and as such it partakes of the contexts and social relations in which it takes place; significant differences in those contexts and relations alter the practice. The act of reading on a computer screen is not the same as reading out of a book; the pragmatics of reading—the speed of our reading, when we pause, how long we can concentrate, how often we skip over material or jump back and reread what we have read before, and so forth—are clearly going to be different, and these differences affect how we interpret, understand, and remember what we read (Bruce 1995).

At the same time, there must be some continuity between

this emergent practice and other, related practices with which we are familiar—it is *reading*, after all. Hence questions about whether it is 'new' or 'the same' miss the point, which is to analyse at the concrete level the various roles that familiar elements of reading play in 'hyperreading' (Burbules & Callister 1996a), *and* how they should be reinterpreted in light of the changing pragmatics of reading in hypertext environments such as the World Wide Web. The volume of information that can be accessed, the speed with which it can be accessed, the structure of the Web as a series of interlinked textual points between which one moves with the click of a 'link', are not the same (despite our use of familiar metaphors, like 'pages', to describe them) as with other texts.[1]

Printed texts are by nature selective and exclusive. Any page, any volume, can contain only so many words; it can refer to other texts, but accessing those involves activities such as reaching to a shelf, purchasing the book, going to a library, and so on; activities that are not themselves reading, activities that require energy, time, and sometimes money that a reader may not have to spare. Hypertexts on the Web are by nature inclusive: texts can be almost any size one wishes; any text can be linked to a virtually unlimited number of other texts online; the addition of new links does not in any significant way detract from the text at hand; and accessing any of these textual links requires little time or effort.[2]

The key element in this hypertextual structure is the *link*. In this chapter I consider some of the different things that a link can be; I explore some of the ways in which a linked textual environment works, in the practice of hyperreading; and I claim that hyperreading can promote a significant kind of critical literacy, once the apparently neutral character of a 'link' has been problematised. My hope is to invert the order of how we normally think about links and information points, nodes, or texts: usually we see the points as primary, and the links as mere connectives; here I suggest that we concentrate more on links—as associative relations that change, redefine, and enhance or restrict access to the information they comprise.

What is a link?

The significance of links in a hypertextual environment is often underestimated; the textual points or nodes are assumed, and the links are regarded simply as matters of preference or convenience. Their ease of use makes them seem merely short-cuts, and subservient to the important things: the information sources that they make available. Their speed in taking a user from one point to another makes the moment of transition too fleeting to merit reflection; the link-event becomes invisible. Their familiarity can be deceptive, and I shall discuss three important aspects of links that need to be brought to the surface in order to counteract their apparent naturalness.

The first is that, although all links in a hypertext work in the same way, involve the same act (clicking on a highlighted word or icon), and end with much the same result (a new screen appearing), all links are not the same, and do not imply the same type of semic relation. Below I will describe a menagerie of links, coding them in terms of some standard categories from rhetoric. Here I simply want to make the point that links are not all of the same type, and that selecting and following any particular line of association between distinct textual points involves an interpretation of the nature of the association this link implies. Sometimes this association involves our own idiosyncratic way of making sense of the connection; sometimes it is prefigured by certain familiar conventions (such as the nature and purpose of footnotes) in the context where we encounter the link; sometimes it involves our attempt to guess why the hypertext designer/author made exactly this link in this location between these two items.

This leads to a second point: in our ordinary encounters with links, they are already made. Readers can certainly design/author their own hypertexts, writing their own texts as well as incorporating or modifying material from other textual sources; and, increasingly, Web browsers will allow readers to add their own customised links to the hypertexts designed/authored by others. Nevertheless, the initial contact users have with hypertext—and for most, even now, the only contact—is with materials created by unknown persons whose reasons, biases, motivations, and credibility are also almost entirely unknown. The use and placement of links is one of the vital ways in which the tacit assumptions and values of the designer/author are manifested in a hypertext—yet they are rarely considered as such.

Third, and at a more subtle level, the act of a link is not simply to associate two givens (Burbules 1996). Beyond this, links change the way in which material is read and understood: partly due to the mere juxtaposition of the two related texts (how will a jump from a page on teenage drug-use statistics to a page on rock music affect how the rock music page is read?); and partly by the implied connection that a link expresses—though it is far from inevitable that the connection a designer/author intends is the one that readers will necessarily draw. Moreover, links are (generally) only one-way: of course we can return from a page we visit to the page from which the link originated, but the semic significance implied by the link from A to B does not necessarily accompany the return from B to A; nor is such a relation, so far as it exists, necessarily reciprocal.

The link, then, is the elemental structure that represents a hypertext as a semic web of meaningful relations. Every text, or set of texts, can be read hypertextually (what I have been calling 'hyperreading'); this involves the reader making connections within and across texts, sometimes in ways that are structured by the designer/author (for example, following footnotes or quotations), but often in ways determined by the reader. In online texts, links define a fixed set of relations given to the reader, among which the reader may choose, but beyond which most readers will never go. Moreover, links do not only express semic relations but also, significantly, establish pathways of possible movement within the Web space; they suggest relations, but also *control access to information* (if there is no link from A to B, for many users the existence of B may never be known—in one sense, the link *creates* B as possibility). The assumptions and values implied by links, where they allow one to travel and where they do not, and the boundaries tacitly limiting this particular semic space will appear for most readers; or, if readers do recognise that such choices have been made, they will regard them as authoritative, since in most cases the ability to create such pages—the knowledge of the code—will give the invisible author a certain status: readers tend to assume that someone knowing and caring enough about the topic to create the hyperdocument must have greater than average expertise on the subject. Now, of course, these assumptions are not inevitable, and many readers are more sceptical: a few will know as much or even more about the subject than the hypertext designer/author does; others will find particular links problematic, and thereby learn not to take other links for granted. On the other side, as more and more people develop the skills to create such documents—or as new generations of HTML editing/word processing software make their creation a seamless part of text creation itself—the credibility of any particular hypertext on the Web will diminish, since there will almost certainly be more garbage than work of quality in this Brave New Self-Publishing World (Burbules & Bruce 1995; Callister & Burbules 1996).

What is different about reading or writing a web?

The conventions of reading, like those of writing, have grown out of the structure of sentences flowing into paragraphs, paragraphs flowing into pages, pages followed by other pages. These conventions began with scrolled parchment, and were later adapted to the codex volume (Bolter 1991): they assume a fundamentally linear and hierarchical organisation of information, with passage following passage in a sequence governed by (a) relative importance, formalised in the discipline of the Outline, and (b) the narrative structure of argument, formalised in the discipline of the Syllogism. These two disciplines have constituted the primary form and rhetoric of academic writing, in particular, for centuries in the West. Certain texts and styles of writing resist these disciplines, and contemporary post-structural theories in particular have directly criticised them. Nevertheless, the force of these habits is so strong that most readers tend to impose such a pattern on textual material in the process of reading, even when the content resists it.

It is not clear how these habits will now begin to change with the spread of hypertextual materials; but there is nothing about the form of such materials that *insures* more perspicuous readings or new ways of organising information. Yet we see an enthusiastic conviction that new technologies, including the capabilities of hypertext, will usher in a wave of educational innovation and reform (Means 1994). In part, this enthusiasm is understandable, for web-like textual systems are much more flexible than traditional resources, such as books: they can accommodate all the textual forms that paper and print can, and more. Where text is linear, hypertext can be lateral as well. Where traditional conventions of writing and reading depend on (or create artificially) hierarchies of importance, hypertext can also represent more complex, 'rhizomatic' relationships between ideas (Burbules & Callister 1996a). Where traditional text depends upon the disciplines of the Outline and the Syllogism, hypertext opens up the additional textual possibilities of Bricolage and Juxtaposition: *assembling* texts from pieces that can be represented in multiple relations to one another. These two new disciplines, it should be seen, are still disciplines themselves, contrasting in certain respects to the traditional pair (Outline versus Bricolage; Syllogism versus Juxtaposition), but as *supplements* to them, not necessarily *replacements* for them. Bricolage and Juxtaposition, more suited in some ways to the forms of hypertext, less linear, more lateral, have their own advantages and disadvantages, as the Outline and Syllogism do.

In general, then, hypertext seems to *add* dimensions of writing, and to that extent may encourage new practices of reading as well: ones that might prove more hospitable to alternative, non-traditional points of view and more inclusive of cultural difference. Yet all this remains to be seen; the development of new practices of reading, as I have stressed, depends upon much more than just changing characteristics of

107

text—indeed, traditional text can be read hypertextually and hypertexts can be read quite traditionally.

Early indicators of such a new orientation to textual materials are mixed at best. A few fairly typical reactions to hypertexts suggest, far from a new critical approach to hyperreading, a much more sobering image of the future.

The first element that indicates a new orientation is *surfing*.[3] We see this phenomenological orientation not only to online texts, but to other multi-channel resources as well (remote-controlled cable television, pop radio stations with push-button station-shifting, CD sampling, leafing through ad-laden glossy magazines, etc.[4]) With a surfeit of stimuli competing for people's attention, they are, on the one hand, becoming more adept at screening information very quickly, making rapid judgements about whether it is desirable, and 'parallel processing' different materials simultaneously. On the other hand, their capacities for sustained attention to any single textual source are affected as a consequence. Moreover, in a competitive market for time and attention, we can expect a premium to be placed on the catchy, instantly appealing 'hook', rather than such interest or subtlety as can only emerge over time. The content of textual materials and media is being changed with the assumptions that interest must be seized and held quickly or an audience will scroll past without stopping, and that few readers will be willing or able to follow the text closely all the way through from start to finish. This leads to an increasing fragmentation of content. Again, these trends have been at work for a long time, in popular culture, in the political sphere, and elsewhere—my analysis here is hardly unique or original. But the structure of hypertextual (and multimedia) resources on the World Wide Web is already taking a shape that acknowledges such readerly dispositions.

Second, and related to this first point, is a growing *consumer orientation* toward information. The habits of mind encouraged by mainstream media (most newspapers, magazines, and television news and documentaries) have tended to level, in most people's minds, all sources of information. A general suspicion of traditional authorities and the emergence of fictionalised, hybrid news/entertainment features has tended to blur distinctions of relative credibility and has made all sorts of information merely grist for the mill of gossip, sensationalism, or opinion formation. As a result, the processes of selection, evaluation, and interpretation that develop information into knowledge and understanding are atrophying for many readers (or are not being developed in the first place). We see this trend epitomised in the Web, and discussions about the Web, which, as Marshall (1996) points out, tend to conflate 'information' with 'knowledge'. The bulk of the Web is organised around information sources: facts, statistics, lists, charts, visual data, and so forth. Once accessed, it is usually up to the reader to judge what it means, or if it means much at all. Unfortunately, this second-order reflection is discouraged by the levelling effect that puts all information points on the same level of accessibility and all designer/authors on the same level of credibility. Links, once again, are part of what can turn information into knowledge, suggesting causal associations, category relations, instantiations, and so forth; but when a link is not evaluated as such, an opportunity to translate information into knowledge of some sort is lost. Hence we need an alternative analysis that highlights the cognitive importance and potential of links (Jones & Spiro 1995).

Third, an intimate connection must be drawn between the general use of computers, including Web browsers as well as other applications, and the use of computers specifically for playing *games*. For many users, especially those who are growing up with these technologies, many of their first experiences with computers involve playing electronic games. This experience develops certain orientations to the machine. Some of these can be considered beneficial since they provide general proficiency with the technology: the user develops technical skill with keyboard and cursors; learns to deal with complex environments; develops skills at navigating, and exploring unfamiliar pathways; and adopts an experimental, trial-and-error approach to the unexpected and difficult. Other consequences of a 'game-like' orientation to new technologies may be less beneficial. Rather than becoming critical and

109

discerning, the author may develop a certain trivialising attitude to what is encountered in virtual space (including particularly, but not only, violent events); an ability to focus extensively on game-like activities, but one that develops at the cost of his or her capacity to concentrate on less stimulating projects; and a tendency to take for granted the terrain and structures of tasks, viewing them as simply the parameters of another computer challenge. Other computer software, and particularly operations of the Web, have come to adopt some similar game-like programming elements, and these can be 'fun' and interesting (e.g., current graphics programs for drawing and painting). However, they may also transfer to other writing, drawing, and reading activities the *attitudes* and *habits of thought* developed in game environments, many of which reinforce a 'surfing', casual, uncritical approach to computers and what one creates—for example, the Internet is used for pornography and for writing or acting out violent fantasies within a 'safe' virtual space, as if these were without serious consequence. Part of this uncritical approach involves *using* links without *reflecting upon* them.

Some different types of links

Developing a more reflective and critical approach to the World Wide Web and the information found on it includes learning to read the subtle and not-so-subtle implications that links make through association. A thoughtful hyperreader asks why links are made from certain points and not others; where those links lead; and what values are entailed in such decisions. But beyond this, links *create* significations themselves: they are not simply the neutral medium of passing from point A to point B (Burbules 1996).

Part of developing this critical discernment, I suggest, is to consider how links are tools of rhetoric (for alternative treatments of this subject, see Brent n.d. and Lanham 1993, pp. 127–9). In the same way that links carry readers from text to text, so also do tropes or other rhetorical turns of phrase associate words and concepts ('metaphor' derives from the Greek words to 'carry over'). By examining a menagerie of such tropes, I intend to illustrate a kind of analysis that could be carried further: I call this a menagerie because the list of items I am discussing is not meant to be systematic or exhaustive; indeed, there can be no exhaustive list of tropes, because they are artefacts of the creative potential inherent in language itself (Lanham 1991). But as examples, I hope that they can help us to consider links as something quite different from what they appear to be.

Metaphor

The term 'metaphor' can be confusing because it is sometimes used to refer to tropes and figurative language generally, and sometimes to one particular type of trope. In the narrower sense, metaphor is a comparison, an equation, between apparently dissimilar objects, inviting the listener or reader to see points of similarity between them *while also inviting a change in the originally related concepts by 'carrying over' previously unrelated characteristics from one to the other*. Like simile, metaphor asks us to see one thing *as* another: 'my beloved is a rose', 'the city is a cesspool', 'school is jail'. Note that, like Web links, these relations tend to be unidirectional, though the second concept (e.g., 'rose') is also changed to some degree by its relation with the first.

Web links can be read as metaphors when apparently unrelated textual points are associated: a link from a page listing Political Organisations to a page on the Catholic Church might puzzle, outrage, or be ignored—but considered as a metaphor it might make a reader think about politics and religion in a different way.

Metonymy

A second trope, often paired with metaphor as comprising the two overarching forms of figuration, is metonymy: an association not by similarity, but by contiguity, relations in practice.

111

Baseball and football have affinities by both being sports; baseball and hot dogs (or hamburgers) have a metonymic affinity only because in American culture they often appear together.

A Web link, almost by definition can become metonymic, with repetition. Most users no longer have to be told that clicking on a pentagon-shaped icon will take them 'home', to the index or entry-page of a set of interlinked pages. The icon could just as easily be, for example, a pyramid shape and the language of return would be less domestic, and more vertically connotative. A page labelled 'Vacation Spots' may take you to 'How to Avoid Pickpockets'. On a broader scale, the increase of clickable icons sponsored by private companies, crowding the screens of pages that have nothing to do with their product, creates a metonymic space that continually reminds the user that the Web is for sale, and that commercial interests (by far the fastest-growing category of Web page producers) under-write more and more of what is presented there.

Synecdoche

Other tropes have a more specific function: synecdoche involves figurations where part of something is used as short-hand for the thing as a whole or, more rarely, vice versa: 'the moustache came back to the bar and asked for another beer; he already had a six-pack inside him'. In the context of Web links, this trope is particularly influential in identifying, or suggesting, relations of categorical inclusion: a list of 'Human Rights Violations' may include links to pages dealing with corporal punishment in schools, or vice versa.

This relating of categorical wholes to particular instances, or of parts to wholes, is vitally important. The power to register superordinate categories to which particulars are sub-sumed is a special way of influencing people's conceptual and normative thinking. Because different categorical wholes are always possible, clustering and organising things in different ways, and because identifying and adjudicating particulars *as* instances is a way of regulating them, such determinations

112

must be recognised as such and brought into question. Links make such associations, but do so in a way that is seldom made problematic: yet because such categorical links are often the gateway that controls access to that information, clustering and relating items in one way rather than another is more than a matter of convenience or heuristic—it becomes a method of determining how people think about a subject.

Hyperbole

One of the more familiar forms of figuration may be hyperbole, exaggeration for the sake of tropic emphasis (or its opposite, understatement, for the same effect): 'my office was flooded with mail'; or 'it was a little warm in Egypt when we visited'. Anyone who spends much time browsing Web sites will recognise these as designer/author tactics to attract attention. But on a more subtle level, the dynamics of the World Wide Web are essentially hyperbolic (starting with its name): each collection, each archive, each search engine, tacitly implies a degree of comprehensiveness beyond its actual scope. For all its wealth and complexity, the Web comprises only a fraction of culture, society, and politics, worldwide; its omissions are often quite glaring, but nothing in its self-descriptions or link attributes—'Movie Guide', 'Dining in San Francisco', and so on—suggest that what is not included may be more important than what is.

Antistasis

A less familiar trope involves the repetition of a word—the 'same' word—in a different context ('whenever I fly in an airline I feel trapped, as if I were a fly in a bottle'). Many Web links work this way: using a particular word or phrase as a pivot from one context to a very different one. Key-word search engines are based almost entirely on this principle. For example, in reading someone's online article about their vacation to San Francisco, the term 'North Beach' might be linked to a page of information about Italian Restaurants, to another

113

on strip bars, and to another about the Beat Poets from the 1960s; the 'same' North Beach in one sense, but in another sense very different, separated in time and spirit. The effect of such links, especially when the differences in context and significance are not made explicit, is to put all phenomena within the same semic space, eliding time, space, and discursive context, making all these information points simply grist for the contemporary reader.

There is a metonymic element at work here as well; as in those encyclopaedias or calendar programs that connect together everything that happened on a particular day in history ('September 24: on this day, the President signed the Voting Rights Act into law; the Baltimore Orioles beat the New York Yankees 4–2; the movie *Singing in the Rain* opened in Los Angeles; a housewife in Akron, Ohio won the Betty Crocker Cookoff with her recipe for Upside-Down Blueberry Cake; in Pakistan government troops used clubs to disperse a crowd of protesters; a panda bear in the Peking zoo became the first to give birth in captivity, etc.'). As noted previously, one of the primary effects of the Web is this juxtaposition of apparently unrelated points of information and the reduction of all to the same superficial level of significance: a bricolage of elements, mixing the momentous and the trivial, the local and the global, the contemporary and the historic; inviting multiple—and frequently untestable—interpretations of significance that can be as personal and idiosyncratic as you like. As such points of information all pivot on a particular date, location, or word, they are brought into an association that may seem either trivial or thought-provoking; at the same time, the impact of the pivotal word or concept shifts and broadens. Antistasis invites such connections by invoking 'the same' in a way that reveals difference.

Identity

It may seem strange to include identity as a trope, but it is included here as a companion and contrast to antistasis. In associations of identity, the 'same' linking point is used to

114

highlight points of commonality, not difference. Whereas other tropes, such as metaphor or simile, invite comparisons of similarity across different items, identity denies difference and emphasises equivalence ('the woman who came into the office this morning is the surgeon who operated on my son last year'). Such relations typically depend on realist assumptions about co-referentiality or on logical tautologies; but here I want to emphasise the tropic effect of such assertions in practical contexts, including the Web.

Unlike antistasis, which tends to highlight the ways in which terms or concepts change significance in different contexts, identity tends to hypostasise meanings, to freeze them, by suggesting that core meaning resists changing context. On the Web, such associations tend to draw lines of connection *through* pages, from different people or institutions, different cultures, or different countries, like a net unifying the surface multiplicity of Web content and contexts. Beneath the particular instantiations of such an association is a figure of interwoven unity and commonality—one image of the Web, but one that excludes and obscures at least as much as it highlights.

Sequence and cause-and-effect

These tropes, too, could be given a very literal and non-figurative interpretation: that they indicate *real* relations, not simply allusive ones. But without engaging that dispute here, there is an effect of such associations, whether based on 'real' relations or not, that may be indistinguishable from the reader's side. Links that suggest 'this *and then* that' or 'this *because of* that' (for instance, the previous rock music/drug use example) do much more than simply associate ideas or information points; they assert, or imply, beliefs about the world outside the Web.[5] But because they do not specify or explain such connections, but simply *manifest* them, they are more difficult to recognise and question; often they simply carry the reader with them to inferences that could just as well be drawn quite differently, or could be criticised and rejected.

Catechresis

This trope is in some ways the most interesting of them all. Though sometimes characterised as a 'far-fetched' metaphor, or as a strict misuse of language ('the belly of the river'), catechresis is the recognition that such apparent 'misuses' are how many tropes originally begin—and that these novel, strange instances might spark reflections just as revealing and delightful as those one recognises more readily (if a river can have a mouth, why not a belly?—perhaps the belly of the river rumbled—perhaps it is the point where the river bends—perhaps it swelled, pregnant with fish). At a deeper level, catechresis is the originary form of changes in language generally: 'far-fetched' uses of familiar words in a new context; slang; accidental malapropisms; street patter that uses coded terms to elude or mislead authorities ('horse' for heroin, etc.)—over time, such uses become familiar and normalised, become 'literal' (is 'the hands of a clock' metaphorical or literal, today? (see Burbules, Schraw & Trathen 1989)).

Catechresis on the Web becomes a trope for the basic working of the link, generally: *any* two things can be linked, even a raven and a writing desk, and with that link, a process of semic movement begins instantaneously; the connection becomes part of a public space, a community of discourse, which, as others find and follow that link, *creates* a new avenue of association—beginning tropically or ironically, perhaps, but gradually taking its own path of development and normalisation. It could be that, before long, a new word processor will be called, jokingly, 'Raven'; or someone will hand-carve a desk out of black wood, using bird shapes as a decorative feature; or the word 'raven' will be used casually to refer to office furniture in general ('I wish these ravens would fly up here themselves so I did not have to call the movers'). Far-fetched or not, such developments are indistinguishable from examples that we do not see any longer as 'far-fetched' at all. Two key points follow: first, *we never can know* which uses will become accepted and standardised, so it is impossible to separate in any strict way proper uses from misuses (it may be simply a judgement made from a particular time-frame); second, the Web, because of its global and cross-cultural span, because of its linked architecture, and because it usually requires the filter of a common language, English, is becoming a major new avenue in which malapropisms, slang, and far-fetched associative links will become familiar and, before long, normalised.

What does it mean to hyperread critically?

I am using the language of tropes, tropically, to describe different sorts of links in order to highlight their variety and non-neutral signification. I want to show links as rhetorical moves that can be evaluated and questioned for their relevance. They imply choices; they reveal assumptions; they have effects—whether intentionally or inadvertently. Judging links, then, is a crucial part of developing a broader critical orientation to hyperreading: not simply to follow the links laid out for us, but to interpret their meaning and assess their appropriateness (on such critical Web literacy, see also Bigum & Green 1993 and Peters & Lankshear 1996).

What I have called the disciplines of Outline and Syllogism have their own sort of deceptive naturalness: as if information had an inherent organisation to which it must fit; as if good arguments necessarily always lead in one way. These disciplines, so much a part of writing and reading generally, imply tacit values and assumptions that should not escape critical reflection. The disciplines of Bricolage and Juxtaposition— more typical, I have suggested, of the rhizomatic character of the Web and the way its links are established—may appear more undisciplined, offering more latitude for interpretation and less designer/author prerogative. However, exaggerating this difference is mistaken both ways: first, because the Outline and the Syllogism are just as much rhetorical forms as are metaphor or hyperbole; and also because Bricolage and Juxtaposition imply just as much responsibility for selecting and ordering information in particular ways, inviting certain inter-pretations and excluding others.

The credibility of designer/authors, then, is continually open for question and challenge by hyperreaders, not only through the standard criteria of expertise, impartiality, and other infor-mal standards of credible authority—important as these are—but also, now, as creators of a semic system: their own pages initially, but then also the larger semic Web from which their pages draw connections and to which they provide (or restrict) access. This latter sense of 'credibility' goes beyond simple authority in the subject matters at hand, to responsi-bility for the particular links they create, where and how they create them, and the larger network of information sources to which they are related. An assessment of personal credibility or responsibility becomes implicated, then, in a larger assess-ment of how the Web works. To carry out such assessments, readers should be discouraged from a simple consumer orien-tation to the Web; to learn to distinguish simple information from *linked information*, which (as I hope is clear by now) implies a host of other assumptions and values; and to resist and suspect the seductive character of multimedia Web design, much of which (such as animated icons, snatches of music/Muzak playing in the background of Web pages, or links that flash on and off) has more to do with attracting and holding the flagging attention of casual users than with com-municating anything useful.

A crucial aspect of developing this capacity for critical hyperreading is, I suggest, to learn about the mechanics of Web design/authoring itself. Just as specialists in other fields (from poetry to acting to political speech writing) can be the sharpest critics of other practitioners because they know the conventions, tricks, and moves that establish a sense of style and elicit particular responses from an audience, so also should hyperreaders (whether or not they actually design/author ma-terial for the Web themselves) know what goes into selecting material for a page, making links, organising a cluster of separate pages into a hyperlinked Web site, and so forth. The more that one is aware of *how* this is done, the more one can

118

be aware *that* it was done and that it *could* have been done otherwise. This discloses the apparent 'naturalness' or invisibility of such designer/author choices, and grants the hyperreader the opportunity to stand outside them—to question, criticise, and imagine alternatives. Links are made, and they are made by specific individuals and groups according to their own assumptions, prejudices, and limitations.

Another dimension of this critical reading is to recognise that however flexible a structure the Web might be, it still has particular organisational and connective features. For one thing, these will not be equally hospitable to all cultural groups and individuals; like any other medium, the Web advantages certain voices and perspectives and disadvantages others. Moreover, as an outgrowth of certain AI (artificial intelligence) assumptions about the way thinking works (*or should work*), the structure of the Web does not simply represent externally the way (certain) people think; ironically, the tool we have created to serve us actually shapes us. However, users aware of this can make it a tool of resistance (for example, by pointing out these structural features and perhaps playing them off against themselves).

Finally, critical hyperreading also includes an apprehension of the *limits* of any organisation of information. As large and inclusive as the Web is, it excludes certain important things to know or care about, and this will be true no matter how 'World Wide' the Web becomes.[6] Because the Web is a complex, interlinked semic network, one can move almost infinitely within it without ever encountering an explicit 'edge' or limit: like physical space itself, the Web curves in upon and contains itself. Yet even though there are no edges, there are limits and these are very difficult to determine *from the inside* (Burbules 1996). It is a special skill of hyperreading to be able to recognise this, to imagine what is not or may not be there (the dog that does not bark), to read the absences as well as the presences of information—in short, to *think differently*, to be able to stand outside the particular set of associations and assumptions that define the information space one occupies. Every link excludes as well as includes associative points; every path leads away from other avenues as it opens one passage; every trope conceals as it reveals. Appreciating all this is a feature of critical reading generally; yet because of the apparent inclusiveness of the Web and because of the apparent neutrality of the associations it establishes, such an awareness must become a particular virtue of hyperreading. With such capabilities, the Web can give readers an enormous opportunity for discovery and synthesis. Without such capabilities, the Web can be a frightening medium of manipulation and distortion— all the more effective for its flashy, user-friendly facade.[7]

Notes

1 Here, as in other work, I use the word 'text' broadly, to encompass other sorts of information media (sound, video, graphics), all of which can be 'read'. A more complete treatment of 'hyperreading' would cover the related, and distinctive, aspects of reading these different materials, and how one integrates information from different media sources.

2 However, for users accessing the Web via commercial service, and using a modem, there is a non-trivial cost difference, compared to those of us who have the privilege of free, unlimited access. Significant equity issues are implied by these different levels of access (see Burbules & Callister 1996b and Burbules & Callister forthcoming article).

3 Noel Gough suggested to me that 'surfing' is a term that alludes to a group of users defined by a specific gender, class, region, and culture; he suggests an alternative term, 'cruising', although that term, unfortunately, is particularised in its own way, too. The point is not to find the perfect term, but to realise the potential slant of any particular term. Thanks to Noel for raising this crucial concern.

4 Or, as is becoming more and more prevalent, doing several of these at once.

5 Yes, there is such a thing.

6 The issue of distorted or slanted content is gaining prominence with increasing trends towards globalisation and the spread of the Web as a medium through which more and more cultural groups and individuals are trying to express themselves.

7 Previous versions of this chapter were presented at Edith Cowan University and Deakin University in Australia. Thanks to participants in those seminars for feedback that helped me to improve this chapter. Thanks especially to Ilana Snyder for her useful suggestions.

References

Bigum, C. and Green, B. 1993 'Technologising literacy: or, interrupting the dream of reason', *Literacy in Contexts*, eds A. Luke and P. Gilbert, Allen & Unwin, New South Wales, Australia, pp. 4–28

Bolter, J.D 1991 *Writing Space: The Computer, Hypertext, and the History of Writing*, Erlbaum, Hillsdale, NJ

Brent, D. n.d. 'Rhetorics of the web: implications for teachers of literacy', <http://www.ucalgary.ca/~dabrent/webliteracies/pointer.html>

Bruce, B.C. 1995 'Twenty-first century literacy', Technical Report no. 624, Center for the Study of Reading, University of Illinois, Urbana/Champaign

Burbules, N.C. 1996 'Aporia and knowledge: passages of learning', Keynote address to the Philosophy of Education Society of Australasia, Oct

Burbules, N.C. and Bruce, B.C. 1995 'This is not a paper', *Educational Researcher*, vol. 24, no. 8, pp. 12–8

Burbules, N.C. and Callister, Jr., T.A. 1996a 'Knowledge at the crossroads: alternative futures of hypertext environments for learning', *Educational Theory*, vol. 46, no. 1, pp. 23–50

——1996b 'Issues of access and equity for new educational technologies', *Insights: A Publication of the John Dewey Society for the Study of Education and Culture*, vol. 32, no. 1, 11–14

——'Access to new educational technologies: democratic challenges', *Critical Forum* (forthcoming)

Burbules, N.C., Schraw, G. and Trathen, W. 1989 'Metaphor, idiom, and figuration', *Metaphor and Symbolic Activity*, vol. 4, no. 2, pp. 93–110

Callister, Jr., T.A. and Burbules, N.C. 1996 'Public spaces and cyberspace: issues of credibility in educational technologies', *Insights: A Publication of the John Dewey Society for Education and Culture*, vol. 32, no. 1, pp. 9–11

Jones, R.A. and Spiro, R. 1995 'Contextualisation, cognitive flexibility, and hypertext: the convergence of interpretative theory, cognitive psychology, and advanced information technologies', *The Cultures of Computing*, ed. S.L. Star Blackwell, Cambridge, pp. 146–57

Lanham, R.A. 1991 *Handbook of Rhetorical Terms*, 2nd edn, University of California Press, Berkeley

——1993 *The Electronic Word: Democracy, Technology, and the Arts*, University of Chicago Press, Chicago

Marshall, J. 1996 'Education in the mode of information: some philosophical issues', *Philosophy of Education 1996*, ed. F. Margonis, Philosophy of Education Society, Urbana, Illinois (forthcoming)

Means, B. 1994 ed. *Technology and Education Reform: The Reality Behind the Promise*, Jossey-Bass, San Francisco

Peters, M. and Lankshear, C. 1996 'Critical literacy and digital texts', *Educational Theory*, vol. 46, no. 1, pp. 51–70

Snyder, I. 1996 *Hypertext: The Electronic Labyrinth*, Melbourne University Press, Victoria, Australia

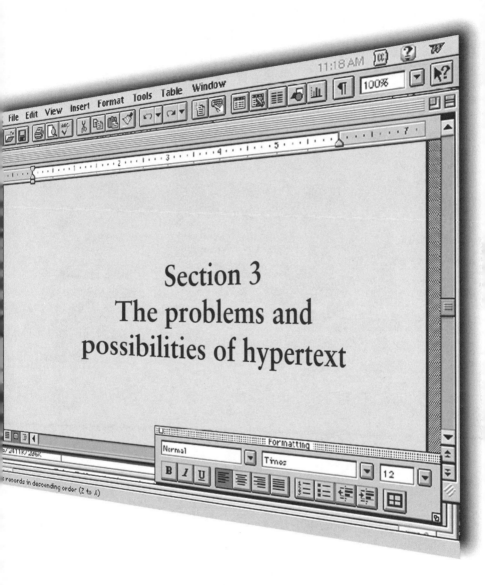

Section 3
The problems and
possibilities of hypertext

6
Beyond the hype: reassessing hypertext

ILANA SNYDER

Many readers will remember when computers first arrived in schools in the late 1970s. There was a little scepticism and a lot of euphoria. In the context of language and literacy education, the cries of the pessimists who warned of the technology's inevitable dehumanising effects were rapidly drowned out by the enthusiastic rhetoric of techno-evangelists who believed that simply giving students computers to use as writing machines would improve the quality of their writing. These responses to the introduction of a new technology—that the technology itself would alter social and cultural practices—influenced the kinds of questions researchers asked for much of that first decade of research into literacy and technology. I was one of the researchers who investigated in an elaborate study what now seems a somewhat naive question: 'Does the use of computers for writing improve the quality of students' texts?' (Snyder 1993a).

Perhaps, not surprisingly, even with data from hundreds of studies exploring similar kinds of questions, the findings were equivocal. Yes, with computers students wrote longer texts and with fewer errors. It proved difficult, however, to establish whether the texts they produced were actually better and, even if they were, whether that improvement could be attributed directly to the use of computers. There was a growing awareness by the late 1980s that the cultural context of the classroom, which includes at the very least teachers, students, teaching and learning practices, hardware and software, influenced in very complex ways students' literacy practices and the texts they produced. To attribute the relative quality of students' writing to the machine alone came to be seen as a reductive interpretation of research data. Today, more cautious and carefully qualified claims about the potential of word processing in literacy contexts dominate the research literature.

What is hypertext?

Before I draw some parallels between the expectations of the use of hypertext in literacy contexts and those that arose with word processing, it is worth offering a non-technical explanation of the technology. Hypertext is an information medium that exists only online in a computer. A structure composed of blocks of text connected by electronic links, it offers different pathways to users. Hypertext provides a means of arranging information in a non-linear manner with the computer automating the process of connecting one piece of information to another. When the structure accommodates not only printed texts but also digitised sound, graphics, animation, video and virtual reality, it is sometimes referred to as 'hypermedia'. 'Multimedia' is often adopted as a marketing term by computer manufacturers, software developers, publishers and others to describe both hypermedia content and the hardware or software that embodies it. Hypertext is my preferred term. I use it to represent both the structure and the content of this type of information technology (Snyder 1996).

A hypertext is constructed partly by the writers who create the links, and partly by readers who decide which threads to follow. Unlike printed texts, which generally compel readers to read in a linear fashion—from left to right and from top to bottom of the page—hypertexts encourage readers to move from one text-chunk to another, rapidly and non-sequentially. Hypertext differs from printed text by offering readers multiple paths through a body of information: it allows them to make their own connections, incorporate their own links, and produce their own meanings. Hypertext consequently blurs the boundaries between readers and writers. These differences help support the view that the use of hypertext affects how we read and write, how we teach reading and writing, and how we define literacy practices.

Hypertext is essentially a network of links between words, ideas and sources, one that has neither a centre nor an end. We 'read' hypertext by navigating through it, taking detours to 'footnotes', and from those 'footnotes' to others, exploring what in print culture would be described as 'digressions' as long and complex as the 'main' text. Any other document can be linked to and become part of another text. The extent of hypertext is unknowable because it lacks clear boundaries and is often multi-authored.

Such features appear to constitute the generic characteristics of hypertext, but it is just as difficult to talk of 'generic' hypertext as to talk of generic print. Not all printed texts appear in books, for instance, nor for that matter as literature. Similarly, hypertext systems are not used exclusively for scholarly purposes in cultural and literary studies: in fact, they are used more widely in applications such as aeroplane-repair manuals. As with print, the projected audience for hypertext largely determines the system's characteristics. So instead of trying to discern its generic qualities, it is more helpful to identify the principal types of hypertext. For example, standalone hypertext systems such as Hypercard differ from networked or distributed hypertext systems such as the World Wide Web, in which digitised text and other data can be manipulated simultaneously by many users. We can also differentiate between 'read-only' hypertext like CD-ROMs (in which readers' contributions are limited to choosing their own reading paths) and hypertext in which users can add text, links or both.

These definitions provide a convenient and useful framework for understanding the full range of forms that hypertext systems might assume. We can think of this range as comprising a continuum. At one extreme, a hypertext document may be so restrictive that readers find they have no more (and perhaps even fewer) navigational choices than they would with a linear version of the text. At the other extreme, a hypertext document may be so open, interconnected and reader-controlled that users could be overwhelmed by the multiplicity of choices.

Ascribing power to technology

Hypertext appeared in school and post-school literacy contexts in the mid-1980s. Like word processing, enthusiasts endowed it with utopian promise. The idea that hypertext linking is so revolutionary that it enhances whatever the author is writing about is like the belief that simply giving a writer a word processing machine improves writing. Such an attitude overlooks the fact that, although the technology may assist in particular ways, it does not perform all the writer's tasks. The writer still has to pay attention to important matters of rhetoric, organisation and so on.

Notwithstanding, hypertext is often discussed in a celebratory if not hyperbolic manner. We read that hypertext is replacing linear writing in an evolutionary step toward perfect communication technology; that the mere act of linking multiple interpretations and voices results automatically in better communication; and that hypertext is transforming society and education systems, democratising the academy, and promoting the breakdown of artificial divisions between the disciplines. Others claim that although hypertext is still in its infancy, it may influence intellectual development as profoundly as did the invention of alphabetic writing in the thirteenth century BC or the printed book in the fifteenth century AD. Hypertext and the other electronic reading and writing technologies are seen as having reached that critical mass which will enable them to supersede the printed word as the dominant means of enculturation and communication.

In a similar fashion, those with dystopian views draw our attention to what they describe as the insidious invasion of electronic communications and information processing technologies. They warn that it is easy to be so dazzled by hypertext that critique is relegated to the margins. Perceiving the new technologies as technocratic by nature and potentially dominant, they express grave concerns for what it means both for individuals and our culture to submit to a dominant technocratic force. As they see it, the threat is a totalitarian nightmare. These critics implore us to ask whether improved technology enhances moral values, if innovations in technology embody our choice of a future, and whether we should be according technology the significance of national progress. They point out a paradox—that at a time when all other meta-narratives are being scrupulously questioned there are those who would propose a grand narrative of technology-as-progress. Also deplored is the fetishisation of novelty—critics question whether the technology should be hailed as culturally and educationally valuable just because it is new. And, at a more particular level, critics draw on a few negative aspects of hypertextuality itself when they argue that the use of the technology offers users nothing but confusion and cognitive overload.

The battle lines are drawn. Those who speak with excitement and wonderment of the powers and possibilities of the new technologies are demeaned by detractors as uncritical, naive enthusiasts, engaged in a 'Faustian pact' (Birkerts 1994, p. 210), a battle between 'technology and soul' (p. 211). Those who lament the alteration of the literary engagement, represented by the displacement of the page by the screen, are reviled by their opponents as technologically primitive, Luddite and conservative in the image of the National Rifle Association (Birkerts 1994). There is mutual disdain; each camp holds the other in contempt with accusations of retarded intellect. However, whether exultant or dismissive, I argue that any extreme appraisals of the technologies' powers are problematic. What

129

seems imperative is to assess both positions. If as educators we are engaged in analysing our social, political and ideological identities, then we must examine carefully how these new technologies affect our culture. Aligning ourselves with one side or the other in this debate seems self-defeating. Yet on the other hand, it is rather unrealistic to imagine that such divergent views of these technologies can be reconciled. Indeed, tensions between different positions can be both salutary and generative. What we must avoid is the descent into no-win slinging matches between the lieutenants and the generals of the opposing armies. But before elaborating further the dangers of polarising the debate, the following examples are included to suggest the kinds of responses to hypertext technologies represented in the literature.

Ted Nelson (1992), who coined the word 'hypertext', connects hypertext directly with social and cultural change. He expresses somewhat fancifully his vision of Xanadu—a networked, universal system:

> Our objective at the Xanadu project has been not to fulfil the needs of industry, or to make things happen a little faster or more efficiently. Ours has been the only proper objective: to make a new world . . . Open hypertext publishing is the manifest destiny of free society. It is fair, it is powerful, and it is coming. (pp. 56–7)

In formulating the notion of Xanadu, Nelson poses a rhetorical question:

> Is it mathematically possible to supply billions of readers at screens with the exact paragraph, sentence, fragment, illustration, or footnote, photograph, or piece of movie that each requires, immediately? Even if the number of the stored documents and the number of links between them grow into trillions? (ibid. p. 52)

Nelson continues to believe that it can be done:

> I have a vision for the year 2020; I like to call it the 20/20 vision. Think of everyone at screens: a billion around the planet. And each person at a screen will be able to extract

from a great common pool any fragment of whatever is published, with automatic royalty and no red tape. (ibid. p. 44)

Despite his confidence, Nelson's Xanadu is probably not feasible because 'there are insurmountable political and social obstacles to a universal system' (Bolter 1991, p. 103). It remains an unachievable vision bearing the trademark of utopian excessiveness.

Another celebrant of hypertext is Lanham (1993) who hails 'the coming of the electronic word, the movement from letters printed on paper to digitised images projected onto the phosphorous screen of a computer' as a momentous transformation of literary studies. He argues that the fixed printed surface becomes 'volatile and interactive' (p. 73), while the immutable text upon which our culture has been built is called into question.

Balestri (1988) and Joyce (1995) see hypertext as offering opportunities to alter the nature of the academy and its traditional kinds of writing practices. They use an idealistic rhetoric of 'community' and the 'democratisation of the academy'. Both Balestri and Joyce suggest that 'our new understanding of textual authority must be centred not on singularity, consistency, and closure, but on difference, multiplicity and community' (Moulthrop 1991, p. 267). They argue that 'we must reconceive writing not as a private activity eventuating in a public product, but as a process of revision or construction that is itself shared between writers and readers, or among reader/writers' (p. 267).

By contrast, when Bigum and Green (1993, p. 4) write about 'technologising literacy', they aim to offer 'an alternative view, one that is much more sceptical and socially critical than is usually the case in discussions of educational computing and literacy pedagogy in Australia and elsewhere'. They question the position that accepts the computerisation of literacy as 'a *progressive* feature, a way of moving into the future'. Their critique focuses on 'the dark side' of 'the American Dream' as embodied in 'the internationalisation of techno-capital'. Bigum and Green regard that prospect as 'less and less fanciful as we look increasingly to the new technologies for our salvation and our solace in a time of crisis and change' (p. 5). Although not writing directly about hypertext, their words reflect the attitude of those who question our allegedly unthinking cultural embrace of computer technologies such as hypertext. In the tradition of postmodern pessimism, such writers reject the romance of Progress, but they should not be seen as wholly negative. Although they fear a diminished sense of human capacities, 'the replacement of the impossibly extravagant hopes that had for so long been attached to the idea of "technology" by more plausible, realistic aspirations may, in the long run, be cause for optimism' (Marx 1994, pp. 255–6).

These examples demonstrate the strains of technological determinism that permeate academic discourse about hypertext. By 'technological determinism' I mean the assumption that qualities inherent in the computer medium itself are responsible for changes in social and cultural practices. The perception of technology as 'an independent entity, a virtually autonomous agent of change' (Marx & Smith 1994, p. xi) is not new. Indeed, assigning technology this role 'pervades the received popular version of modern history' (Marx & Smith 1994, p. x). The compass and other navigation equipment are seen as having made possible Europe's colonisation of the world; the printing press is acknowledged as the cause of the Reformation; and the invention of the cotton gin is similarly linked to the American Civil War. Such popular narratives convey a strong sense of 'the efficacy of technology as a driving force of history' (Marx & Smith 1994, p. x). Unlike more abstract forces such as sociocultural and political formations, the tangibility of mechanical devices seems to make it easier to assign them determinative power.

The popular discourse of technological determinism is typified by sentences 'in which "technology", or a surrogate like "the machine", is made the subject of an active predicate: "The automobile created suburbia" . . . "The Pill produced a sexual revolution" '. And in the case of hypertext, where the views are most often endorsements: 'Hypertext democratises the academy'; 'Hypertext liberates the reader/writer'; 'Hypertext transforms education'. In each example, a complex event is made to seem the outcome of a technological innovation. 'Many of these statements carry the further implication that the social consequences of our technical ingenuity are far-reaching, cumulative, mutually reinforcing, and irreversible' (Marx & Smith 1994, p. xi).

It should be apparent by this stage of my argument that I believe that grandiose claims about the influence and power of any technology, and in the context of this chapter, hypertext, must be interrogated assiduously since they build on the spurious premise that technology is directly responsible for changes that inevitably affect social relations. Overlooking the human agency integral to all technological innovation, they rely on an interpretative frame in which any notion of control over technology disappears. When examining the problems associated with technological determinism, Stoll's notion of 'silicon snake oil' (1995, p. 50) is both evocative and useful. It signifies the need to query the 'technocratic belief that computers and networks will make a better society'; that access to information, better communications, and electronic programs 'can cure social problems' (p. 50).

The functions of hypertext are not wholly determined either by technology or society. As Selfe and Selfe (1994, p. 482) point out, 'computers, like other complex technologies, are articulated in many ways with a range of existing cultural forces and with a variety of projects in our educational system . . . that run the gamut from liberatory to oppressive'. Moreover, seeing that the humanities and the social sciences have been using hypertext technology for only ten years or so, claims about its impact can be only provisional. To hail its advent as the beginning of a social and educational revolution is politically naive. It is similarly naive to connect the invention of hypertext directly and causally with the demise of print culture, if, indeed, we are witnessing such a phenomenon.

Hypertext's educational potential

Although writing concerned with the educational promise of hypertext often has an ebullient flavour, not all claims for the value and use of hypertext can be dismissed as the product of techno-narcissism. One commonly identified advantage of using hypertext is that it simulates and subsequently clarifies some of the most significant ideas of postmodern literary theories. A number of hypertext theorists, including Landow (1992), Bolter (1991), Lanham (1993) and Johnson-Eilola (1994), agree that the parallels between hypertext technology and postmodern theory are so strong that the two fields have 'converged' (Landow 1992, p. 3). Bolter finds it 'uncanny' that many of those postmodern pronouncements which scandalised print-bound readers seem no more than descriptive of the properties of computer-generated hypertext. Lanham argues that hypertext replicates the logics of postmodern thought by 'literalis[ing] them in a truly *uncanny* way' (1989, p. 287). Johnson-Eilola (1994, p. 203) believes that hypertext helps us to 'revise theories of reading, writing, and literacy in key ways by making various traits of these theories visible' (p. 203). In another article, he explains that the text can be 'deconstructed [not only] in the reader's mind or in a secondary, parasitical text, but also visibly on the computer screen' (1993, p. 382). More than any previous text technology, argues Johnson-Eilola, hypertext 'encourages both writers and readers . . . to confront and work consciously and concretely with deconstruction, intertextuality, the decentring of the author, and the reader's complicity with the construction of the text' (1993, p. 382).

Hypertext is seen not only as valuable in literalising postmodern theories; other claims are made about its educational potential. Although some seem quite appealing, many are yet to be verified by systematic studies. The most extravagant, however, smack of technological determinism and utopian myopia. When Lanham (1993, p. 107) argues that '[d]igitisation of the arts radically democratises them', he places himself firmly in a long tradition of technological utopianism that has made similar claims for the railway, the telephone and the car. Although not always an advocate, Tuman (1992, pp. 4–5) perceives electronic technologies in general and hypertext in particular as 'the source of a possible cultural reorientation as profound in its implications (for literacy education and practically everything else) as the industrial revolution of the last two centuries'. Landow (1992, p. 160) is convinced that 'even the comparatively limited systems and bodies of literary materials thus far available demonstrate that hypertext and hypermedia have enormous potential to improve teaching and learning'. Nevertheless, Lanham, Tuman, Landow and others focus on important aspects of teaching, learning and the curriculum that may be affected by the use of hypertext. These include the promotion of more independent and active learning, changes to teaching and curriculum practices, and challenges to our assumptions about literacy and literary education.

Hypertext is both a teaching and a learning tool. If teachers are prepared to transfer to students much of the responsibility for accessing, sequencing and deriving meaning from information, hypertext can provide an environment in which exploratory or discovery learning may flourish. Hypertext users participate actively when locating information: students become reader-authors, either by choosing individual paths through linked information, or by adding texts and links to the network. Hypertext systems seem to foster an implicit, incidental and contextual kind of learning, which is widely regarded as more enduring and transferable than direct, explicit teaching.

A hypertext classroom can change the role of the teacher. Since some of the power and authority is transferred to the students, the teacher becomes something like Bruner's (1986) coach, 'more an older, more experienced partner in a collaboration than an authenticated leader' (Landow 1992, p. 123). Students can become correspondingly more independent as active shapers of the knowledge they acquire. Hypertext is equally appropriate for both individual and collaborative work. Because hypertext easily accommodates interdisciplinary approaches to literary studies, teachers can use it to develop and extend their students' ability to think critically and make connections between discrete bodies of information. The electronic facility to make such connections speeds up the development of skilled reading and creative thinking. The instantaneity of hypertextual links also permits and encourages sophisticated forms of analysis. Hypertext enables students to assimilate large bodies of information while simultaneously developing those analytic habits they need for thinking critically about the information.

Hypertext can also meet the needs of students with differing abilities. Since educational materials do not have to be pitched at a particular standard of ability, verbal and non-verbal materials of varying levels of difficulty can be interwoven, and self-paced learning encouraged. Furthermore, students who are less comfortable with the printed book than with alternative information media respond well to hypertext. The technology provides the means of redefining the textbook by renegotiating 'the traditional ratio of alphabetic to iconographic information' (Lanham 1993, p. 106). Hypertext also provides an alternative means of participation for students who may be inhibited or shy, enabling them to 'contribute' to class discussions by adding to or commenting on an element of the hypertext.

Other kinds of student may also be provided for in a hypertext classroom. For distance-education students, hypertext combines the reader's control with the virtual presence of a large number of authors, and thus 'frees the student from the need to be in the physical presence of the teacher' (Landow 1994, p. 12). It also offers an environment that encourages both the individualist and the autodidact.

Common claims made about hypertext in the teaching of writing 'include the possibility for promoting associative thinking . . . collaborative learning . . . synthesis in writing from sources . . . distributing traditional authority in texts and classrooms . . . and facilitating deconstructive reading and writing' (Johnson-Eilola 1992, p. 96). It is difficult, however, to produce research data that support these claims. Research on hypertext runs into much the same problems as research on word processing: different programs, for example, may elicit different types of responses from users (Snyder 1993b). The hypertext software found in the academy and schools has been designed primarily for creating technical and functional documents, and not for educational purposes. At present, information about the connections between hypertext and the development of writing still largely depends on anecdote and prediction.

The use of hypertext in literary studies is not as yet widespread. Some advocates argue, however, that its impact cannot be ignored when it is integrated into a literature program. In their view, hypertext far exceeds the contextualisation, formal recognition and annotation that have long been the backbone of literary education. For Tuman (1992), hypertext represents a radically new way of conceiving text, and (with the integration of graphics) of organising knowledge itself. Just as the word processor is more than a turbo-charged typewriter, Shakespeare on CD-ROM is more than an efficient vehicle for traditional literary scholarship. In fact, literature courses need not be limited to 'all English literature', since hypertext enables the teaching of literature to become interdisciplinary: all texts—literary or otherwise—may be interconnected. Accounts of literary courses that use hypertext technology in creative ways are now beginning to appear.

It seems clear that these and other educational uses of hypertext will expand in the coming years, yet as Burbules and Callister point out:

> . . . the growth of hypertext has not always been accompanied by a critical reflection on its assumptions about cognition and learning, about its possible consequences for attaining certain educational benefits at the expense of other aims, or about its implications for issues of equity. (1996, p. 24)

Expunging the hype

In this chapter I have argued that there are alternatives to adopting the characteristic stance of the enthusiasts who embrace the computer as a tool that can become a vehicle of human creativity, or of the critics who warn that computers have penetrated not only our social relations but also our personalities and culture. It seems futile to either exult or deplore the influence of electronic mediations on everyday life. Instead of celebrating or demonising computer technology, it seems more productive to try to widen our understanding of developments such as hypertext in order to exploit their educational potential. We have to look critically at assertions that the technology will either radically transform or degrade and diminish the social interactions intrinsic to effective teaching and learning.

I have also argued on behalf of the educational value of the connections between definitions of the postmodern text in contemporary literary theory and the physical characteristics of hypertext: because hypertext *embodies* postmodern theories of the text, it makes it easier to understand them (Snyder 1996). Some critics, however, are sceptical. Douglas (1993, p. 423), for example, observes that hypertext apologists' use of postmodern literary theory is honorific in that it serves 'to make preliminary descriptions of the new environment appear more substantial by anchoring them to a large and highly esteemed body of critical writing'. By claiming that Barthes (1979) and Derrida (1976) 'uncannily anticipated' (p. 423) electronic text in their definitions of the postmodern text, Douglas argues that theorists can place hypertext in a discursive continuum from the spoken word right through to hypertext itself.

On the other hand, if by pointing to these connections we can help students understand such theories, then it becomes a useful exercise. More problematic is the way hypertext theorists use literary theory 'to make predictions about the social impact of hypertext' (Douglas 1993, p. 423). We need to examine very carefully how 'embodiment' arguments are used to support a technological determinism that presents hypertext as something that inevitably transforms both society and its education systems. We need a critical perspective to understand

138

that 'many of the assessments of the potentially "revolutionary" impact of hypertext on society are overly simplistic' (p. 417).

Both Landow and Lanham enthusiastically advocate the benefits of hypertext for education in the humanities and social sciences. Landow claims that hypertext challenges conventional assumptions about teachers, learners and institutions, and reconfigures everything. But he is not optimistic that this will happen in the immediate future, given our technological conservatism and lack of concern about pedagogy. He is also careful to qualify the importance of links between hypertext and literary theory, preferring to view the text produced as a site on which the accuracy of these theoretical concepts can be tested. By contrast, Lanham predicts that hypertext will result in a far-reaching social revolution that will radically democratise education and the arts and enfranchise minority groups. The problem with such claims is their assumption 'that society will be shaped largely by the widespread use of hypertext technology, not that the developing technology will be moulded by social interests' (Douglas 1993, p. 421). Lanham's perspective is technocentric in that it . . .

> . . . permits theorists to make judgements about the type of interactions readers and writers will have with hypertext as well as predictions about its effects on the institutions of publishing, education and government—all based on the physical characteristics of hypertext as an environment for discourse. (1993, p. 423)

Incipient technological determinism is discernible in many evocations of the educational possibilities of hypertext and manifests itself in 'propositional statements that ascribe agency to technology itself' (Grusin 1994, p. 470). It is present also in claims that the electronic media and network technologies could have deleterious effects on human consciousness and culture by isolating groups and individuals (Bigum & Green 1993). Technological determinists who predict the social consequences of hypertext tend to rely vulnerably on either a utopian or a dystopian view of the future. But because hypertext can be used for all sorts of purposes, it can both 'liberate' and 'constrain' educational and social practices. It 'can be an enormously liberating innovation or a powerful system of ideological hegemony' (Burbules & Callister 1996, p. 43).

Hypertext certainly has the potential to affect the cultures of learning in significant ways. No technology, however, can guarantee any particular change in cultural practices simply by its 'nature'. A hypertext classroom can be used either to support new theories of reading and writing or to promote traditional approaches to the study of texts. Teachers who are neither trained in nor sympathetic towards hypertext pedagogy will either ignore or subvert its potential. The use and effect of a technology is closely tied to the social context in which it appears. Hypertext will succeed or fail not by its own agency but by how people and institutions use it. Every evolving technology is socially constructed by the interests and assumptions of particular social groups.

If our concern is the enhancement of our students' and our own literacy practices, then Umberto Eco's (1995) warning is well worth heeding. He argues that the concept of literacy comprises many media and that an 'enlightened policy on literacy must take into account the possibilities of all these media'. He also cautions us not to fight against false enemies: 'Even if it were true that today visual communication has overwhelmed written communication, the problem is not one of opposing written to visual communication. The problem is rather how to improve both' (p. 91). But just as we should not fight against false enemies, we should not endorse false friends. These technologies may be able to enhance learning but at the same time they also have the power to manipulate and control, a potential built into all technological systems (Burbules & Callister 1996). We must retain, against all odds in this rapidly changing literacy landscape, a position of informed scepticism.

At this point in the history of our profession's engagement with the new technologies, it is time to move beyond the limitations of polarised responses to them; neither uncritical enthusiasm nor effete repudiation are adequate any more. We must admit that technology is composed of both good and bad, generative and repressive influences. Indeed, Foucault's (1979) notion that all our explanations of power and the technologies of power are inevitably partial—neither wholly good nor wholly evil—is clearly a more useful stance from which to explain technologies and their influences.

It will be interesting to see how teachers in the humanities and social sciences who are concerned with literacy issues respond to the possibilities and problems that hypertext presents. What we have at this moment is an intriguing technology whose operations compel us at the very least to revise our print-derived notions of reading, writing and text. But at the same time, perhaps the technology will also influence the cultures of teaching and learning in ways we cannot yet imagine.

References

Balestri, D. P. 1988 'Softcopy and hard: word processing and writing process', *Academic Computing*, vol. 2, no. 5, pp. 14–17, 41–5

Barthes, R. 1979 'From work to text', trans. J. Harari, *Textual Strategies*, ed. J. Harari, Cornell University Press, Ithaca, NY, pp. 73–81 [Fr 1971]

Bigum, C. and Green, B. 1993 'Technologising literacy: or, interrupting the dream of reason', *Literacy in Contexts: Australian Perspectives and Issues*, eds A. Luke & P. Gilbert, Allen & Unwin, Sydney, pp. 4–28

Birkerts, S. 1994 *The Gutenberg Elegies: The Fate of Reading in an Electronic Age*, Fawcett Columbine, New York

Bolter, J. D. 1991 *Writing Space: The Computer, Hypertext, and the History of Writing*, Lawrence Erlbaum Associates, Hillsdale, New Jersey

Bruner, J. 1986 *Actual Minds, Possible Worlds*, Harvard University Press, Cambridge, Massachusetts

Burbules, N.C., and Callister, T.A. 1996 'Knowledge at the crossroads: some alternative futures of hypertext learning environments', *Educational Theory*, vol. 46, no. 1, pp. 23–50

Derrida, J. 1976 *Of Grammatology*, trans. G. Chakravorty Spivak, Johns Hopkins University Press, Baltimore, Maryland [Fr 1967]

Douglas, J.Y. 1993 'Social impacts of computing: the framing of hypertext—revolutionary for whom?', *Social Science Computer Review*, vol. 2, no. 4, pp. 417–29

Eco, U. 1995 *Apocalypse postponed*, ed. R. Lumley, Flamingo, an imprint of Harper Collins, London

Foucault, M. 1979 *Discipline and punish: the birth of prisons*, trans. A. Sheridan, Vintage, New York

Grusin, R. 1994 'What is an electronic author? Theory and the technological fallacy', *Configurations*, vol. 3, pp. 469–83

Johnson-Eilola, J. 1992 'Structure and text: writing space and storyspace', *Computers and Composition*, vol. 9, no. 2, pp. 95–129

——1993 'Control and the cyborg: writing and being written in hypertext', *Journal of Advanced Composition*, vol. 13, no. 2, pp. 381–99

——1994 'Reading and writing in hypertext: vertigo and euphoria', *Literacy and Computers: The Complications of Teaching and Learning with Technology*, eds C.L. Selfe and S. Hilligoss, Modern Language Association of America, New York, pp. 195–219

Joyce, M. 1995 'Siren shapes: exploratory and constructive hypertexts', *Of Two Minds: Hypertext Pedagogy and Poetics*, M. Joyce, University of Michigan Press, Ann Arbor, pp. 39–59

Landow, G.P. 1992 *Hypertext: The Convergence of Contemporary Critical Theory and Technology*, Johns Hopkins University Press, Baltimore, Maryland

Landow, G.P. 1994 'What's a critic to do? Critical theory in the age of hypertext', *Hyper/Text/Theory*, ed. G. P. Landow, Johns Hopkins University Press, Baltimore, Maryland, pp. 1–48

Lanham, R.A. 1989 'The electronic word: literary study and the digital revolution', *New Literary History*, vol. 20, pp. 265–90

——1993 *The Electronic Word: Democracy, Technology and the Arts*, University of Chicago Press, Chicago

Marx, L. 1994 'The idea of "technology", and postmodern pessimism', *Does technology drive history? The dilemma of technological determinism*, eds M.R. Smith and L. Marx, MIT Press, Cambridge, Massachusetts, pp. 237–57

Marx, L. and Smith, M.R. 1994 'Introduction', *Does technology drive history? The dilemma of technological determinism*, eds M.R. Smith and L. Marx, MIT Press, Cambridge, Massachusetts, pp. ix-xv

Moulthrop, S. 1991 'The politics of hypertext', *Evolving Perspectives on Computers and Composition Studies: Questions for the 1990s,* eds G.E. Hawisher and C.L. Selfe, National Council of Teachers of English, Urbana, Illinois, pp. 253–71

Nelson, T.H. 1992 'Opening hypertext: a memoir', *Literacy Online,* ed. M.C. Tuman, University of Pittsburgh Press, Pittsburgh, pp. 43–57

Selfe, C. L. and Selfe, R.J. 1994 'The politics of the interface: power and its exercise in electronic contact zones', *College Composition and Communication,* vol. 45, no. 4, pp. 480–504

Snyder, I.A. 1993a 'The impact of computers on students' writing: a comparative study of the effects of pens and word processors on writing context, process and product', *Australian Journal of Education,* vol. 37, no. 1, pp. 5–25

——1993b 'Writing with word processors: a research overview', *Educational Research,* vol. 35, no. 1, pp. 49–68

——1996 *Hypertext: The Electronic Labyrinth,* Melbourne University Press, Melbourne and New York University Press, New York

Stoll, C. 1995 *Silicon Snake Oil: Second Thoughts on the Information Highway,* Macmillan, London

Tuman, M.C. 1992 'First thoughts', *Literacy Online,* ed. M.C. Tuman, University of Pittsburgh Press, Pittsburgh, pp. 3–15

7

Will the most reflexive relativist please stand up: hypertext, argument and relativism

JANE YELLOWLEES DOUGLAS[1]

Is it significant that for the classic philosophers (for instance, Plato, Kant, Hegel, Aristotle) discussion continues, even after centuries, about what claims and arguments are being made in their texts? The enduring significance of their works does not rest on their ability to support absolutely univocal claims, but on their opening up new territory for thought. Questions outlast the answers with which they first came, and hypertext is very good for asking questions. (David Kolb 1994a, p. 340)

The explicit presence of more than one voice reminds the reader (and the writer) that interpretation goes on all the time, that the idea of one reading a singular correspondence between text and meaning is illusory. In particular, the dialogue is one way of introducing some instability into the presumed relationship between text and reader. I am reminded of the rather nice phrase by Woolgar: 'We need to explore more forms of literary expression whereby the monster [reflexivity] can be simultaneously kept at bay and allowed a position at the heart of our enterprise.' (Woolgar & Ashmore 1988, p. 4)

A decade ago, you could probably fit everyone on the planet who knew anything at all about hypertext onto a single bus. Five years ago, you could probably accommodate everyone who had ever heard the buzzword inside the Hollywood Bowl. Today, there are probably as many people using hypertext routinely—largely in the form of links on the World Wide Web—who have ever heard (or heard of) the Beatles.

First invented to make documentation more accessible to a variety of users, hypertext is a computer-mediated form of writing enabling authors to construct texts that can be read in a variety of orders, suitable for different audiences with widely divergent interests and even reading skills. Hypertext could, as novelist and hypertext writer Michael Joyce has argued, enable you to write a book that would never read exactly the same way twice. Today, hypertext is the 'glue' that holds the Internet together, linking a travel company's page on escorted tours of Istanbul with a page on the history of Istanbul's Hippodrome or a chronology of Byzantine history supplied by a university department of history.

On the World Wide Web, hypertext is largely about making information accessible, its links enabling vast bodies of information to be wired together to form a cross between an encyclopaedia, the yellow pages, and just about every reference and guide book published—and a good deal of material no publisher would ever be caught dead putting into circulation. Yet the initial buzz of excitement about hypertext was about more than simply making information apparently endlessly accessible to the wired; it was about an emerging technology that promised to enable its writers and readers to do things with words, with argument, with representation, far beyond anything possible within the confines of print. Ironically, the exposure hypertext has received through the World Wide Web has obscured its more radical and far-reaching possibilities for providing writers with alternatives to linear and singular arguments, particularly for all the philosophers, scientists, educators, and sociologists who long ago rejected objectivism for relativism and who do battle with the monolithic constraints of the printed word on a regular basis.

We might logically assume that academics writing on rhetoric or the teaching of writing or the nature of text would be those most likely to be fascinated by the possibility of new forms, new technologies, new ways of arguing that may not seem particularly like the arguments we know. But in Anglo-American universities, surprisingly few teachers of English seem particularly self-conscious about the relationship between the structure of their arguments and the nature of the arguments themselves, while departments of sociology tend to be veritable hotbeds of reflexivity where writers constantly mull over the constitutive nature of genres and conventions, fretting over the similarity between the structure of their own arguments and those of the theorists they tackle.

Sociologists interested in reflexivity—the practice of examining the way one's own argument is constituted, generally using the same approach or method one uses on the topic or discipline under scrutiny—tend to engage in rhetorical callisthenics over the relationship between the methods and generic conventions they have chosen and the constraints these choices impose on what they can actually say. The reason is simple: most sociologists who are determinedly reflexive in their writing are either social constructivists or relativists—neither of them positions notably well served by the conventions of print.

Constructivists insist that the things we tend to think of as 'hard' or 'real', regardless of whether the subject is a bridge or an ultrasound image, are the product of complex social, economic, and political relationships. A bicycle, for example, has symmetrical front wheels and pneumatic tires due to a number of interrelated factors, among them concerns about safety, a smooth, comfortable ride, the desire for speed and Victorian squeamishness about women taking up bicycling. Relativists go one better, believing not only that everything man-made is socially shaped but that it is almost impossible to arrive at a single interpretation, a solitary reading of an object, its function, its effectiveness. 'It could always be otherwise', is the relativist credo.

All this would merely amount to a series of reasonably interesting arguments about technology, if it were not for the particular quandary relativism and constructivism pose for writers—it is infinitely easier to represent singularity and certainty, a single correct answer, the final verdict, than it is to

146

do justice to a complex web of factors, influences, and forces so dense that no-one can arrive at a single interpretation or, at least, stand by one with anything resembling certainty.

How to read a bridge: treating technology as a text

Of all the brands of relativism in the world, it is difficult to imagine a group more forthrightly relativistic than those sociologists who study technology from a constructivist perspective and who insist that the operation, use, and even the design of technologies are shaped by an entire conglomeration of social practices. In perhaps the most famous example of a constructivist argument, 'Do artefacts have politics?', sociologist Langdon Winner (1986) seizes on bridges constructed by New York's most fervid city planner, Robert Moses, as examples of technological artefacts that served an infinitely more insidious purpose than merely routing roadways around natural or man-made obstructions. The parkway bridges Moses constructed, Winner argues, were engineered to ensure that buses—and their inner-city working-class passengers—could not venture onto the magnificent park system he had constructed on Long Island.

Like any good constructivist, Winner knows how to use irony rather adroitly. First, he chooses an artefact which, to anyone studying it, would appear perfectly unremarkable, even banal. Second, he introduces evidence from Moses' biographer that the city planner harboured some rather rabid race and class prejudices. Third, he then forges a causal connection between items one and two to arrive at a judgement on the effects of the technology under scrutiny: Moses deliberately constructed bridges too low for buses to pass under them, thereby making the Long Island beaches and parks accessible only to white, middle-class New Yorkers with cars.

For Winner, technology can be read like any other text: you read it; you interpret it; you write an academic article about it. Yet, as many other constructivists have pointed out, reading itself is not as easy as all that: the interpretation of a

147

mute artefact embedded in a complex system requires a bit more in the way of flexibility before it can be introduced to the whole equation. Further, being a relativist—as sociologist Steve Woolgar (1991) has pointed out in a critique of Winner's methods and general lack of reflexivity—also entails scrutinising your own interpretation, your own system of representing Robert Moses and bridges and the parks system with the same beady eye that you cast over the issue of artefacts and politics in the first place. Thorough-going relativism entails being reflexive about your own process of representation, as Woolgar has noted about the area from which most relativist-constructivists had recently migrated, the sociology of scientific knowledge:

> Epistemic practices include visual and textual representation, argumentative discourse, making interpretations, knowing, being certain, explaining, understanding, using evidence, reasoning, and so on. Since such practices are (reckoned to be) foundational to a huge variety of actions and behaviour, the significance of SSK [the sociology of scientific knowledge] clearly goes beyond its ability to enlighten us about science. Its significance lies not just in providing more or different news 'about science' but in its potential for reevaluating fundamental assumptions of modern thought. (Woolgar 1991, p. 25)

By being insufficiently reflexive in his reading of Moses' bridges, Winner himself produces an artefact, a text, that lays itself open to the same brand of ironic interpretation that he himself used on the parkway bridges. If we are going to rely on the metaphor of technology as text, Woolgar (1991, p. 39) reminds us in 'The turn to technology in the Social Studies of Science', that we should realise that the arguments we construct are themselves texts that should be as open to relativist readings as the technologies they study.

The chief difficulty with the reflexive relativist agenda, as Woolgar himself recognised, is that, while print conventions can comfortably accommodate an unequivocal Winner-type response and even a more flexible, interpretative reading—one open to a variety of ways of accounting for the shaping of an

148

artefact—the rhetorical conventions for representing the sort of fairly radical work that relativist-constructivists do cannot comfortably accommodate the application of relativist-constructivist methods to their own texts. In other words, if you are going to employ dollops of irony to your reading of how Long Island's rustic stone bridges function, you must be equally generous with irony when it comes to representing your own stance. Woolgar (1991) insists:

> If current conventions of explanation constrain our attempts to explore the ramifications of relativist arguments, we need to consider what is being gained by modifying our reliance upon these conventional forms. It is this line of argument that provides a rationale for recent textual experiments, "new literary forms", and other explorations in reflexivity (p. 25).

Of course, you can be as reflexive as you want in print—at least in theory because the written or printed word, as any good practising relativist-constructivist will tell you, lends itself to a broad spectrum of uses, including articles that are the literal equivalent of the familiar Escher drawing of two realistic-looking hands, each pencilling in the details of veins and shadow on the other. In practice, however, it is another story, one that strikes at the very raison d'être for writing itself.

The rhetoric of print

Whether one is writing documentation for a word processor or a chapter for *Page to Screen: Taking Literacy into the Electronic Era*, writers rely on the written word to represent a single way of thinking about something. In this sense, all forms of non-fictive writing can be described as inherently persuasive, since their authors aim to convince us to share their perspectives on particular subjects. Writing extends the reach of our voices beyond their physical limits in space and time, yet, as Plato (1973) reminds us in *Phaedrus*, the written word is infinitely more vulnerable to misunderstandings because we are no longer present to control the way in which our messages are received:

149

> [O]nce a thing is committed to writing it circulates equally among those who understand the subject and those who have no business with it; a writing cannot distinguish between suitable and unsuitable readers. And if it is ill-treated or unfairly abused it always needs its parent to come to its rescue; it is quite incapable of defending or helping itself. (p. 97)

To be a persuasive writer according to the rhetoric of print, you must convince your readers, as hypertext theorist John Slatin (1990) has noted, not simply that you have forged the best of all possible connections between your scraps of evidence, but that you have discovered the only possible way of integrating them coherently. Which is one reason why writers like Woolgar would have felt compelled to evolve their own 'new literary forms' to help them represent reflexivity within relativist-constructivism. Unfortunately, the conventions governing the printed word make linear, singular, objectivist representations into arguments that we readers recognise as convincing; everything else comes across like shoddy rhetoric or a writerly game that leaves its readers scratching their heads and wondering what conclusion they were supposed to have reached. Or something still more insidious—an argument that is playful and reflective about its own constitution but ends up pushing a singular, unequivocal way of viewing things after all, in spite of all the reflexive hand-waving.

Representing relativism in print—the writer's quandary

Relativist-constructivists insist that all technologies are, by their very nature, underdetermined and tend to ironicise their peers' accounts by pointing out that 'it could always be otherwise'. So it could be argued that, for example, Moses' bridges could have been designed to make it well nigh impossible for buses to pass easily under them because his parkways scheme prohibited all commercial traffic and aimed to capitalise on the pleasures of country-like drives for what was then newly car-mad America. Or that Moses' bridges were simply designed to the same standard—and heights—as the Lincoln,

Holland, and Brooklyn-Battery tunnels and the rest of the infrastructure in greater New York. Or possibly that Moses failed to foresee the growing height and width of American buses. Or even that Moses simply intended to build the legislative prohibition of commercial traffic on his parkways into the very design of the bridges themselves, so that buses and trucks would be never be able to use the likes of the Cross Island and Palisades Parkways, regardless of what the city or state legislatures did to the traffic laws. Technologies, relativist-constructivists argue, evolve from ideas into designs into prototypes into usable entities through a dense network of social, political, cultural and economic pressures. Ideally, the buck stops nowhere, but is continually passed on from one culprit to another, leaving traces on every pair of hands it passes through.

But the rhetoric of argument prefers the linear to the multiple, proof to speculation, the line to branches, so all this reflexivity, all this determined relativism generally concludes with a singular, satisfying bottom line, an argument that, stripped to its essentials, ends up recapitulating the same rhetorical strategy that Woolgar (1993) examined in Winner's work: (a) the intentions of the author are first rendered consistent with the effects of the argument; (b) the effects of the argument, however, can be discovered, on close reading, to diverge from the author's intentions, so that, finally, (c) a whole series of different possible effects can be said to stem from that argument. In this instance, it is not that Long Island bridges reveal that Moses is a covert racist but that Winner's reading of these mute artefacts shows that, while Winner may pass muster as a constructivist, he stumbles coming out of the gate in the relativist stakes. The cruel irony of reflexivity is that the conventional linearity of print rhetoric drives even the most rigorous reflexive relativist-constructivists through the exact same gyrations as the sociologists they are busily attempting to discredit. One of the chief problems with linearity is that it generally leads to something singular.

As Bruno Latour (1988) has pointed out, the power of arguments can be traced to an equation between explanations and things to be explained. Economy on the explanation end of things and a profusion of things explained makes for stronger arguments, while a single explanation that accounts for the greatest number of things to be explained makes the strongest argument of all. To fly in the face of this equation, this convention that dictates which arguments we will find the most satisfying, is probably to condemn yourself to being published solely on your own World Wide Web homepage for the rest of your days—although it is still not certain whether this means your argument is likely to be encountered or at least skimmed by far more readers there than if it appeared in, say, publications of the Modern Language Association.

Must a claim be the demand to affirm some proposition?

> I use 'reflexive' to denote any text that takes into account its own production and which, by doing so, claims to undo the deleterious effects upon its readers of being believed too little or too much . . . [W]e have to write stories that do not start with a framework but . . . end up with local and provisional variations of scale. This also means that stories which ignore cause and effect, responsibilities and accusations, will be unfit for the normal mode of denunciation, exposition, and unveiling. Our way of being reflexive will be to render our texts unfit for the deadly proof race over who is right. (Bruno Latour 1988, pp. 166, 174)

> A text can still make a claim on you even if it does not argue for a particular proposition. The text could claim your acknowledgement. For example: that a certain question or option is live, that this is who you are, that this is where we live, that these are connected, that there are more possibilities here than you thought. While such claiming can be reported in propositions, there need be no such propositions explicitly argued for in the text, and yet the claim may be made on you. (David Kolb 1994b)

If the linearity of argumentative print convention is anathema to certain sociologists of technology, it is the governing principle behind philosophical argument. As philosopher David

Kolb (1994a) points out, philosophical arguments link premises and conclusions, and students in introductory philosophy courses are taught to make sense of Locke or Kant or Dewey by first pouncing on the conclusion, then outlining the text's structure, working backward to investigate how well the line of argument connects beginning and conclusion, premise and proof. In light of this relentless linearity and Latour's politics of explanation, it is hardly surprising that for many philosophers the singular and austere mathematical proof represents an argumentative ideal.

Yet, as Kolb goes on in his hypertext *Socrates in the Labyrinth* (1994b), in spite of philosophy's reliance on clearly defined and conclusively established claims, what has kept the works of philosophy's pantheon alive is neither the arrow-like straightness of the argumentative line nor the limpid clarity of their conclusions but, instead, the continuing and often heated debate over just what the likes of Plato, Aristotle, Kant and Hegel were claiming. Philosophy's exemplary texts, moreover, are hardly textbook examples of linear, analytic reasoning. Plato's dialogues replicate the give-and-take of conversation, and, if they end up settling on a definitive reading of, for example, the effect of the written word on memory, they often get there by visiting a welter of tangential spaces and by pausing intermittently to reflect on the journey itself.

Hegel decried the use of geometric diagrams that supposedly displayed relationships between ideas. He claimed that ideas were connected by interdependencies and mutual constitutions too complex to be represented adequately by illustrations that depicted merely simplified relationships such as inclusion, exclusion, and one- or two-way relationships (Kolb 1994a, p. 332). And, most famously, Wittgenstein believed that forcing his ideas to fit into the unified, linear form of analytic arguments would infinitely reduce their complexity—he preferred to treat philosophical topics as if they were features of a detailed landscape. To ensure that his landscape would not be merely a matter of lines and planes, Wittgenstein promised, in his preface to *Philosophical Investigations* (1958), to crisscross it in a multitude of directions, so

153

that the same sketches of specific cases would reappear in multiple contexts, analysed from different perspectives. Perhaps what Wittgenstein and Woolgar have in common is a knowledge of the full repertoire of strategies for arguing in print and all the limitations those conventions imply—and a desire to express degrees of complexity, contingency and indeterminacy that cannot be represented by something as linear and determinate and conclusive as an argument governed by the rules governing things that appear in print.

Like Wittgenstein's forays across a landscape, a hypertext argument could represent multiple constructions of a single object, like Moses' bridges, that yield radically divergent interpretations depending on which path you trace through the text. The text that insists that you understand that Moses was a racist could also lead you to another textual path that 'walked' you through maps of the hundreds of playgrounds, swimming pools, and public parks the New York powerbroker installed in some of the city's most blighted neighbourhoods, many of them home to largely minority populations. Or it could shunt you down a trail of evidence that disassembled Winner's argument itself, pointing out that Winner's evidence is predicated solely on two sources in Robert Caro's monumental biography of Moses, *The Power Broker* (1974): one source ostensibly came from an unreferenced interview with a city planner who once worked for (and was most likely stymied by) Moses; the other was based on interviews with a former Moses lieutenant who was not particularly fond of his boss, and whose statements were made long after Moses' death.

The text could take you on a virtual tour of bridges, tunnels and roadways throughout New York's five boroughs, focusing on tunnels with height restrictions identical to those imposed by Moses on his parkways, and on Interboro Parkway bridges of the same specifications and construction which were designed to connect economically underprivileged, primarily black communities. Our hypothetical hypertext could even construct yet another path that turned the same sceptical eye on its own evidence and arguments and convince us that it, too, is merely one of many possible ways of thinking about these technological artefacts. Even if we never stumble across this last path, however, the hypertext, with its capacity to represent a single artefact in a myriad of different contexts and argumentative constructions, will have been working to illustrate its gist rather literally even if we never reach the part where the authors get their spanners out and dismantle their own argumentative lines.

The beauty of hypertext is not that it obliterates what Robert Coover (1992) has dubbed 'the line', but that it propels us from the straitened 'either/or' world that print has come to represent and into a universe where the 'and/and/and' is always possible. It is an environment more conducive to relativistic philosophy and analysis, where no single account is privileged over any others, yet, because hypertexts are constructed from strings of code, writers can ensure that readers traverse some bits of the argumentative landscape more easily and more frequently than others; or that readers are left to make their own connections between one bit of text and another. Hypertext writers can also ensure that readers may latch onto some sense of the argument's outlines by constructing a cognitive map of the territory, claims, evidence, and conclusions still to be encountered.

If this seems all terribly revolutionary for philosophy or sociology, it may help us to turn to yet another philosopher discontented with the constraints of representing his ideas in print: Martin Heidegger. Heidegger (1950) used the word *Holzwege* (Woodpaths) as the title of a collection of essays, as Kolb (1994b) notes in his hypertext *Socrates in the Labyrinth*, because the word referred to . . .

> . . . fragmentary paths found in the forest, leading nowhere, not converging, but opening up the dark woods in one another's neighbourhood. That plurality of paths seems an appropriate image for the paths we may write in hypertexts, and for thought as seeking what is to be said, with neither atomistic disintegration nor final unity . . . A French translation of that title was *Chemins qui menent nulle part*, ways that lead nowhere. (*Holzwege*) (Kolb 1994b)

155

One of the prime insights of relativism is that reality is something negotiated, not given; it is something filtered, organised and rearranged by institutions and individuals, artefacts and arguments alike. The difficulty with representing a relativistic stance or world is that print conventions have evolved so that writers use them almost solely to toy with their readers or send them down narrow rhetorical alleys, like scientists directing a pack of lab rats through a maze, where wayward rats blundering into the cul-de-sacs get shocked, and those rocketing to the centre get a slab of cheese.

A little over a century ago in *The Experimental Novel*, Emile Zola (1971) suggested that novelists could conduct their own experiments into the constitution of human character by testing the mettle of characters like Cousin Bette with a series of moral challenges—with everything, of course, created utterly by the author. But Zola never intended us to be any more ambivalent about his characters than he himself was. His experimental novel never tried to represent a system, a psyche so complex, so ingrained with cultural, social, economic, historical influences that its readers oscillate between interpretations, discovering multiple, mutually exclusive readings like readers poring over ambiguous figures, seeing first the rabbit, then the duck, then the rabbit again, but never both at once. So what is a relativist to do? How do you enable readers to negotiate meanings without organising your material to yield singular readings? And, if you attempt to marshal all your sources, quotes and citations so that your readers can blaze their own trails through them, how do you avoid saddling your readers with all the cognitive overhead that you have already poured into your research?

Kolb suggests that hypertext is best suited to representing certain types of arguments, and that building particular arguments into one of a series of distinctive rhetorical shapes enables writers to guide readers through claims, evidence and analysis in an order that maintains a sense of both structure and coherence. In fact, hypertext is brilliantly suited to precisely the kind of argument Kolb himself puts forward in both the print and hypertext versions of *Socrates in the Labyrinth*—

one that allows for the possibility that hypertext is both continuous and discontinuous and can still carry the rhetorical traditions of philosophical argument which can raise as many questions as answers.

Readers may emerge from Kolb's hypertext buzzing with ideas for experimenting with the rhetoric of argument, or with a somewhat tetchy response to some of his assertions, but not with a sense that Kolb has made a case for a singular way of thinking about or using hypertext. Rather than establishing a single line and arguing it through to the end, Kolb's work instead lays open a field of possibilities that makes claims upon us as readers but does not necessarily claim to be anything like a proof, truth or even a set of unified conclusions.

As is only fitting for a medium that is virtually defined by its multiplicity, hypertext has a seemingly endless capacity to accommodate a variety of argumentative possibilities, enabling readers to experience an article or segment of an argument in its entirety before or after they encounter a critique of it. Yet, to a relativist-constructivist, even this can still seem merely a way of resituating arguments that unfold awkwardly in the dimensions of print—presenting the kinds of argumentative stances the likes of Winner and Woolgar might adopt in the context of the materials that informed their construction.

Hypertext can, Kolb insists, accommodate types of arguments we would never encounter within the confines of print, enabling writers to make associative connections between diverse disciplines and genres, to set up arguments that discredit themselves through their proliferation, to keep argumentative possibilities open and accessible even after others have been explored. Hypertext can enable us to offer our readers texts that are thematically unified without being organised linearly, statements that metamorphose into questions or a series of qualifications, connections between the universal and the familiar that become problematic the deeper we delve into a text (Kolb 1994b, 'philosophical hypertext actions'). And writers can continually remind us of just how deeply we have ventured into the hypertext by nesting qualifications within examples within propositions, its virtual three-dimensional structure assigning significance to certain levels of text according to their position: propositions may float relatively close to the surface of the hypertext, while definitions and examples may occupy places several levels below them, and qualifications may await readers in the text's virtual basement level—or vice versa.

Perhaps most strikingly, hypertext can show us that context is everything. In Michael Joyce's ground-breaking *afternoon, a story* (1990), the first hypertext novel, readers encounter a single space repeatedly in widely divergent contexts, and the text in that space, although it remains constant, seems to change each time they encounter it; only the most careful readers who scrutinise the text line by line will realise that this is the same fragment of text they have already encountered two or three times before. When the height of the parkway bridges is read in the context of Moses' racist remarks to his associates or his desire that his beloved Jones Beach remain untainted by hordes from lower Manhattan, we may be easily convinced that these scenic, rustic bridges built from native stone truly are particularly sly forms of social engineering. Encountered along a path where we learn the established height of the bridges and tunnels surrounding Manhattan and see that the bridges are simply meeting the prevailing standard height specifications, however, the bridges become merely vehicles for carrying the traffic of local roadways over the parkways without interruption. The meaning of an artefact in an argument, as in life, is embedded in the context constructed around it. Hypertext, you could say, is the ultimate relativist medium.

Unlike print, however, hypertext has few fixed conventions to let writers know precisely which effects will lend themselves to which interpretations by their readers. While Kolb tries to codify some of the ways in which philosophical hypertexts might be organised—constructed as pyramidal texts attached to an outline, or multiple arguments leading to joint or related conclusions (Kolb 1994b, 'philosophical hypertext organisation')—there are few codes that writers of hypertext generally observe. So that nesting conclusions deeply within the hypertext structure may not necessarily lead readers to recognise them as conclusions, any more than attaching a critique to the full text of the argument it examines is any guarantee that your readers will read all of it. The conventions of print arguments took hundreds of years to evolve into their present state, and even television took several decades to get from the electrified vaudeville of Milton Berle and its other early stars to the intricate narrative lines and multiple perspectives embodied in series like *Hill Street Blues*, *ER* and *Law and Order*. Each new use of hypertext defines the medium, which is also still evolving as a technology that could one day use fuzzy logic to accommodate the intricacies of the text to the interests and knowledge of each reader—and end up delivering multiple, relativistic texts that are transformed into singular, positivistic arguments in order to meet the expectations or needs of their readers.

Reflexive relativism in print

Of course, print itself is malleable, fluid, as perfectly capable of representing a relativistic stance as a positivistic one—provided the writer is willingly to fly in the face of a few hundred years of established conventions, as well as the politics and economics of publishing. Bruno Latour, one of the luminaries of reflexive relativist-constructivism, recently published *Aramis or the Love of Technology* (1996), a work that mingles a detective-like quest by a fictional engineer-cum-sociologist investigating the demise of an innovative Parisian transit system, interviews with all the participants involved in the now-defunct project, press clippings, outrageous and wholly imaginary reports of press conferences, metacommentary on all the above—even a sort of j'accuse that issues from the now-dead Aramis itself. To keep his strands (rather like hypertext paths) separate, Latour sets them off with distinctive typographic styles and leads us to no fewer than twenty-one separate conclusions about the demise of Aramis, although he cannot quite resist concluding that the real culprit was lack of unity among the network of forces conspiring to bring Aramis to life. Just when we might think that Latour is succumbing to the print line, however, he whirls back around on us, with the investigator's mentor musing on the book he would like to write about the whole shebang:

> . . . in which there's no metalanguage, no master discourse, where you wouldn't know which is strongest, the sociological theory or the documents or the interviews or the literature or the fiction, where all these genres or regimes would be at the same level, each one interpreting the others without anybody being able to say which is judging what. (p. 298)

To which the investigator, who tells us his story in the first person, replies by chiding him:

> You're about to embark on another Aramis project, another wild-goose chase. As infeasible as the first one. Remember the lesson of Aramis: 'Don't innovate in every respect at once.' Your book is just one more rickety endeavour, ill-conceived from birth, a white elephant. (p. 298)

Playfulness and reflexivity on Latour's part, doubtless, with perhaps just a tinge of anxiety thrown in, since he is, after all, dealing with audiences weaned on the rhetoric of print arguments. Clearly, both Kolb's print *Socrates in the Labyrinth* and Latour's *Aramis* are evidence of a way of using print to stake out a field of possibilities and tensions, artefacts and debate that exceed traditional argumentative conventions. Print is, after all, every bit as flexible a tool as hypertext is—as any good relativist-constructivist can tell you.

But the conventions of print have already been socially negotiated and, while the existence of Latour's price-tagged book on a bookstore shelf argues for the malleability of those established conventions, the single most attractive feature of hypertext is that it has none. When you spin an argument in hypertext, you can choose to represent a world that is strictly 'either/or' or one that is 'and/and/and'. As we write and read with it, we ourselves become part of the influences that will determine whether it becomes a refuge for relativists weary of doing print callisthenics to avoid being taken for realists—or decidedly unreflexive relativists, which, as far as relativist-constructivists are concerned, may well be the same thing—or whether it remains merely a handy way of linking data on 'Langdon Winner' with 'Moses', 'bridges' and 'Woolgar'.

Notes

1 An earlier version of this chapter first appeared as an article in a special issue on literacy and technology of *The Australian Journal of Language and Literacy* (1996, vol. 19, no. 4).

References

Caro, R. 1974 *The Power Broker: Robert Moses and the Fall of New York*, Vintage, New York

Coover, R. 1992 'The end of books', *New York Times Book Review*, 21 June, pp. 1, 23–5

Heidegger, M. 1950 *Holzwege*, Klostermann, Frankfurt

Joyce, M. 1990 *afternoon, a story*, computer disk, Eastgate Systems, Cambridge, MA

Kolb, D. 1994a 'Socrates in the labyrinth', *Hyper/Text/Theory*, ed. G.P. Landow, Johns Hopkins University Press, Baltimore, pp. 323–344

——1994b *Socrates in the Labyrinth: Hypertext, Argument, Philosophy*, computer disk, Eastgate Systems, Cambridge, MA

Latour, B. 1988 'The politics of explanation: an alternative', *Knowledge and Reflexivity: New Frontiers in the Sociology of Knowledge*, ed. S. Woolgar, Sage, London, pp. 155–77

——1996 *Aramis or the Love of Technology*, trans. C. Porter, Harvard University Press, Cambridge, MA

Plato 1973 *Phaedrus*, trans. W. Hamilton, Penguin, London

Slatin, J. 1990 'Reading hypertext: order and coherence in a new medium', *College English*, vol. 52, pp. 870–3

Winner, L. 1986 *The Whale and the Reactor: A Search for Limits in an Age of High Technology*, University of Chicago Press, Chicago

Wittgenstein, L. 1958 *Philosophical Investigations*, Blackwell, Oxford

Woolgar, S. 1991 'The turn to technology in social studies of science', *Science, Technology & Human Values: Journal of the Society for Social Studies of Science*, vol. 16, no. 1, pp. 20–50

——1993 'What's at stake in the sociology of technology?', *Science, Technology & Human Values: Journal of the Society for Social Studies of Science*, vol. 18, no. 4, pp. 523–9

Woolgar, S. and Ashore, M. 1988 'The next step: an introduction to the reflexive project', *Knowledge and Reflexivity: New Frontiers in the Sociology of Knowledge*, ed. S. Woolgar, Sage, London, pp. 1–12

Zola, E. 1971 'The experimental novel', *Critical Theory Since Plato*, ed. H. Adams, trans. B.M. Sherman, Harcourt Brace Jovanovich, New York, pp. 647–59

8

New stories for new readers: contour, coherence and constructive hypertext

MICHAEL JOYCE

In November 1995 I was discussing N. Katherine Hayles' (1993) essay, 'Virtual bodies and flickering signifiers', with my Vassar first-year students. We were talking in room 006, the computer classroom where IRL, or 'in real life' as the computer jargon has it, some of my students were actually present. Others, however, were in their dorm rooms or the library. I myself was seated before a brimming ashtray of someone's cigarette butts and the palaeontological crusts of someone's pizza at a computer in the basement of an art museum in Hamburg, Germany, attending the Interface3 symposium on the nature of the body and human community in cyberspace. The room 006 where my students and I met and talked was also in cyberspace, at Vassar MOO, the mirror world of a student-created, increasingly rich verbal representation of the Vassar Campus as a textual virtual reality.

In the midst of our class discussion the computer in Hamburg beeped to tell me I had new mail on my account at Vassar. It was from Kate Hayles, the author of the piece we were discussing in the MOO class, firming up details for a talk she gave later that month as part of a Vassar Library lecture series on women and technologies. Somewhere in the shifting space of the infoscape, the present and the future, as well as the present and the absent (or what we have come to call the real world and the virtual world) had briefly merged.

What is most amazing about these stories of technological presence and multiplicity is how used to them we are. A week or so after I returned from Germany, I gave two workshops at the University of Missouri Institute for Instructional Technology (MUITT) at the invitation of Eric Crump, a moving force in the computers and writing community. I was in my real office at Vassar but speaking in the virtual MUIIT seminar room located IRL at ZooMOO on a computer in Missouri, 'speaking' to conferees in three states. As yet another instance, in 1994 members of my hypertext rhetorics and poetics class became annoyed with a text about media philosophy, *Imagologies*, co-authored by Mark Taylor (1994), a philosopher at Williams College. Without consulting me, a woman in my class invited Taylor by email to meet the class on Vassar MOO and within two weeks he was 'there' (or here), standing up to a barrage of incisive questions about his text. I am quite certain that most of us knew the difference between meeting Taylor on the MOO and meeting him both IRL and FTF (computer jargon for 'face to face'), but I am likewise certain that none of us thought we were merely continuing to read in this lively yet utterly textual encounter with him.

The computer, like our classrooms, becomes a theatre of our desires as well as of our differences. Although we are becoming so used to stories of technological presence and multiplicity, our profession as teachers and writers is predicated upon a necessary and creative scrutiny of the things we are used to, especially those to do with our understanding of differences: between the virtual and the embodied, between the lasting and the transient, between the rare delights of human community and presence and the universal promise of access and equality.

In coming to teach with and talk about electronic forms of writing and discourse we must be aware of our desires and wary of what we are rapidly becoming used to in their representations, for what we are used to we too often become used by. In this chapter I discuss those representations and then suggest how we and our students can become unused to what merely passes as the new and so avoid becoming used by passing technologies. Finally, I suggest a new voice for our interactions: one that evokes age-old values and a forgotten syntax, but promises to redeem us from the game of technology, creating instead a real space for the play of self and community, a middle voice where we begin to see ourselves in where we are.

Increasingly, where we are is on the web. The truth is that I don't enjoy the world wide web very much, except (and I don't mean this to be a punch line) when I am there for some reason or in the company of others, my students or my sons. Likewise I don't particularly regard it a place as much as a utility, and not so much a medium as the virtual machine which people like Netscape's Marc Andreeson and Bill Gates of Microsoft have begun to acknowledge it as: the ur-computer which contains and enacts a dazzling but often alienating set of representations and practices. The web is a virtual machine in an actual machine, a shared and imaginary computer which contains virtual visions of actual us and often disseminates others' actual plans for a virtual us.

The web puts me at a loss and I do not know exactly why. Sometimes I fear mine may be simply the reaction of someone with a minor reputation elsewhere who feels himself passed by in this new set of practices. It is, ironically, the pure boundedness of the linked space that will distinguish my field, hyperfiction, in the age of the web. Thus I write a passing form in an uncertain medium. 'Passing' since in hypertext the word is likely to have to renegotiate its relationship with images and audience, and 'uncertain' because there is no guarantee that any of these works will survive the shift from virtual machine to machine as computational platforms change (in a process like the shift from clay tablet to parchment).

I suppose my resistance to the web could be a hypertextier-than-thou reaction to the failure of the web to take the form I imagine it should have taken, yet the fact is I don't know what form the web 'should' take. In fact, I am quite fond of Rick Furuta and Cathy Marshall's (1996) caution to the hypertext community that it is less important that we ask why the web has not paid heed to the decades of research into hypertext as it is to ask what makes the current forms so attractive.

And yet even as I say these things, I am suspect. I am aware that the phrases 'the truth is' and 'in fact' in what I've said already may suggest that I may be deluding myself. The truth is probably something I cannot see and the facts are somewhere beyond my saying. What we are used to we too often become used by and so we must begin to see ourselves in where we are.

I am afraid that one of the things making the web in its current form so attractive is that so many of us are afraid and lonely and do not know what to think or who will hear us. The web does strike me as a lonely pursuit, something which douses the crispness of difference and community in a salsa of shifting screens. It encourages pecking orders and hierarchical thinking. Our culture has slipped the web over our heads as a lonely guy slips on a tee-shirt from the Hard Rock Cafe. The web privileges the culture of brand names and corporate logos over the weave of our own multi-threaded culture and history. Like the lonely guy in the Hard Rock tee-shirt we haven't any place to go. The old places seem either deserted or dull and the infoscape seems paradoxically crowded and lonely, already mapped by somebody else and often without a clear place for us. The web too often packages rather than represents the shape of our desires; and doesn't yet manage to show us what we really see there.

It is no revelation to suggest that the web is more hierarchical than hypertextual. That is, it is paradoxically and inherently (if sometimes innocently) hierarchical as a cost of its platform-independence and server-based links. If I move from your page to a certain site you point to, I am obliged to come back to your page if I wish to visit another of the sites you point to. In the process of doing so I begin to construct a contour which represents at very least the momentary ranking of my own interests and curiosity and, at worst, my lonely

166

reading of what I think to be what you value. You cannot yet easily point me from your page to another site and lead me back to a second page of yours. There is as yet no way to shape a reading of successive spaces, whether visually, socially, or through sequenced links to and from exterior sites. It is a rhetoric of an empty room, the eye listening for a voice, the ear seeking a shadow.

At this point in most discussions of the web someone (on my campus it is often me) rushes to say that all this is, of course, changing. Throughout the world, web researchers and developers are busy developing social and sociable interfaces, Java applets and CGI scripts, which will allow us to map, share, and shape journeys through webspace. Web conferences and ACM meetings buzz with technical papers from information warriors with contending models for changing everything, while high above the battlefield public relations barrages from Microsoft and Netscape and America OnLine (AOL) burst into clouds of bankable smoke, casting shadows on everything below. Sometimes the new actually falls like rain in something like AOL's wet-behind-the-ears version of the WOO (the web plus MOO), a chat room strapped to a web browser.

What we are used to we too often become used by. The web, like most technologies, encourages a constant hunger for newness without a taste for detail. The eye gets tired of watching passing patterns and we settle into a commercial glaze. In that way it reminds me of watching cars as a kid in the 1950s when we prided ourselves on our eye for model years, telling a '54 Chevy from a '53, a Hudson from a Studebaker, with an eye for the broadly iconic which probably owed more than we could imagine to a generation of fathers trained to recognise danger or salvation in the silhouette of an airplane, a Nazi helmet, or Betty Grable. It is the same eye I use now to hit the stop button in Netscape at the point where the ad is about to load on the *Hotwired* screen or as someone's over-graphicked homepage is about to hatch its ostrich eggs.

We are so used to thinking something new will come, and so tired of seeing only patterns, that we never really see or settle into the particularity of where we are. We are discouraged from valuing our own culture and history and representing the shape of our desires for ourselves. This is ironic in a medium whose very stuff is represented history and where everywhere there are remnants of what we once desired to know. Netscape litters our hard-drives with the dutifully coded titles of the pages in its cache; we paper our own interfaces with the hotlist or bookmark and strew our own hard-drives with the curiously named information farms created by the Eastgate web squirrel. Search engines list page-on-page of hits, mental footsteps we sometimes mistake for our minds. Some evidences we collect and save, in a process that mimics memory, like snapshots of where we once walked. Others dissolve in the formless track of a Go list, like a walk through a snowstorm, in a process that mimics consciousness.

Meta-sites (the best-ofs, worst-ofs, top 100s, worst 500s, Alta Vista, Lycos, Yahoo, Excite, and so on) have moved from utility to commodity and seem poised to become the medium itself. Everywhere there's a cry for better filters as if the point of making coffee is to keep out the grounds, not whether it tastes any good. People read links rather than sites. At first this development seems alien, as if *The Reader's Digest* suddenly became *The Reader's Table of Contents*. In fact, however, there is nothing particularly new in this. What's new is how clearly we can see on the infoscape something previously invisible or (what is the same thing) something we became used to.

Almost invisibly in the past, for instance, most library patrons read much more of the online or card catalogue entries, book spines, and tables of contents than they read from the volumes themselves. People have only so much time. They can't read everything and so they depend upon others to link them to what they need or wish to read. The notion that editors are 'necessary' to filter out the mass of information, of course, insists upon a hierarchy of information and implies one of human beings; it suggests an immanence of cultural values rather than a culture constructed by human presence, discussion, and community. As meta-sites become the medium, neutral tools and interface aspects are not merely programming in the sense of computer instructions but are the same programming that spews from the box of televised light on the wall.

And yet the proliferation of electronic discourse can refresh our cultural sense of the value added by human community and may point to a future where the net (in whatever form) confirms our sense of community. For as editorial filters, search engines, and software agents themselves proliferate, we will more than ever need a community (that is, an embodied presence among others) in which to discuss and agree upon the usefulness of these tools. It has been argued that it was a web of coffeehouse culture and public spaces which led to the emergence of 'readable' editorial sensibilities and publishing houses in the eighteenth century. Whether a newly resocialised web of virtual public space can invert cultural evolution and reverse the degeneration of editorial sensibility into tradestyle, or publishing house into branded conglomerate, remains, quite literally, to be seen.

In so saying I want to begin to turn away from the litany of my own unease and examine how we can begin to see ourselves in where we are. As I make this turn, however, I want to be clear that I have not 'svenned' myself, I'm not doing a 'half-Birkerts' from the high board, not suggesting that we 'Stoll' the car and go back to the future, when books was hypertext and Christopher Lloyd drove the car and the quaint band of Swiss physicists built their first hyperlinks in numbered items that riddled a screen of text like holes in cheese. You can't stop the music, thank God, and even when you think you can the kids slip outside into the Delorean and sail away to the land of Studebakers. We have lived through the failure of so-called 'critical thinking' and the media courses which meant to inoculate us against buzzwords but failed with all but the words 'media', 'buzzwords', 'critical' and 'thinking'. The truth is, everything is abuzz.

Neil Postman wanders Newton Minow's desert looking for the oasis while, between issues devoted to giving Nicolas Negroponte more episodes than *Nicholas Nickleby*, *Wired* interviews a fictional Marshall McLuhan. Bob Dole praises

Arnold Schwartzenegger's family values and the German pornography industry does more than NAFTA ever could to teach us and Compuserve the meaning of protectionism and global economies. Meanwhile some of us delude ourselves into thinking that, because Louie's Pizza Palace-dot-Com can put up a homepage with full colour anchovies on a $15 a month site offered by his local internet service provider, this suddenly puts Louie on the same footing as MacDonalds whose bandwidth is wider than the Red Sea and whose daily Macmuffin cashflow alone would wash Louie's feet from under him in a tsunami of melted cheese. Louie, like all of us, is caught between a Hard Rock and Melrose Place. If we want to begin to see ourselves where we are, we will have to find ways to say exactly what we are seeing.

To begin with, where we are is in multimedia and what we are seeing is television, a profoundly simple point which Stuart Moulthrop makes so brilliantly that it baffled at least one audience we shared. There is hypertext (which includes hypermedia) and there is multimedia, Stuart suggests. The former is what we do as teachers, writers, artists, learners, the latter is a variety of television.

Despite my already averred fondness for Furuta and Marshall's (1996) cautions to the hypertext community, it is arguable that visually the web sets hypertext back at least ten years. The Netscape <frame> structure recapitulates the typical Hypercard interface of 1986 which itself was a version of the typical television interface of the preceding forty years—that is, a box of image (often blond wood) surrounded by tuning buttons. The Hypercard interface in turn almost immediately became a multimedia design cliche in CD-ROM where each screen featured a box and buttons (often very like a TV) inside the putty box of the monitor, a scheme which, soon thereafter, itself re-infected television as well so that one now faces the prospect of seeing a box with buttons inside a box with buttons inside a box with buttons. The whole thing becomes what the hypermedia video artist Grahame Weinbren (1995) calls 'the pit of so-called "multi-media", with its scenes of unpleasant "buttons", "hot spots", and "menus", [which] leaves no room for the possibility of a loss of self, of desire in relation to the unfolding drama'.

Netscape's frames promise central, supposedly 'open' and 'changeable' spaces surrounded with immutable (or at least filtering) interface structures that define and mediate the changing experience. You can change the channels but not the commercials. Marshall McLuhan is famous for saying that the subject of every new medium is the medium it displaces. These new media are in the business of displacing themselves—not hour-by-hour in the TV way, but cycle-by-cycle, thirty times a sec, in the way a television screen rewrites itself—and so their subject (happily for them, it is what they know best) is themselves. If what we are viewing is, as some commentators suggest, the marriage of television and the computer, a web is an apt place for it. Like the spiders whose copulation the *New York Times* Science section gleefully reported, they are willing to prolong their pleasure by allowing their mates to devour them in *flagrante dilecto ad mortem con pesto*.

Every space is for sale. Cable networks brand the bottom corner of their images with see-through logos, sports network screens carry textual infomercials along their edges as simultaneous contests compete for the viewers' attention in the split frame. CNN Headline News does the news in review in the form of a little on-screen shadow play in which an unseen mouse summons story videos from a drop-down menu via a disembodied on-screen arrow; MTV lets geeked boys play Beavis for a byte, by broadcasting music viddies on a split screen over the real-time scrolling transcript of adolescent wit and uppercase cool from their online chatroom.

What's going on here is the familiar encrustation of images dogging the steps of any holy war, whether they be mandala, marriage of heaven and hell, World Wrestling Federation, religious icon, American Gladiators, or the matching bibs and banners of the medieval Crusaders. Umberto Eco (1994) gained a great deal of media play and mail-list reposting from a piece of journalism differentiating the Mac and IBM as Roman Catholic and Protestant respectively, thus building a pleasant little religious farce. Eco was right about the wrong

171

platforms. The current war is between a ragtag group of quasi-Calvinist sentence-diagrammers, strict constructionists, logical positivists, taxonomists, mark-up militia and bibliographic fundamentalists, the Taggers, versus their Romish antagonists the Flaggers. Taggers believe that revelation came down from heaven with a TEI header and an SGML DTD and favour baptism through total immersion in platform independence. The Flaggers, an extravagantly baroque group of admen, anchormen, cereal salesmen, and scanner-laden Wired-boys, spend most of the day blurring away their blemishes in Photoshop. They believe in transubstantiation, insisting that the image of themselves is in the centre of what we see. Because the Flaggers tend to think that literature goes back as far as Bruce Sterling, and that history started with *Star Wars* (the movie, not the delusion of Ronald Reagan), they have ceded control of literature, history, and in fact all archives of everything that doesn't matter (i.e., what's out of copyright or what Bill the Gatekeeper doesn't want on his castle wall) to the Taggers and to Sir Henry Chadwyck, the proprietor of all English poetry before Princess Di's phonemail.

The web's become a zombie news-stand filled with news from the front where lots of glossy things wave in the light like Victoria's not-so-secret. It may seem in the interim that the homespun sense of what any of my first-year students know about hypertext—that a new way of thinking and communicating emerges—is lost in the glitter of the war bounty and web booty. It may seem that at this news-stand we don't stand a chance.

Yet because the web is by nature (since it must be writable to be readable) partly constructive, and since anyone experiencing hypertext constructs the contour of her own text regardless of the caret-bracketed <frames> which tag and hold her or the trademarked Adobe Acrobats which tumble before her, the possibilities of hypertext will eventually (even in Mr Bill's market economy) out. It is not simply that, like Louie's Pizza-dot-com, we get to pin up our own shiny fishy things on the news-stand. Rather that for Bill the Bettman to sell us his archive of our images in one-mil increments, or for

Hotwired to sell demographic nine-digit chunks of zipcoded human genome to Saturn and Sun, or for Netscape to send its paying customers our address in a Magic Cookie, we have to be able to write back, if only in some perversely inverted version of the letters from camp or college, that is, 'Dear Dad having fun, wish I were here, I'll send money, signed Someone'.

The truth is that we stand a chance. New technologies foster highly articulated horizontal target markets even as they attempt to target and homogenise them. This suggests that eventually a consuming culture can sustain itself only by providing access across a wide social and economic spectrum. This sort of thinking informs what *Wired* so breathlessly terms Esther Dyson's radical rethinking of intellectual property as a trade-off of content for market segment; it likewise inevitably informs the so-called utopian vision of the United States Secretary of Housing and Community Development, Henry Cisneros, who suggests turning public housing into information campuses, and it surely drives the info-industry rush to develop the Yugo computer, the dollar-an-interactive-channel $500 cable modem souped-up TV for home-bound shoppers and popcorn aficionados. Ironically, by asserting themselves as a populist/utopian community, web users become an identifiable target market, that is, an audience with definable (populist/utopian) attributes and a hunger for continued access.

To win them you merely have to trade an upstream soda straw for a downstream sewer pipe. It's a pissing contest in which info-marketeers are sure they can prevail. And should the info-communards be flooded from their quaint sewerside homes, they can easily parlay soggy populism into lovely parting gifts, for instance, a lifestyle and a tee-shirt, or a search engine and a channel guide. Even so it's a game of give and there is space enough to give ourselves to, space enough to stand a chance.

We stand a chance if we create a pedagogy and foster writing geared to making something more than page layouts as game boards with links, something more than house-of-mirrors screen shots of putty-coloured boxes and animated buttons. There seem to be two general approaches to doing

173

so. The first (and one I am guiltiest of) is a consciously experimental, stir-fry pedagogy. We treat the classroom as a vast and virtual wok and throw in a mix of web pages, MOO and WOO sessions, hypermail, interchanges, IRCs, Storyspaces, mail-lists, and a pinch of Quicktime, then serve (sometimes, as I do, all at once) with a cup of steaming Java. Sometimes each ingredient keeps its particular flavour, texture and colour; sometimes it is subgum.

There is an inherent representational problem in an experimental approach since it suggests that someone approaches writing (or any task) with a sense of being experimental, traditional, or what-have-you, doing so in the way you choose tee-shirts or a radio format. Although perhaps some people *do* intend to write in a particular fashion, this intention is political and not artistic or intellectual, and only history can decide whether the effort was experimental, radical, traditional, and so on. Something like this realisation led my Vassar student, Josh Lechner, to ask author and critic Jane Yellowlees Douglas, after a talk she gave on hyperfiction: 'If, as everyone seems to want to suggest, hypertext approximates the way our minds work now, would it be fair to call it the new realism?'.

Even so, there are advantages to a stir-fry approach to teaching, especially one that insists that synchronous and asynchronous, written and oral, face-to-face and virtual discourses can be integrated with the spatial, analytical, and the visual by using hypertext and graphical tools. So stirred, we see writing as spatially as well as temporally represented while remaining aware that closure and coherence are only local and contingent representations. We begin to see ourselves in where we are. We experience writing as what the poet Charles Olson called 'field composition'.

The second general approach to teaching electronic writing is a consciously theoretical one, a sort of rotisserie pedagogy, where writing is put on the spit and turned slowly over a theoretical fire until, one hopes, the fat drains off while the muscle remains moist. The problem with this approach is that to get the fire you have to burn up the furniture. For the distinction between writing and theory is truly only a matter

174

of furniture arrangement, a convention of academic institutions, course descriptions, and chapter headings. Most writers write conscious of the writing at hand; and theory (only another name for this consciousness of what is at hand) has no greater or lesser place than it does in any other kind of writing. In some sense there is never theory, only writing.

A theoretical approach, of course, also has its advantages. It is rather like consciously thinking about your tongue; at a certain point, you either choke or laugh or shift to thinking of your toes. To the extent that hypertext blurs artificial, institutional boundaries it enables a kind of writing which, even in a theoretical approach, chokes and laughs and wiggles its ears, one which from moment to moment is more and less consciously theoretical, whimsical, practical, lyrical, parodical, and what-have-you—that is, one in which these terms oscillate as what Kate Hayles (1993) calls 'flickering signifiers' (p. 71).

I want to suggest another approach, not the inevitable dialectical third, but a middle way, something which plays in the space between and among us, a self-sufficient sensibility given over to others, a lasting presence of particularities which persists beyond the newness we are becoming all too used to and too often used by. To do so I propose that we appropriate as a model for our writing—including and especially those special cases of writing which interaction and collaboration represent—an obscure and foreign sense, the middle voice of the classical Greek verb. The middle voice in Greek is neither active nor passive, yet it offers us a way to see where we are. In the middle voice the subject performs the action, but the action somehow returns to the subject, that is, the subject somehow has some special interest in the action. In Greek, the middle voice can turn the meaning of the verb 'take' (*airo*) into 'choose' (*airoumai*), and turn the meaning of 'have' into 'keep close'. In Greek, the verb 'perceive' (*aisthanomai*) is always in the middle voice, always something one does consciously.

The middle voice is a solitary but not a lonely pursuit, what Cixous (1993) calls 'walking through the self toward the dark' (p. 64). In interaction the middle voice returns person to the self, the reader whose experience itself creates the meaning of a new form. In collaboration, the middle voice maintains the continuity of the self as something with a voice and name: the writer, a self-sufficient sensibility given over to others. Simultaneously making the action serve the self and the self the action, the middle voice is a voice of coherence, offering us a lasting presence of particularities as a strategy against the fragmentary plenitude and multiplicity that faces and effaces us. The middle voice is a voice given over to coherence: swimming rather than surfing, or, if surfing, body surfing. It has seemed to me for some time that reviving a discussion of coherence as Peg Syverson does (Syverson *et al.* 1996) might add to our understanding of electronic discourse. If we begin with the thesis that coherence can be seen as partially meaningful patterns emerging across a surface criss-crossed with potential meanings, then coherence distinguishes itself against other possible coherences, in meaningfulness not meaninglessness. Better still, coherence no longer, if it ever did, distinguishes itself against but rather within. Not against chaos and the random but in recurrence and the flickering.

More recently as I came to collaborate with Peg Syverson, Carolyn Guyer and Marjorie Leusebrink (in press) over thinking and writing about coherence, it seemed important to consider the vernacular sense of coherence. In everyday usage coherence remains relatively undetermined and yet admits to inner and outer representations and recognitions (perhaps the same thing in our time). In this sense it offers an intuitive term for the distinctive experience most people report in coming to electronic forms as they feel themselves in a different relationship to text and image and with a different understanding of how text and image make meaning.

Coherence has an everyday vernacular sense whose formal qualities are appropriately multiple and morphogenetic (form-making). We say of someone, 'He doesn't seem coherent' and in some sense mean this to refer to an unspoken and yet recognisable notion of coherence. There is no inclination (as with logic or argument) to test it against axioms, relations, or systematic measures. Yet we also use the word 'coherence' easily and self-referentially. 'This coheres for me' is a statement which the *American Heritage Dictionary* definition, 'a mass that resists separation,' captures well. Coherence in this vernacular sense is very close to what I understand catastrophe theorists to mean by a singularity or phase change: a recognisable shift in which something amorphous takes on form defined by its own resistance to becoming anything other than its own new form. Coherence is the middle voice of consciously making sense for oneself and yet among others.

But this is an area which in my experience troubles many of us teachers. We long for a shared coherence, for formats and practices (not to say standards) held in common and for common competencies (not to say requirements) which might inform reading and writing in these new forms. While I am inclined to any conversation about what is common among us, I am less inclined to think that even improvisational commonalities will or should emerge in an electronic age. Here, I think, there is an actual newness upon us. In the place of competencies and commonalities electronic spaces offer the swiftly shifting and easily shared particularities of the middle voice. Instead I would suggest that we reassess coherence in terms of the successive attendings to persisting forms.

During our English department hypertext seminar my colleague Donna Heiland asks me how I help my students make their hypertexts more coherent:

> It is so seductive to write these lyric fragments and link them like music. Some of the most interesting hypertexts have a sort of senseless but shapeful beauty and play. I worry that my students will lose their ability to read closely or to argue or to theorise, or at least that they won't be as willing to.

I am midway through an almost unconscious discussion of how we talk about and model hypertext forms in my class (e.g., projecting the hypertexts on the screen, discussing the way the Storyspaces cluster, then looking at series of links to see if they provide a model of some sort) when Donna and I each realise (a foolishness dawning over each of our faces) that such a discussion may merely be marking the limits of our own literacy. I stop mid-sentence and we say (I do not recall which of us said this): 'It may be that we cannot see the truly new forms of rhetoric and theory that are emerging. What we see as senseless beauty may be the emergence of as yet unrecognisable new ways of making sense'.

As if in confirmation, one afternoon almost a year to the day after Donna and I talked, I had three successive meetings with students writing hypertextual senior theses. The first, Shaz, was writing on hypertext and french feminist theory and she has created a four-pole structure, a cluster of thematic tensions (the rational, the natural, arrogance and boundlessness). Shaz is worried lest each of the sections seem to be too coherent, she doesn't want to be bound by sense, doesn't want the reader to believe that she has escaped the tensions she discovered and established as the contrary movements in her text.

Heather, the second student, was writing on contour and consciousness, the nature of authority in texts and the construction of reader communities and their relationship to feminist discourse. Her writing focused on Nabokov's *Pale Fire* and Shelley Jackson's (1996) hyperfiction *Patchwork Girl*. She wanted to learn how to do random links so that the text alternates beginnings with each reading and she wanted to show me how she had established zones of colour in the Storyspace where the thinking of certain theorists (e.g., Cixous 1993; Deleuze & Guattari 1987) prevails though it may or may not be directly quoted or attributed.

The last of the three, Noah, was writing an extraordinary hypertext narrative of gender construction, a story of a boy growing up in a world of women and a place of presence and multiplicity, of difference and desire. He explicitly rejects the fiction of guard fields and shaped contours exemplified in the Eastgate fictions (especially *afternoon*) in favour of a fiction of 'slippages', 'narrative traction' and 'release'. He wants readers to be free to choose and is experimenting with ways to confront them with this freedom at each turn. He is never unaware of the paradoxes. He writes:

There will come a point in the narrative, when the page return will no longer yield as the default reading often encourages a reluctance to engage with the form, the skittish bob of the RETURN [sic] key. This turn constitutes the first narrative 'release' after which the narrative explodes, or dissolves, depending upon how one looks at it. I've intentionally disarmed the 'default reading' of its dissuasive availability. In my opinion the page return ought not to encourage the decision not to choose.

I have written elsewhere, in response to those who claim that the so-called MTV generation has no attention span, that in an age like ours which privileges polyvocality, multiplicity and constellated knowledge, a sustained attention span may be less useful than successive attendings. Already in 1934 the poet Ezra Pound felt what we might call the hypermediated urge to 'charge language with meaning to the utmost possible degree' (p. 34) including sound, and vision, as well as what some have lately and stupidly taken to calling content. Pound's notion of phanopoeisis, the play between the image as written and read, attends to the oscillation between representation and world—what Kate Hayles (1993, p. 71) calls 'flickering signifiers', as well as the process of confusion and exhilaration as we shift between them. The cave myth in Plato's *Republic* is as much concerned with what Socrates calls 'an art of bringing about [vision]' as it is to the painful and ultimately impossible task of turning from the shadows to the 'dazzle and glitter of the light'. Hyperfiction embodies this art learned in turning, an art of the interstices.

We experience hypertext fictions as wayward, embodied and illegitimate. This is the cyborg consciousness, what Donna Haraway (1991, p. 177) calls 'an argument for pleasure in the confusion of boundaries and for responsibility in their construction'. Hypertext, even on the web, both embodies and is itself solely embodied by what in print is an invisible process of nonetheless constant waywardness. The reader of a hypertext not only chooses the way she reads but her choices in fact become what it is. The text continually rewrites itself and becomes what I term the constructive hypertext: a version of what it is becoming, a structure for what does not yet exist.

As more and more becomes linked, it is arguable that what is passed over becomes more strongly linked on that account. For instance, because the web links edgewise, it suggests that every screen is linked to another; hypertext links thus become the severing of one screen from another (much as each time we read, our eyes clip words in sequence). Exclusion and inclusion interact, the outside defines the centre; and so communication involves no longer so much the substance of what we say, but more of its expression and construction.

It seems to me that these three young Vassar College writers each has a distinct sense of the shared particularities that construct and communicate vernacular coherences. They are creating texts which require and welcome successive attendings and whose coherence distinguishes itself within other possible coherences, in meaningfulness rather than against meaninglessness. They each insist in undoing the ways they are used to reading hypertexts. They each expect a reader reading for herself, a reader less concerned with knowing than knowing about.

Teaching and writing in a middle voice reminds us that we have always been less geared to knowing than knowing about. The poet Robert Duncan used to give his students a survey which included the question: Name ten masterpieces of literature which you haven't read and know you will never read that nonetheless influence your life as a poet. Years ago I heard someone ask Jean Luc Godard about the source of the rich literary allusion pervading his films. He claimed that he absorbed these things while working at a Paris bookstore in the instant between taking a patron's book to the cash register and putting it in its sack. These are descriptions of matrices of meaning. Whether the web or what comes after it will become the poet's bookshelf or the filmmaker's Paris bookstore remains to be seen. We are in the midst of making a new culture, one we will make as much out of persistence as of newnesses.

Yet we cannot let persistence become habit lest we become used by what we are used to. Nor can we let the allure of newness blind us to seeing ourselves where we are. We need to bring to our tasks a new and persistent voice, one neither active nor passive, but rather the middle voice my student Heather Malin invokes in one of the random beginnings that alternate in her hypertext of contour and consciousness:

> To begin and end with consciousness, to ask questions that will not yield answers. This is the way to enter into the movement, to allow room to stretch and become blind, to hear and feel the things that our common sense denies. This is how I come to know the bodies and waves, how I get to the place where my language is really mine, and where I do not worry that I will not be understood. The closure is not the issue, but the (not) getting there. And this is how it begins.

Notes

Parts of this chapter were originally given as a talk, 'Writing in the middle voice: vernacular coherence or seeing ourselves in where we are', *Plenary talk for the Mid-Atlantic Alliance for Computers and Writing Conference*, 9 February 1996, George Mason University, Virginia. I wish to thank Sharon Dolente, Heather Malin and Noah Pivnick, Vassar College '96, for permission to quote from their theses and to recount our discussions.

References

Cixous, H. 1993 *Three Steps on the Ladder of Writing*, trans. S. Cornell and S. Summers, Columbia University Press, New York

Deleuze, G. and Guattari, F. 1987 *A Thousand Plateaus: Capitalism and Schizophrenia*, trans. B. Massumi, University of Minnesota Press, Minneapolis

Eco, U. 1994 'La bustina di Minerva', *Espresso*

Furuta, R. and C.C. Marshall 1996 'Genre as reflection of technology in the World Wide Web', *Hypermedia Design, Proceedings of the International Workshop on Hypermedia Design (IWHD'95), Workshops in Computing*, eds S. Fraïssé *et al.*, Springer, New York

Haraway, D. 1991 'A cyborg manifesto: science, technology, and socialist-feminism in the late twentieth century', *Simians, Cyborgs and Women*, Routledge, New York

Hayles, N.K. 1993 'Virtual bodies and flickering signifiers', *Oct* 66, Massachusetts Institute of Technology, Cambridge MA, pp. 69–91

Jackson, S. 1996 'Patchwork Girl', computer disk, Eastgate Press, Cambridge, Massachusetts

Pound, E. 1934 *ABC of Reading*, New Directions, New York

Syverson, P., Guyer, C., Leusebrink, M. and Joyce, M. (in press) 'Walk four ways one time: narrative coherencies', *PRE/TEXT (A Journal of Rhetorical Theory)*

Taylor, M.C. and Saarinen, E. 1994 *Imagologies: Media Philosophy*, Routledge, New York and London

Weinbren, G. 1995 'In the ocean of streams of story', *Millennium Film Journal*, no. 28, Spring, Interactivities, pp. 15–30. Online version: http://www.sva.edu/MFJ/GWOCEAN.HTML

9

Living on the surface: learning in the age of global communication networks

JOHNDAN JOHNSON-EILOLA

Most of us see the world through two separate, contradictory philosophies: time and space. Part of us lives at the chronological nexus uniting what once was with what is becoming. Living in time, we think of our history as building us in a slow, steady accretion of experiences, a small version of cultural history moving toward a perfect existence. We pass stories down, from grandparent to parent to child to grandchildren-to-be. This was your grandfather's watch; this quilt I save for my children, and their children's children.

But another, more recent part of us lives in space, in a place where things happen on the surface in a state of continuous stimulation. We experience things not at depth but on the surface; not a slow accretion but an everything-all-at-once shout. We do not pass tales linearly, but experience them multiply, simultaneously, across global communication networks.

Many adults are terrified of this place; many children live there happily. Those of us raised in the modernist first world tend to deride the second, postmodernist world as superficial, artificial, and dehumanising (Bloom 1987; Heim 1987; Hairston 1992). We have lived through the shift, and are unfamiliar and uneasy (at best) with what we experience. Surface seems shallow, easy, hollow, flashy. History offers a sense of *depth* (we think, without irony), of genealogy and belongingness, of seriousness. Understandably, we attempt to teach our children to value history over the easy seductions of space.

Our panic intensifies when we are confronted by communication technologies such as computers interconnected on a global scale. In these articulations, postmodernism abducts modernist technologies: the computer, a device originally constructed to calculate weapons trajectories, is reconstructed and redistributed to provide a fluid, flowing space where users experiment with multiple subjectivities; where stories lose concrete beginnings, middles, and ends; where the rules of games shift, are overwritten, and sometimes even disappear. We, who Foucault (1986, p. 22) once termed 'the pious descendants of time', do not understand or relate to these networked spaces in the same ways that our children and students do; we tend to criticise them unfairly.

Such critiques are understandable, but misplaced. Although we think we are helping our students and our children learn mature, complex thinking processes, in many cases we are also trying to tie them to a way of seeing the world, a way that is no longer feasible; in more ways than one, we hold them back. Certainly we should continue to be concerned about 'traditional' issues such as the quality of work we and our students do online and about the consequences of our actions there in terms of others. But we need to re-understand many of our traditional ways of working and thinking as well; we need to be open to possibilities.

Most of my thinking in this chapter has grown out of informal observations of children working and learning in these new spaces. Like many parents and teachers, I have watched children and young adults use computers in ways that seem alien to me. My initial response included many of the tendencies mentioned above: annoyance or patronising amusement. But over the past few years, in watching and discussing these games with my 8-year-old daughter, I have changed my position on the value and focus of interactions between children and computer interfaces. The transcript here, in which Carolyn explains to me how to play the game *Per.Oxyd* (1995), discussed in more detail later in this chapter, suggests some of the ways in which users such as Carolyn are not merely passing time or learning traditional skills. Speaking both literally and metaphorically, the rules of the game are changing:

Carolyn: I know what to do. I've done this hundreds of times.

Johndan: How do you know which blocks to hit?

C: I just . . . hit them.

J: Just for . . . How'd you figure out to hit them? [pause] Tell me which blocks you're going to try to hit next.

C: Trying to hit the corner ones.

J: Why? The corner ones better?

C: Yeah . . . sometimes.

J: Sometimes?

C: Hey . . . Where'd the other one . . . Where's the other one?

J: It went away . . . the corner one again. You just hit them until . . . two of them match?

C: Yeah. And then it won't have a question mark like that.

J: Oh . . . the question marks mean they don't match yet, huh? Oh . . . they flash the question mark and then something else.

C: See?

J: Can you get two round ones to match?

C: I already got them.

J: So you make the things bounce on the screen?

C: Yeah. But this is . . . this is just the first level. They're all different.

J: Wow.

C: And it can go to a hard part of a level.

J: So how do you figure out what the rules are?

C: Just play.

J: Just play? And then what happens?

C: You just . . . play.

* * *

187

J: What's this level?

C: Some . . . not very good level.

J: No? Just dull? Why's it dull? What do you have to do?

C: I have to . . . bang those things so that I can push those things up so that I can put the bigger ones . . . I need to put the biggest ones on those flashing lights and then do it like that and then put those ones.

J: How'd you figure out you had to do that?

C: Just did.

J: How?

C: I just played the game and found out that was what to do.

To someone raised in an historical worldview—one valuing linearity, genealogies, tradition, *rules*—Carolyn's explanations of the game sound haphazard, unplanned and immature. But to someone familiar with global information spaces such as the World Wide Web, games such as these provide environments for learning postmodernist approaches to communication and knowledge: navigation, constructive problem-solving, dynamic goal construction. There is a profound cultural shift here which, as educators, we cannot simply reject but must work with and beyond, using powerful methods for constructing new literacies and ways of living. We cannot retreat nostalgically to a modernist era; that time is no longer available to us in the way it once was. But we can make this a celebration, and a remaking, rather than a lament.

Technology and culture: an incomplete introduction

One of the primary difficulties of moving beyond our normal conceptions of communicating in surface environments lies in our understanding of how technologies operate. To many people, technologies are instruments for accomplishing predetermined ends. A typewriter is a tool for placing letters on a page in order to write sentences or fill in forms. An automobile is a tool for moving objects and/or people from one place to another. Technology critic Andrew Feenberg (1991) terms this view 'instrumentalist', because it presents technologies as simple tools. Opposing this concept, Feenberg identifies the 'substantive' view, which holds that in some cases technologies have power over developers and users, who become destined toward certain ends merely by choosing to handle technologies such as guns or nuclear weapons. As some critics of nuclear power would argue, the mere decision to develop this technology puts humanity on a specific path—toward destruction, for example. Indeed, many of the most intractable arguments over technological development and use polarise as instrumentalist versus substantive views of a technology. The debate over handguns in the United States, to take one extreme case, often pits instrumentalists (who believe that guns protect law-abiding citizens, and that safety lies in education) against substantives (who believe that weapons designed to kill will eventually be used to kill).[1]

Surface versus depth arguments tend to look at technologies in these all-or-nothing ways: print and literacy are typically considered mature, historical technologies while television is marked as immature and surface level. From another perspective, print is an instrument that a mature person learns to wield, while television is a technology that taints and damages every thought or communication it touches. While such analyses are certainly satisfying in a visceral way, technologies are much more complex than this. At one level, it is profitable and productive to think of our technologies as tools: if we do, it follows that we should take responsibility for our use of them. But at another level, contemporary systems of technological development and use are so intricately meshed that it is impossible to tell where one single, concrete technology use ends and another begins: not every technology affords every sort of activity completely. A relatively low resolution of a television screen makes it worse for extended text communication than a book; the fixity of a printed page makes it less open to animation.

It is easy to see why both the instrumentalist and substantive views are so popular: each works to explain powerful

189

aspects of technology use. But these views are dangerous when we use them as alibis for our own cultural positions. In use, technologies are neither completely neutral nor all-powerful—they are somewhere in between and beyond. Those of us raised in history are uneasy with computer technologies because we attempt to do things with them as if they were simple tools; our ways of working and living do not fit. We need to admit that other ways of working with these same technologies open different doorways.

New literacies: modernism, postmodernism and interfaces

This chapter explores different ways of understanding contemporary interface design that are more in tune with surface ways of thinking and communicating. Far from being isolated, neutral objects, computer interfaces play out a range of assumptions, authorisations, and challenges to literacy practices. Interfaces provide interesting objects of inquiry because they act as the nexus between people and computers (and networks); they include not only visual screen displays but other points of contact, including keyboards, mice, trackpads, sound waves through speaker and microphone and more. In addition, 'interface' as noun gives way to verb, in the actions of users who interface with computer spaces in a temporal sequence of actions and reactions.

Before examining computer interface design as a cultural and educational object, I shall begin by considering the postmodernist world in which these interfaces are designed and used. The distinction between modernism and postmodernism is notoriously complex and interpretations of it highly variable, but for our purposes in this chapter we can adopt Jean-François Lyotard's (1984) version, which describes postmodernism as the loss of belief in 'grand narratives' and the consequent disintegration of communication into 'language games'. In other words according to Lyotard we can no longer believe in foundational cultural stories about history and progress. These stories used to anchor our everyday lives and our positions in the world. Without unproblematic grand narratives, we must resort to local agreements about what counts as valid statements or 'moves' in a language game; these rules vary from site to site. In this situation, there are no longer universal truths on which participants in language games can rely; instead, they find themselves increasingly involved in manipulating information according to local rules of admissibility and purpose. Furthermore, distinctions between appearance and substance start to collapse, because ranking one before the other demands an impossible search for universally true meanings.

Developments in software design over the last decade illustrate many of these postmodern tendencies: a lack of depth, an emphasis on contingency and multiplicity. Those developments have taken place in response to (and sometimes in anticipation of) users learning new ways of relating to information and communication—this is not a cause-and-effect relationship, but a mutual construction. A quick glance at software from a surface orientation highlights some of the key skills we need before we can work productively in a world of global computer networks. The chapter continues by analysing two types of skills or approaches fostered in some forms of children's software: the ability to process multiple streams of information simultaneously and the propensity to experiment in free-form, ill-defined problem domains. Although these skills are sometimes considered unimportant or immature, they are becoming vital for learning and working in global information spaces, as evidenced by an examination of current and experimental interfaces in World Wide Web spaces.

Simultaneous, parallel reading

Examining computer interfaces can help us understand the potential shape and direction of changes in the way we and especially our students and children are adapting to this type of space. Computer games, both educational and entertainment

191

Figure 9.1 **Screen from *Oregon Trail II*, showing active map; status bars for temperature, climate, date, and distance; buttons for guide, diary, party health status and supplies**

(sometimes combining as 'edutainment'), provide some significant examples of these changes.

Consider an educational program such as *Oregon Trail II* (1995). Briefly, the game involves children in a quest to guide a wagon train across nineteenth-century United States. In key ways, this narrative mimics those enacted by children for generations. So at first glance, the game seems to exemplify a traditional approach to learning.

Figure 9.1 includes a map indicating the wagon train's progress across the frontier. At the bottom of this screen children follow real-time updates on landscape, date, temperature ranges, and distance travelled. Buttons to the right of the status bar open a guidebook, an editable diary that automatically tracks key events in the trip, and display windows for tracking and adjusting critical elements such as supplies (Figure 9.2) and the travellers' health.

Figure 9.2 **Screen from *Oregon Trail II*, showing a portion of the supplies list and controls for different activities**

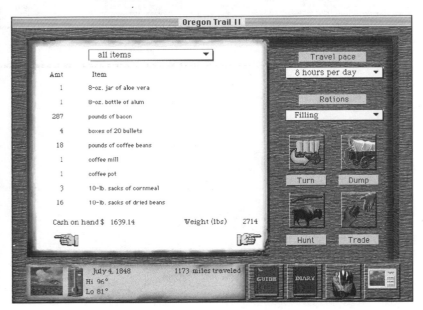

At critical points in the journey, the map in Figure 9.1 is replaced by graphical views of towns, stores, liveries, rivers to ford, or by animated screens synchronised to audio tracks for interacting with other travellers, local inhabitants, or (for vital decision-making) members of the party offering advice, sometimes contradictory or argumentative (Figure 9.3).

The traditional content of *Oregon Trail II* (1995)—its genre is one that children have played in one form or another for generations—only partially masks its postmodern nature. The game, like many contemporary computer games, is somewhat overwhelming to anyone not conditioned to process and manage multiple, parallel displays of information. The interactive and dynamically updated interface panels require players to monitor and manipulate not merely one source of information, but often up to five or more, making rapid (sometimes parallel or connected) decisions based on options and data offered in those panels.

**Figure 9.3   Screen from *Oregon Trail II*, for conversation
(synchronised with audio)**

Simulation and experimentation

Games such as *Oregon Trail II* also encourage (even require) users to open themselves to change and experimentation. Although traditional games routinely rely on chance in their play, they typically do so in limited and clearly demarcated ways. For children, modernist games propel them relatively powerlessly along a gameboard according to the roll of dice or the spin of a wheel, learning to happily accept their position in a larger plan of historical progress (a common thread running through many stories backing technological development, capitalism, religion and socialism).

Contingency is a valuable quality in contemporary computer games, but it is a chance of a radically different sort: the pace and structure of such games require children to accept chance and to learn to work with it, actively rather than passively. To cope with environments such as those offered by simulation games, users learn to juggle multiple, dynamic

**Figure 9.4   Screen from *Per.Oxyd*, a complex game
                 encouraging experimentation**

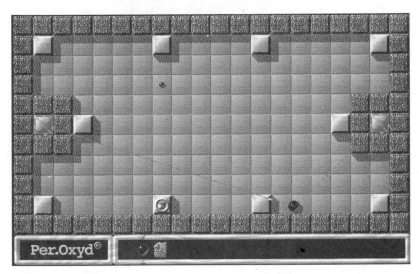

vectors of information without attempting to understand them
fully. Instead, they play out multiple hypotheses about connections among numerous symbolic forces. A game such as
Per.Oxyd (1995) (see Figure 9.4) gives no clear, explicit rules
or objectives, beyond the simple display of sequential levels
(which itself is apparent only after a user has passed from level
one to level two).

Simultaneity and contingency in global communication networks

This emphasis on taking action and representing knowledge
across broad, flat surfaces is a repudiation of historical distinctions between appearance and true content, a hallmark of
postmodernism. Children learn here to deal tactically with
contingency, multiplicity, and uncertainty. Where modernists
are compelled to understand the rules before playing a game—
or at best, must be able to discern simple, clear rules by trial
and error—postmodernists are capable of working such
chaotic environments from within, moment by moment. Their

Figure 9.5 **Variety of onscreen controls In *Microsoft Word*, including: Standard toolbar (top); Database toolbar (centre right); Formatting toolbar (bottom); as well as context-sensitive and popup help (yellow rectangle in Database toolbar and status line at bottom of screen)**

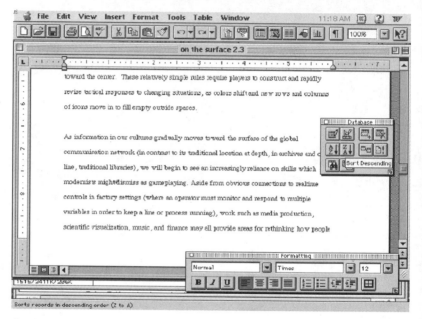

domain is space rather than time. They exist with time, dancing across it, rather than being subordinated to it.

It is easy to dismiss these examples of the skills fostered in some game software as juvenile or immature: after all, this has long been the way modernists view postmodernists. We must remember that these shifts in the kinds of skills required to function in global information spaces are part of a broader movement, bringing information to the surface not only in children's educational and entertainment software, but in computer interfaces in general, including such core 'productivity' applications as word processors and databases. Programs such as *Microsoft Word 6.01* (1995) provide increasing amounts of surface information in the form of button bars and contextual online help (see Figure 9.5).

In Figure 9.5, operations and assistance in the program are raised from previous positions that required users to move down through menu trees to execute commands or access assistance. Graphical User Interfaces (GUIs) such as those popularised by the Macintosh and now adopted by Microsoft Windows provide a general instance of such surfacing: GUIs bring to the surface instructions on how to operate the computer, giving users two- or even three-dimensional visual cues; on older, command-line systems such as MS-DOS and BSD UNIX, users were required to memorise complex verbal commands to type, one letter at a time, into the command line of the interface. In other words, users of graphical interfaces operate in the visual present while users of command-line interfaces operate serially after the long-term learning of hidden system logics.

This tendency to bring information to the surface is increasing with the popularisation and growth of global information spaces. Rapid increases in the use of computers and in the degree of interconnectedness between traditionally discrete computer systems is creating a new space for communication and learning. It is certainly possible to continue using these spaces in modernist ways that emulate the linearity and temporality of traditional communication media (one-to-one, serial communication or one-to-many broadcast media). But these spaces are also the scene for the development and use of postmodern interfaces that draw on many of the characteristics highlighted above in terms of children's software.

Collections of addresses to World Wide Web sites, for example, are typically stored and accessed in ways that reflect a position in the boundary between modernist and postmodernist worldviews: linear-hierarchical or database. The linear-hierarchical list, a staple of print culture, requires storing mass information in a somewhat structured, retrievable format. Print texts are a response to early scrolls, which were accessed more or less linearly: even if a user understood that the required material was near the end (inside) of the scroll, they had to spool off all the early material to reach the end. Scrolls are firmly entrenched in time; they do not attempt to lay out

197

Figure 9.6   Linear-hierarchical list of addresses on the World Wide Web

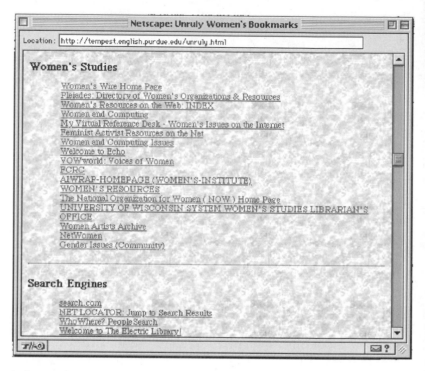

information in a two-dimensional fashion. Printed and bound books, however, construct the possibility for a more complex hierarchy. Although the linear ordering of pages still gives a strong sense of progression, Tables of Contents simultaneously organise that information into hierarchical levels. Rather than rely on the reader's progression through a set of ordered pages, the hierarchical organisation provides a single master-plan for putting each element in its proper place beneath the top level of the hierarchy, the main point, the thesis, or the broadest idea. Alphabetical indexes and more recent hypertexts exist at the boundaries between linear and network text, in some cases asking users to unravel a thread through an unseen (but implied) network structure, sometimes offering readers the network structure as a directly manipulable reading and

198

Figure 9.7 **Search and Response screens in YAHOO (Yet Another Hierarchically Organized Outline) World Wide Web index**

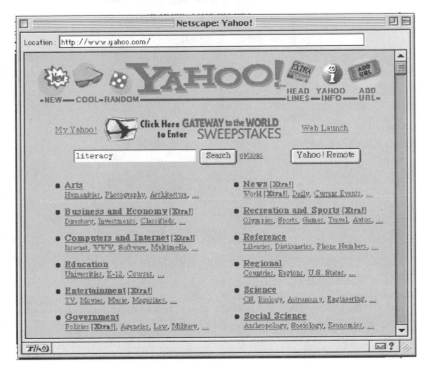

writing space. This boundary condition helps to explain why hypertext operates in such a wide range of manners, from fast-access information retrieval for on-line help to experimental postmodern fiction.

Most small sets of addresses on the World Wide Web retain the hierarchical-linear structure (Figure 9.6), allowing users to skim hierarchical lists and click on a relevant entry to jump directly to that site. As Jay Bolter (1991) correctly points out, literacy technologies each construct a 'space' for writing and reading. Linear-hierarchical structures offer a tree of knowledge, with each specific bit of knowledge possessing its own proper place within the global system. In other words, linear-hierarchical ordering should connote a sense of place, a modernist universal ordering for knowledge.

Figure 9.8   YAHOO database translated into *Project X* file

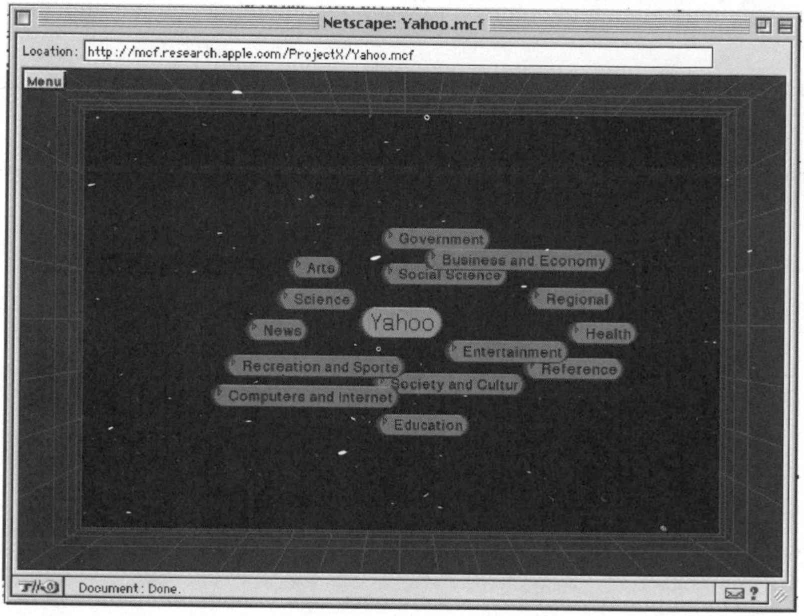

As the amount of information to be searched on the World Wide Web has risen, the linear-hierarchical ordering no longer suffices: users' queries range too widely to be anticipated and new sites are added too rapidly to be integrated into the neat tree structure. The construction of large databases such as the popular Alta Vista and Yahoo (Figure 9.7) acknowledges that no single tree can keep up.

The early WWW index Yahoo constructs multiple, overlapping hierarchies that are displayed to users on demand. Alta Vista, more postmodernist, offers a flat space of freely searchable information. The very invisibility of the database on which the searches are run demonstrates that there is, from a modernist standpoint, too much information. It can no longer be processed by users as a coherent structure, but constitutes a data cloud.

Interface such as the query/response forms in Yahoo or Alta Vista are understandable responses to cognitive overload. But they are not the only nor perhaps the most appropriate

200

Figure 9.9   *Project X* **user flying into dataspace from Figure 9.8**

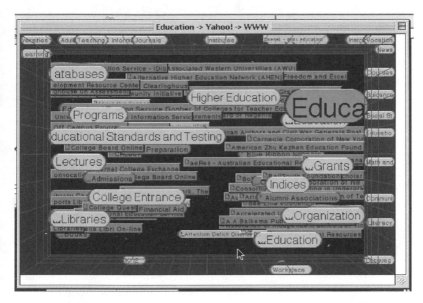

response. The surface and postmodernist tendencies discussed above in terms of children's educational software also show up in recent work on World Wide Web databases. Graphical interfaces such as *Project X* (1996),[2] an Apple Advanced Technology Group project for displaying indexes to World Wide Web spaces, construct masses of information not as ordered lists but as rich visual structures for developers and users to manipulate and navigate. The screens in Figure 9.8 show a large subset of the Yahoo database translated into the *Project X* interface. Users fly (visually and metaphorically) around the space on the screen, zooming in and out to show the data cloud at various resolutions (Figure 9.9) and to connect to individual World Wide Web sites, some of which might themselves hold other *Project X* databases.

At one level, these visualisations do not seem to differ much from the linear-hierarchical index: in *Project X*, the limbs of the tree are spread out and distributed slightly differently. At best, in this interpretation the visual model does not add much

201

to the user's experience: why not make the structure more orderly, more like an outline or an index? But one wrinkle here is in the recursion allowed by the structure: the nodes shown in the visual display may themselves offer competing visual structures. Users flying into a single node may find themselves suddenly navigating a whole new space, or the same space with a radically different organisation, or spaces much larger than the original space.

In addition, the impulse to show the structure graphically distributed rather than to limit users to the query/response screens of Yahoo (Figure 9.7) is due to an understanding of reading multiple strands of information, at the surface rather than at depth. Users comfortable with information-rich screens such as those shown in Figure 9.9 tend to have many of the same habits of thought and understanding as those of users of programs like *Oregon Trail II* and *Per.Oxyd*: the ability (and perhaps necessity) to understand things in multiple, contingent, spatial structures rather than in serial and chronological orders. Interfaces like *Project X* are designed for those who have grown up with interfaces like *Per.Oxyd* and *Oregon Trail II*. In many ways, in fact, *Project X* is only a weak indication of the future of information representation. What sort of interfaces might be developed when productivity programs—word processors, databases, graphics programs—are modelled on action games? A relatively simple game such as *Zoop* (1995) (Figure 9.10), for example, requires users to manipulate a central control in four directions in response to shifting coloured icons around the four perimeters of the screen. The icons move toward the central grid; if they reach it, central control explodes. Players coordinate changes between icon colours and the central control colour by firing light beams. If the central control and the outside icon (or row or column of icons) are the same colour, the icons are removed; if the two are different colours, the central control swaps colours with the icon(s) and the icons continue to advance toward the centre. The game resembles the classic *Tetris*, except that markers in *Zoop* move inward from four sides instead of from only one. These relatively simple rules require

Figure 9.10 *Zoop*, **fast-paced surface-oriented computer game**

players to construct and rapidly revise tactical responses to changing situations, as colours shift and new rows and columns of icons move in to fill empty outside spaces.

As information in our cultures gradually moves toward the surface of the global communication network (in contrast to its traditional location, at depth, in archives and offline, traditional libraries), we will begin to see greater reliance on skills which modernists might dismiss as game-playing. Aside from obvious connections to realtime controls in factory settings (where an operator must monitor and respond to multiple variables to keep a line or process running), work such as media production, scientific visualisation, music, and finance may all provide means for reassessing how people work, think, and communicate. US Labour Secretary Robert Reich (1991) describes a new elite job class of 'symbolic-analytic workers' skilled at manipulating, abstracting, and experimenting with information (pp. 177–80).

At least part of the difficulty in thinking of such interfaces in culturally and intellectually positive ways is perpetuated by a modernist insistence that all subjects experience these spaces in identical ways. This is not at all true. Some of the terror of postmodernism that many of us feel is due to our experiences and habits accumulated by living in a world oriented to the idea of trans-historical truths, a world in which most of us strive for focus and possession. We tend to seek out and create situations that let us concentrate on single elements in sequence: linear narratives in novels, the needle in a haystack of information, the single voice rising above the 'noise'. In this modernist worldview, cognitive overload and contingency are negative, damaging tendencies. In the face of surface-oriented information spaces such as *Per.Oxyd* and *Project X*, history-oriented people attempt to understand these communicative spaces under the old paradigm: they attempt to focus on one element to the exclusion of all others. Understandably, these efforts fail: the mass of surface information and representation crowds in, overlaps, shifts position constantly. In our own interpretations of such spaces, we therefore tend to view them as ineffective and poorly designed, incapable of supporting serious work.

But we need to acknowledge that from a postmodernist worldview, such spaces are experienced in radically different ways. At a basic level, these spaces can be navigated and negotiated from a simultaneous, surface perspective that does not attempt to find single facts or linear structures but has learned to process information along parallel lines without relying on a single focal point or goal.

Post-postmodernism and interfaces: agency within chaos

If postmodern tendencies prevail in contemporary computer interfaces, that does not make them automatically more desirable than older ways of relating to information, knowledge, and the world. In fact, the critiques of postmodernism discussed above contain some elements of truth. Their difficulty lies, as I have argued, in oversimplifying and demonising postmodernism so that they overlook its benefits. They also frequently view modernism nostalgically, and tend to ignore some of the revolutionary potentials of postmodernism. In this section I present a critique of postmodernism that tries to avoid dismissing or negating its potential. The critical aspects of those definitions will then lead, in the final section of this chapter, to a set of tentative guidelines and goals for productive, computer-supported learning that takes advantage of postmodern potentials for learning at the surface without becoming naively celebratory.

If a postmodern stance seems to offer a position from which people can negotiate new understandings and capabilities in computer-supported-environments, this same stance sometimes degenerates into the purely superficial. When surface replaces history as life's organising paradigm, stable identities tend to disintegrate. Traditionally, the weight of history almost literally held us in place: what we were, and who we were becoming, grew out of what our ancestors were. History provided a sense of security which, in breaking the threads of history, postmodernist worldviews dislodge. Security and containment are flipsides of the same coin. In learning to understand communication in terms of simultaneous, contingent streams and structures, users also lose the ability to anchor themselves anywhere with any certainty.

Literary and cultural theorist Frederic Jameson (1991) explains the problem of postmodernism in noting that traditional living occurs in the act of uniting history and future to a shifting present; in other words, at every instant we work to reconcile all the things we have been up until now with what we want to do next. Without history, that effort fails because there is no past out of which to live. This failed historical binding is something cultural theorist Dick Hebdige (1988) says commits postmodernists to an existence in 'the blank, empty spaces of the now' (p. 164).

We understand now why the modernist disdain for surface felt so comfortable: there is little comfort in postmodernism. And there are no guaranteed paths to empowerment; in many ways postmodernism, like its cousin deconstruction, is frequently most valued for its ability to break down entrenched oppressive systems. But we cannot simply reject postmodernism because the world itself increasingly requires postmodernist responses at many levels—from advertising to art, labour and so on. So we need to reach a different understanding of the possibilities of surface; we need to remain critically aware of their shortcomings and drawbacks.

Not surprisingly, we might respond by avoiding a complete rejection of modernism. Instead, we can help students and children to learn to alternate between surface and depth, between history and space. One of the most damaging elements of modernism was its insistence on universal truths. The productive paradox in alternating between postmodernism and modernism lies in its willingness to appropriate aspects of each perspective without allowing the viewer to be completely absorbed by each.

This approach is commonly seen in cultural studies work that attempts to move beyond postmodernism into social change. Theresa Ebert (1991), for example, makes a useful distinction between ludic and resistance postmodernism. *Ludic* postmodernism, the most highly notorious cultural form of postmodernism, demands the free flow of signification and the total breakdown of all stable connection. *Resistance* postmodernism, however, attempts to capitalise on the fundamental rupture by reconstituting social and economic relationships in more equitable ways. Such resistance requires the acknowledgement that even after the breakdown of universal narratives, after the loss of hard-core truths, we must still attempt to recognise that some people have unfair power over others, that some people are exploited or live degrading or painful lives. Reaching these understandings requires something of an epistemological trick: the ability to occupy a position while remaining critical of it. After all, the claim that one person is treating another unfairly seems to resort to universal truths about power and equality. To keep this new stance from fossilising into the foundational truths of modernism or from disintegrating into the celebration of rupture in postmodernism, we must gain (and teach) the ability to look critically at ways of thinking, living, and communicating. Philosopher Seyla Benhabib (1992) provides an account of justice and ethics that is not based on traditional conceptions of universal truth but still admits provisional truths in order to prompt discussion and action. But where a modernist conception of public discussion would focus on critiquing, verifying and improving conceptions of universal truths, Benhabib's model insists that we should focus on a meta-discussion about how truths are admitted to discussions, how they are evaluated, and how they are changed. In other words, Benhabib's model never aims to provide universal statements but founds itself on moving terrain, and then makes that contingency a primary feature.

We must work to develop and teach (and help children and young adults develop and teach with us) the application of these critical abilities to literacy and computers. Earlier, I discussed Feenberg's distinctions between instrumental (neutral) and substantive (all-powerful) technologies, noting that neither position productively or positively explains how users interact with computers and with each other on computer-supported networks. Feenberg's alternative, a critical theory of technology, attempts to help developers and users understand their relations to technologies and to each other in more contextualised, interpersonal ways.

In this view, it is not possible to identify the negative or positive potentials of a technology outside contextualised uses. This contextualisation also helps to explain why history users' interpretations of computer interfaces for children differ from those of surface users: history users do not interact with the programs the way surface users do. The insistence on contextualisation also provides a critical edge to postmodernist, surface uses of technology to prevent users from becoming so detached from their contexts and social responsibilities that they lose the ability to make judgements about social positions and needs. Each interface provides areas for critique; each provides elements that support unequal distributions of power. Graphical User Interfaces, for example, support certain types of uses while discouraging others: the base metaphor of a Western corporate office, for example, affords use by only those who are familiar with the logic of that system, while it discourages those who are not (Selfe & Selfe 1994). The notion of a folder icon as something to store documents in, and open later, makes sense only if the user has learned how to use a folder in other contexts, such as an office.

Other programs, in particular the popular genre of alien invasion, first-person action games, invite critical scrutiny, not merely of the game but of the culture that popularises it. In *Marathon* (1995), players hunt out and destroy various monstrous aliens who have invaded an earthship. When I asked Carolyn why she shot the aliens, she replied that they were going to kill her if she did not kill them first. Interested in this common cultural response ('the best defence is a strong offence'), I asked how she knew this; in every game she played she fired first—perhaps the aliens were the ones shooting in self-defence. Later, Carolyn and I explored a wide range of topics dealing with violence, identity and stereotypes. We talked about the assumptions involved in the technology of the game itself, the fact that the game afforded either shooting at aliens or hiding from them, but not communicating with them. We explored cultural responses to language barriers and how the game might include new features, such as trading with aliens or talking to them.

Certainly such critiques do not completely remove from children the attraction to violence, at least at the vicarious level—such violence is ubiquitous in our culture. But when contextualised, these games do provide the opportunity for a critique that can then be tentatively applied to broader cultural issues. This critical perspective, alternating between surface and depth, is crucial if we are to help children and young adults generate positive responses regularly to such situations. As interfaces present us with more and more surface information, critical skills are necessary for both survival and agency. And as we, the occupants of history, come to understand the possibilities of these environments we will also find that the next generation, surface dwellers, have learned to understand those environments in new ways and have things to teach us.

Notes

1 Feenberg attempts to break this binary by constructing a 'critical theory of technology' that will help re-contextualise technology development and use. At this point in my argument, I am only interested in using the instrumental/substantive binary to identify certain tendencies in looking at computer interfaces.
2 Apple now markets the technology under the title 'Hot Sauce'.

References

Benhabib, S. 1992 *Situating the Self: Gender, Community and Postmodernism in Contemporary Ethics*, Routledge, New York
Bloom, A. 1987 *The Closing of the American Mind*, Simon & Schuster, New York
Bolter, J.D. 1991 *Writing Space: The Computer, Hypertext, and the History of Writing*, Lawrence Erlbaum Associates, Hillsdale, NJ
Ebert, T.L. 1991 'The "difference" of postmodern feminism', *College English*, vol. 53, pp. 886–904
Feenberg, A. 1991 *Critical Theory of Technology*, Oxford University Press, New York
Foucault, M. 1986 'Of other spaces', *Diacritics*, trans. J. Miskowiec, pp. 22–7 (Original work publ. Oct 1984, as 'Des espaces autres', *Architecture-Mouvement-Continuit*)
Hairston, M. 1992 'Diversity, ideology, and the teaching of writing', *College Composition and Communication*, vol. 43, pp. 179–93
Hebdige, D. 1988 *Hiding in the Light: On Images and Things*, Comedia/Routledge, London
Heim, M. 1987 *Electric Language: A Philosophical Study of Word Processing*, Yale University Press, New Haven, CT
Jameson, F. 1991 *Postmodernism: Or, the Cultural Logic of Late Capitalism*, Duke University Press, Durham, NC
Lyotard, J.F. 1984 *The Postmodern Condition: A Report on Knowledge*, trans. G. Bennington and B. Massumi, University of Minneapolis Press, Minneapolis, Minnesota
Marathon 1995 Computer software, Bungie, Chicago, IL

Microsoft Word 6.0.1 1995 Computer software, Microsoft, Redmond, WA

Oregon Trail II 1995 Computer software, MECC Software, Minneapolis, MN

Per.Oxyd 1995 Computer software, Dongleware USA, Cambridge, MA

Project X 1996 Computer software, Apple Computer, Cupertino, CA

Reich, R.B. 1991 *The Work of Nations: Preparing Ourselves for 21st-Century Capitalism*, Alfred A. Knopf, New York

Selfe, C.L. and Selfe, R.J. 1994 'The politics of the interface: power and its exercise in electronic contact zones', *College Composition and Communication*, vol. 45, pp. 480–504

Zoop 1995 Computer software, Viacom New Media, New York

10

Children, computers and life online: education in a cyber-world

RICHARD SMITH AND PAMELA CURTIN

Childhood in a contemporary age

What sort of people are contemporary children compared to those of former generations? The orthodox position in educational theory and teacher education practice suggests that 'kids are kids' and that traditional assumptions about their socio-psychological development in educational settings remain as valid today as they were in the past. In this chapter we challenge this position by arguing that children raised in contemporary Australia are attitudinally and cognitively predisposed to life in general and formal education in particular in ways that make them quite different to children of even a decade ago. Conventional theories about child development do not fully grasp the nature of the social movements of the times. In this respect, a full understanding of the social settings and contents of children's cultures is vital for understanding formal education in today's world.

A number of writers illustrate our point. Smith, Sachs and Chant (1988) argue that young people are culturally positioned by the pervasiveness of computer-based and media technologies. Their research suggests that the use of these electronic technologies is producing a postmodern consciousness of multiple perspectives and 'social saturation' (Gergen 1991, p. 227). In particular, they make a special plea for educators to develop 'technology literacy' programs to assist young people to live in an information-rich technological world. Green and Bigum (1993), in their seminal article 'Aliens in the classroom', argue that young people exemplify an emergent postmodern student-subject with complex multiphrenic subjectivities. They are making what Haraway (1990, p. 203) calls a macro-level cultural shift from 'comfortable old hierarchical dominations to the scary networks' or what Wexler (1987, p. 154) calls the 'semiotic society'. These new kids, living in new times, are described by Green and Bigum as radically different to previous generations. They are 'aliens' in the sense that the intersection of youth culture and global technology is a kind of nature. In this respect, boundaries between humans and machines are blurred and, as a consequence, children have 'new needs and new capacities' (Green & Bigum 1993, p. 119). Green and Bigum call for a reconceptualisation of 'education' for 'aliens' while recognising the complexities of theorising and researching new times from a generational position.

In this chapter we make three claims about children and schooling in new times. First, young children are the first generations to live in an all-encompassing electronic habitat. This requires them to make sense of 'normal' family, peer and school life in a commercialised electronic world of TV, video, radio, cinema, games and computers. Second, to deal with this complex habitat, children develop forms of cognitive and attitudinal organisation that enable them to interpret the world and perform in it. In so doing, children help to shape and change the social world they live in, at both the individual and cultural levels. The third claim is that conventional school curricula and pedagogical procedures are out of step with the cognitive and attitudinal organisation of the young.

We present these claims with the intention of testing the belief that today's children are in fact 'different' to those in the past. We argue for a move away from the existing models of teaching and learning which disregard how the young may be affected by their different, technologically constructed perceptions of the world. To substantiate this argument we draw on data from a study of what young children say about and do with computer and video-game technology (Smith, Curtin & Newman 1995).

Background

Our work is premised on presuppositions about the convergence of historical period, the mode of production and culture or what some refer to as a change of century (e.g., Kinsman 1991). We support Kinsman's claim that there are analogies between the present historical period and shifts from agricultural to industrial production and culture in the eighteenth to nineteenth centuries in Europe. In this historical period, electronic communication and the proliferation of information technologies in general are major forces in the creation of new environments for conducting social life. New technologies intended to simplify or streamline tasks become events in themselves. Of particular importance is the expansion of the term 'information' as the key to contemporary living and society, predicting a new historical period.

As Poster (1990) proposes, new forms of information storage and retrieval affect communication patterns. In turn, new forms of language and behaviour for dealing with information technologies affect social relationships and individuals' psychological construction. Especially significant to the new communication forms into which the young are born and socialised are computers and, in turn, computer-based games. Both are becoming increasingly common in work and leisure pursuits in the home, school and community (particularly in video-game parlours).

Our study suggests that there are special argots and cultural practices for young computer-game players. William Gibson's (1984) notion of the 'cyberpunk' (Cyber = fusion of flesh and machine tech; punk = rebellion against social norms) is not far-fetched. TV series and a host of magazines about computer

213

games, replete with jargon, styles and demeanour, reinforce the cultures of technological communities. Terms such as 'cyberspace' and 'cyberpunk' have become part of the vocabulary of the 'information age'. Computer-game playing is central to the proposition that the young 'live' in an electronic entertainment media world.

Such developments are symptomatic of a shift from face-to-face to symbolic communities, said to be characteristic of the postmodern era (Olalquiaga 1992; Smith & Wexler 1995). For adults and, we daresay, teachers this shift is evidence of the fragmentation of contemporary culture which often leads to feelings of intellectual and practical powerlessness in the face of technology, and to judging the young according to stereotypes emphasising cultural primitivism. In short, there are both social and psychological dimensions to cultural change and history and we focus on computer and computer-game cultures and discourses as prime examples. Our contention is that such cultures and discourses are the socialising context for children: this is where they develop their 'needs and interests' and their conceptions and expectations of the world. An analogy borrowed from Gomila (1995, p. 80) makes our point clearer: a microscope does not modify our visual capacities but its use makes available new kinds of information. Similarly, computers and computer games make new representational capacities available without obliging us to draw on concepts of a transformed learning mechanism (p. 80). If this proposition is correct, the culture of the young is bound to have implications for formal schooling and curriculum.

Computers and computer games

The social context of computer use troubles some researchers, who are concerned that excessive computer use by children replaces human interaction, and that the face-to-face environment of computer use lacks the verbal and non-verbal cues necessary for their development of social and emotional skills.

This is a serious objection that concerns parents and educators. By contrast, Shimai, Masuda and Kishimoto (1990, pp. 771–6) demonstrate that pre-schooler game players showed greater sociability development compared to that of non-players and argue that 'this seems to reflect that children acquired a new repertoire of play from the TV game'. Our interpretation of the research is that human communication skills are fundamental to computer use and that interaction is of prime importance in an Internet environment because people are challenged to communicate with others from many 'cultures'.

Indeed, the interactive nature of the Net allows for new linguistic discourses that reflect social and emotional issues. Electronic messages usually reflect a genre more familiar than the standard letter, and online communications such as Internet Relay Chats (IRC) are more likely to be personable, even intimate. The assumption that the young are losing out on human interaction possibly reflects the ignorance of an older generation and its inability to accept any form of radical change. Social norms and various linguistic socialisation patterns of cyberculture and its subcultures are emerging constantly. 'Appropriate' behaviour is monitored by others in cyberspace. Through the uncontrolled medium of the Web comes a sense of self-government and individual responsibility. Cyber-communities (many who have laughed and cried online would dispute the term 'virtual community' as for them it is often more real than other experiences) can develop strong emotional ties despite their usually transient populations.

Singh (1995) maintains there is a significant strand of research that conceptualises computers and computer games as a threat to theories about agency, emancipation and 'progress'. An important theme of this work is that male characteristics are said to be over-represented in the screen displays and voice emissions of computers and computer games, and that access is restricted by social conventions and structures so that girls are excluded. However, there is evidence that such gender stereotyping may be breaking down as computers change and as new generations of young female and male users perceive the computer as 'feminine' and 'masculine' respectively (Turkle 1995). There may be nothing intrinsic to more sophisticated interactive computing to discourage girls. Cunningham's (1994, p. 13) study of primary school girls suggests that computer-game culture is no longer a male preserve now that it is shifting from 'street culture' in the arcades to 'bedroom culture' in the home, thereby giving girls access and 'permission' to play, unlike practices in other youth cultures.

Haraway's (1990) image of the cyborg challenges women to rethink their existence and to find survival strategies in a hi-tech world. While 'survival' may have been, and perhaps still is, a preoccupation for today's women, the younger female generation seems much less likely to assume that technology is a male domain. If we take the traditional view of women as communicators, it makes sense to assume that computer interaction will be readily adopted by women as a means of communication.

Other writers express reservations, arguing that computer technology has fleeting 'novelty' value, that the costs of such technology are too high for mass use by the young, and that there are limits to the amount of information young users can absorb from technological devices over a limited period. While there are doubts that computer-driven technologies will change conventional educational practices that have withstood other challenges, and scepticism about their educational value, significant research has been made on the valuable contribution that computer technologies can make to existing educational practices (e.g., Wark 1992). Metacognition skills, for example, can flourish in a computer-learning hypermedia setting. Interactive technology is recognised as a way of developing all the senses, and as a way of catering for individuals' different learning styles, pacing and sequencing in a non-threatening learning environment. In a similar vein, research literature on the Internet suggests education benefits but advises teachers to guide students in their computer use so that motivation is maintained, and so that through 'searching' as opposed to 'surfing' students have a sense of direction and purpose.

Work on computers and computer games confirms that

they are extensively used by the young, in the Western world at least, and that use increases with age. Of particular importance are the interactive effects of young people's exposure to and involvement with computer-based perceptual-cognitive-motor stimulation and multiple sources of fantasy. We take Cunningham's point that research must focus on *how* computer technologies such as games are used and less on the fact of their existence. Our own research prompts us to examine this notion further.

Young children and their use of computers

An observation and interview study of fifty-four students in Years 3, 5 and 7 indicated that the participants all know about computers and computer games (Smith, Curtin & Newman 1995). All but a few of the children have direct access to a computer and/or computer game outside school. The few children without direct access to a computer or games are familiar with their peer group's computer and game-playing discourse. These children use computers for entertainment and/or mental stimulation, as a playmate and competitor, to retrieve information and as a word processor for private or school purposes.

According to these young informants, computers are a central feature of their everyday lives. Some have more than one computer in the home and differentiate between 'games' (Nintendo or Sega) and 'computers' (Commodore 64, IBM, or Apple Mac). For the younger children, in particular, a computer in the home is a taken-for-granted household item along with other technologies such as CD players and televisions. It is 'normal' to have the IBM compatible 'in the study' and the Atari 'in my mum's room with the TV'.

Although children report that they frequently play computer games in arcades and shop fronts and that such venues serve as child-minding sites while parents shop, there is evidence that computer-game playing at home is becoming more common. Personal computers enable children freer, more relaxed access and they can play for longer periods. Some spend up to five hours a day in front of a screen and sometimes longer. As one eight-year-old said:

> All day, all night! When I first got it, I was just playing it, and playing it, and playing it. Right until bedtime. When I first woke up I'd get up really early to play the megadrive and when there was lunch or breakfast I'd say, 'Do I have to have it now?' and anyway, when I did have it, I'd scoff it down and then I'd go back and play it again.

The first use of a computer has the status of a milestone not unlike first steps or first words. Most of the children in the sample started playing computer games at age five or six. Similarly, access to a real 'computer' and learning to use it are remembered as important events. For most of the children in our sample, computer use and game playing is part of a 'normal' day.

Dealing with computers and having a liking for them spills over into school use, as this Year 3 child indicates:

Q: Do you like being the computer monitor?
A: Yeah. I like helping people with the computer.
Q: Do you like being with the computer?
A: Yeah. It's sort of like my friend [laughs].
Q: Do children like being the computer monitor?
A: Yeah, they always say, 'I wish I was the computer monitor.'
Q: Why do you think they say that?
A: Maybe they just want to help people on the computer, and probably they want to spend more time on the computer.

For others, school appears to be little more than a minor interruption in the day's computer-game activities. School computer use is regulated, so their resistance to it is established early. At school, children have to take turns and complete tasks within time-lines, whereas home computer use is less restrained.

Our study suggests that the dominant modes for learning how to play computer games and how to use computers are those under the direct control of the learner. Children talked about 'learning by yourself', 'doing' and 'practice', 'trial and error', and 'watching' others play. They confirm the observation that 'kids just do it' rather than having to look up the rules in computer manuals (Turkle, cited in McCorduck 1996, p. 162). The important 'teachers' were older siblings, a parent, especially 'dad', and school teachers interested in computers. With all these teachers the relationship is informal and the instruction experiential and 'just-in-time' (provided as required). This contrasts with the teaching approach that attempts to provide a store of knowledge and skills before practice.

Many of the children discussed the possibility of intervening in the way computers work, especially in commercial games. By Year 5 some children are interested in computer programming and use elementary books in the quest for additional ways of intervening in game software. From the youngest age-groups, instruction manuals and computer magazines are used to find telephone numbers and other sources for short-cuts ('cheat codes') and ways to beat the game and machine.

Q: Do you try and re-program the game?
A1: In my Gameboy I've got this game called Boxall, and there's a section called play, password, select, or create and if you go into 'create' you can create your own maze, and that's good.
A2: Well, most games have got like codes and that and there's certain cheats that you can use to change levels and make bad guys and you can make your own items and that. So that's kind of re-programming it.

In our view, the predisposition to search for ways to make the codes work is a key to judging the impact of computers and computer games. The discovery of codes and user conventions, like cultural mores, leads to the expectation that reciprocity is possible with both machine and game. In this sense, the computer is like a living thing, able to reason and tell one what to do, and able to respond. Moreover, for many of these young users, the computer game can generate, and indeed feel, emotions like 'getting mad' at the user/player. To this extent, the computer and its programs are composed of both syntax and semantics.

An overwhelming impression about children's use of computers and computer games is that it is emotionally charged. In discussing competition with the machine and the game, children's discourse is replete with descriptions of emotional states. Computer-game players are 'mad when you lose' or 'do something wrong' and 'excited when you win'. There is also 'tension'—'holding your breath to finish the game' and playing a game for the first time because 'you just don't know what is going to happen next'. Finishing a game or solving a problem brings 'relief', perhaps because many games take time to progress through the levels, and failure makes you return to the beginning.

The emotional involvement with computers and computer games reaches a peak, perhaps, with the interaction of fantasy and competition. The games these children like best feature fantastic landscapes and they prefer characters such as vampires, dogs, 'bad guys' and mad scientists, but almost any will do as long as they are not conventional 'fairy tale' characters—these are 'dumb'. Our interview scripts clearly indicate that while computer-game characters and plots are seen as fantasy, these children understand the difference between fantasy and 'real' life and that 'in real life you only get one life and you cannot make mistakes with death and then retry . . . the stakes are too high'. These youngsters, unlike older generations, live at the intersection of the technological and the 'real' in a way that combines criteria for judging both.

Although our data on this issue are incomplete, the appeal of the game seems to depend on the total experience rather than any specific part. Thus, there is interactivity generated by the software ('You're something and you've got to do something else. A lot of them are running and jumping'); by the fantasy of the characters in a multimedia setting; and by pitting oneself against the story and the machine ('there's always a really big bad guy at the end of the game that you have to beat').

220

Competitiveness with the computer, the game and its codes, with others who can play the game and with one's own 'levels' of competence and achievement, are all components of the fantasy: winning 'feels good' and losing means 'getting mad', getting 'stressed' and going back to 'bust the computer' (beat the computer), a competitor and above all, one's self. The importance of the total experience is captured in a Year 5 child's remark that 'it's not the story behind [the games] that makes us want to play them. It's what the game is actually like when you play it'. A computer game generates its own experiences and 'pleasures' which need further investigation (Cunningham 1994). We suspect that for these children, winning and beating the machine and the game are crucial elements of self-construction—elements in which human characteristics merge with the technological. It is not difficult to appreciate that as children operate a computer game they try out hunches about how to apply their skills and knowledge. Such characteristics reinforce the very elements of an emergent subjectivity and the notion of 'cyborg'.

Discussion

Our data make it abundantly clear that for these young children, computers are part of the normal day at home with parents and siblings or at school with peers. They are 'ordinary' youngsters attending standard elementary schools of mixed populations. They live a full round of 'normal' family and school activities and are hardly the Compu-Freak stereotype of the mass media. Indeed, the very conventionality and mundaneness of their everyday lives disguises the pervasive use of computer-based devices. In an epistemological sense, they are a whole historical period removed from their parents' and most of their teachers' generations. Their interest in print literacy has waned in comparison with that of former generations and their meta-representation or self-structure is generated by a social context in which electronic media is an organisational principle for social life. The children in our

221

sample are better prepared for dealing with computing concepts, the virtual reality world of cyberspace, the Internet and hypertext than their parents are because they have acquired a repertoire of social practices that link computer-based artefacts to the structure of self. This behavioural flexibility enables the young to colonise the new electronic environments (Brandon & Hornstein 1986). And it is salient to remember that modems and the Internet were generally unknown to the sample of children interviewed, and that they have not yet felt the impact of connectivity, networks and interactivity associated with the exploration of cyberspace.

However, if we are to observe the intense culture developing on the Net we can argue that the notion of 'alien' is likely to be short-lived. Already Webchats are a standard form of communication among people who might otherwise never meet due to physical distance, class, age or other forms of social stratification. Borders are becoming blurred as inhabitants of cyberspace become further absorbed in their computer identities. Teenagers and many adults are engaging in dialogue ranging from politics through to cybersex. In fact our definition of 'computer game' is likely to become confused in this realm as people adopt alternative identities. The fantasies found in computer-game characters are lived out under pseudonyms or 'handles' such as Phantom, The White Tiger, Troll and Sleeping Beauty. It is acknowledged but of no great importance to these 'cyborgs' that they might converse intimately with an individual who has a completely different 'real life' identity. Conversants often ask for 'stats' or information about age and gender but anonymity prevails. The concept of multiple identities is perhaps most prevalent in the IRC environment where players/participants can change handles each time they enter a chatroom.

As we mentioned earlier, the integration of computers has been such that the young can no longer be categorised as computer nerds or freaks. Young people today are more cynical about life's mundanity than their predecessors were, and perhaps this is why so many prefer fantasy and alternative realities. Children today may, in fact, represent a point of macro-scale social transition into computer-based electronic spaces and lifestyles that cross two generations or more, with each successive generation more deeply implicated than the last, a phenomenon not unlike that which is happening in Germany. According to Richard (1996), the differences between youth culture and parental culture have disappeared. Each has similar preferences for leisure activities and youth styles arc not the defining feature that they were even a decade ago. In the dance-culture, for instance, it is style not age that counts. In this transitional period, one set of cultural meanings anchored in print and the industrial age are making way for new cultural symbols and meanings. If we are correct in this surmise, by about 2010 the techno-cultural understanding and practices of the children described in this chapter will incorporate the whole sociocultural space called adulthood so that there is no computer technology 'alien' phenomenon as such. There will be other discontinuities between generations, to be sure, but in our view the shift to the electronic revolution will have been achieved. We contend that these propositions about 'new kids' are well founded in the 1990s.

If the characteristics of the children in our study and the teenage interactivity on the Net are indeed tendencies of a transitional age, then the sophisticated technical ideas of computer games and computing shape how the young think about themselves, while foreshadowing what will be important in our entire culture. Emergent cultural forms and practices have a distinctiveness of their own and foreshadow a different society to that which triggered the changes. As Green and Bigum (1993) remark:

> . . . a fundamental issue is the significance of what is more specifically and appropriately understood as 'techno-popular culture', conceived as more and more the distinctive semiotic space which young people will increasingly inhabit as their natural environment, their proper realm, and the site par excellence of their sovereignty. (p. 127)

This does not necessarily admit that earlier educational concepts and practices are misguided but it does suggest that the novelty in the situation is the changed society with new problems and new tasks. We need to build new assumptions and concepts about 'education' rather than holding on to concepts anchored in a previous epoch with an additional set of morbid symptoms to account for a system under siege. Leaving aside the myriad of other changes that affect education, these generations of the young present an unprecedented challenge that goes far beyond existing programs and practices. It is necessary to deal with education for postmodernity rather than assuming that education in the postmodern era is 'business as usual' with some irritating diversions (Bauman 1992, p. 111).

In the first place, as we have argued, time and memory are composed of traces of experiences that are intrinsic to subjectivity within a culture or a language world (Basu 1995, p. 135). Our data show that the language of these children sets horizons for narrative possibilities about themselves, machines, schools, others, fantasy and so on that mark them off from older generations. In this sense, the cultural learning of the six-year-old to twelve-year-old cohort is, at least partly, an elaboration of experiences expressed in the very language that references their culture. Using computers and playing computer games is always a social act and not simply an 'individual' capacity. The game is part of a larger system of processes used to express meaning. However, through the game we are seeing a development in mental skills. For example, a significant feature of some forms of IRC is the split-second delay before a comment is presented on screen. This means that dialogue does not always flow, and that participants are often involved in several conversations simultaneously. This type of communication is typical of chaotic systems and demonstrates our point that flexible cognitive abilities and behaviours are integral to a postmodern society.

The use of the Internet and increasing immersion in simulation, navigation and interaction will accelerate the creation of new cultures and new ways to see the world. In this sense, the experiences of the young children in our sample signal a subversive form of pluralism which brings new meaning to 'cultural diversity'. Computer use encourages conceptions of a pluralist self and as Turkle (cited in McCorduck 1996, p. 109) says, 'When you can have an instantiation of your body on a computer—this is new.' Moreover, the electronic world opens up the possibility of communication between diverse life-worlds and communities by electronic media instead of formal political processes. Negroponte (1995) argues that the nation state will be both bigger and smaller as digital worlds replace nation states and politics becomes confined to smaller, competing ethnic enclaves. The social dilemma facing institutions like education is how to reassess fundamental concepts such as 'communication', 'difference' and 'curriculum' and how to select and justify 'content' in changed circumstances. To fulfil the requirements of conventional theories of teaching and learning and for the people who say that nothing has changed, the task is to recover the meaning of radically diverse, often 'alien' experiences and reassemble them in curricula and organisational structures designed not only for a different age but also for different mass, system-regulated purposes.

The latter situation will continue but its future is limited because these difficulties are already upon the educational establishment. At every level in educational bureaucracies, vague unease has led to the realisation that authority about what is most worthwhile culturally and the means to get it have slipped away from the traditional gate-keepers and cultural transmitters—schools, teachers, universities, books, libraries. This loss cuts deeply into professional educational traditions and aspirations. Thus, while this is a period of unprecedented cultural consumption in the form of the media, electronic databases and the arts, market agents other than teachers and academics are gaining control of it (Bauman 1992). It presents a complex but decisive challenge to institutional education because educators have always opposed the expansion of public education and easy access to information for the masses. As our data show, 'off-the-shelf' computer technology enables people to enjoy a do-it-yourself home education. There is a sense that the computer use we describe is in the vanguard of a 'cross-over' process to move the

225

province of the school and the academy into homes. It follows, of course, that the current social recognition of teachers' work is undermined by the diversity to which we refer.

The average teacher in Queensland, Australia is over forty years of age and most are likely to face significant professional and personal dilemmas in dealing with the 'alien' children we describe. Moreover, like others in the population, many feel a sense of intellectual and practical powerlessness, an 'unprecedented sense of personal responsibility and individual impotence' (Olalquiaga 1992) as old structures and cultural assumptions break down and new ones emerge. In parallel fashion, younger teachers, like Richard's (1996) subjects, probably have more in common culturally with their students than with the school's academic curriculum or culture. Younger teachers, because of their contact and interaction with the icons and practices of the times, come to recognise their own selves and experiences in the absence of universal and knowable truths and the instability of meanings and institutions. As young graduates enter teaching it is likely that the community of assumptions about the deep values of 'scholarship' that underlie teacher-preparation courses and the school curriculum will progressively decline. It follows that a lack of commitment by teachers to conventional curriculum will intensify the diversity that challenges the 'school' as we know it.

The young children in our study learned to play computer games by entering programs and 'mucking around'. This allows them to explore the context and apply tentative solutions in concrete form. Much of the learning is best described as 'tinkering with intent' where the outcomes are vaguely known and the procedures are largely intuitive, based on experience with similar activities. More generally, there is some evidence that young people today are interested in applying knowledge and skills to everyday life. Developments in computing and communications technologies beyond the school seem to anticipate a learning-by-doing model that links users to the 'real world' (Rothenberg 1994, p. 278).

These elements are strongly represented in early childhood education and are progressively reduced in later years of

226

schooling as children deal with decontextualised knowledge. For example, Cole (1987) believes that beginner readers who fail to progress from contextualised oral language to de-contextualised reading knowledge are marked as having a 'learning difficulty'. Similarly, Clark (1992, p. 552) argues that there is no such thing as the 'general idea' of something and that there is only a large number of minute particulars which, when fully grasped, can be referred to in shorthand by a single name. Possessing the name without mastering the essential particulars is pointless. The only way to grasp those particulars is through personal practical experience and a setting that provides 'bridges'. It underlines the importance of ensuring that children without previous experience can connect their lives to educational requirements. Computer technologies can help here by identifying and filling gaps in knowledge and skills so that teachers can design individual programs.

In this respect, the assumptions and practices of the pre-dominant 'school' and 'university' paradigms of information transmission, processing and accumulation seem vulnerable to the critiques of schooling developed since the 1970s. The dominant paradigm of curriculum and learning is based on 'industrial capitalism and factory-based mass production'—one that presents teaching and learning in a fixed order and on a fixed timetable for the certification of the middle class (Lemke 1997). Schools seem even more quaint and shaky against the backdrop of technology and the new kinds of capacities and needs demonstrated by the children in our sample. These children determine what and when they need to know, in conjunction with knowledgeable specialists such as 'Dad', and they find learning satisfying. For them, participation, individual specialisation and access to information are preferred to the imposition of learning, and their presuppositions are those of 'the people who created the Internet and cyberspace' (Lemke 1997).

The extent of the educational problem indexed by these concerns is daunting. It involves multiple levels of confluence including the relationships between individual learners and teachers; between teachers, learners and knowledge; and the

227

internal cognitive and emotional states of the teacher and the learner. In addition, one must now add the possibility of the flexible delivery of hypertext to multiple sites, AI-based interactive multimedia that is simulation rather than transmission; and educative materials that emphasise outcomes rather than 'doing time' in 'classes'. Moreover, the concepts of 'teacher' and 'learner' will alter in quite radical ways as the 'teachers' are assigned less authority for the transmission and testing of knowledge. Of crucial importance are the individual educational provision and self-managed learning that were unimaginable even in the recent past. In spite of the educational rhetoric about 'individual differences' of the past four decades, computer technologies make it possible for students to learn what they want, when they want, how they want, without schools (Lemke 1997). Such a conclusion carries a host of implications for the teaching force everywhere. While the politics of education are very much the politics of what is possible, the state is unlikely to willingly surrender control over either content or delivery while education remains part of the ideological solution to current economic and political problems. To this extent the emergence of new curriculum models, modified teaching and management skills and a consequential need for a different educational organisation appears inevitable.

Teaching in the new times tends to generate a double sense of crisis and a search for certainty (Andrews 1996). On the one hand, older teachers are faced with an uncertain world, a kaleidoscope of surface features without underlying meaning. Andrews shows that these older teachers seek to recover and re-establish educational concepts and theories that represent the unbreachable order of relationships between schooling and society, teacher and student, knowledge and teaching and so on. On the other hand, younger teachers, forced into the rigidity of a schooling order that seeks certainty, respond by adopting strategies that rely more on presentation styles like visualisation and performance than on printed text. It is not surprising that so many teachers who prefer an open-ended exploratory approach to professional problem-solving favour action research, given its similarity to the tinkering of the bricoleur and the way it conveys an impression of freedom from the orthodoxies of 'research' and top-down advice.

What 'communication' and 'literacy' might mean in this social habitat is of considerable political interest as the number and pervasiveness of national inquiries in Australia make clear. It is widely believed that the ability to read print and the possession of background knowledge that makes reading meaningful are necessary but not sufficient for today's young. The new literacy, referred to by Green (1996) as 'computency' or 'computent', contains a vastly different set of capacities. It demands a style of relating to computers and, moreover, the connection of the technology to 'a constellation of cultural associations' (Turkle 1995, p. 61).

Our sample children's capacity and predisposition to use the materials at hand, and their ease in the electronic environment, suggest that many elements of the new literacy (however it is defined) are already out there in the environments of computer games, the cinema, magazines like *Wired* and Internet sites. We take Martinez's (1994) point that the new literacy is inextricably bound up with technology operating systems and applications, together with more abstract understanding of how information is accessed, managed, manipulated and presented. But at the core of the new literacy are the notions of a 'soft' style: playing with bits of the program and the tasks at hand, having a relationship with the computer or video game, having a conversation with the work materials, dealing with electronic devices as expressive media (Turkle 1995). Already some organisational theorists propose that network proficiency will become a new metric of professional skill in almost all occupations (Reinhardt 1995). Lemke (1997) proposes that the generic literacies of the information age are multimedia authoring skills and critical analysis, cyberspace exploration and navigation skills, thus reinforcing the sense that 'education' is moving to a different kind of intellectual and practical environment.

The challenge for today's educators first of all is to satisfy the print-text literacy requirements of today's students without allowing the ideological battle over literacy and numeracy to obscure their responsibilities. Lemke (1993) suggests a revision of literacy that is at the same time radical yet conceivable. He argues that if we took one step back to a pre-literacy age of images we could move two steps forward thus allowing literacy to become both immersed in and a by-product of images. This is possibly an ideal framework for meeting students' needs and maximising the potential of computers. The second challenge is to ensure that current debates over literacy and numeracy do not prevent educators' involvement in determining the role of skills such as information analysis, evaluation, prediction and communication in any version of self-managed learning. If state education in Australia continues to demand 'performance standards' then computer use must prove itself by meeting the prevailing criteria and benchmarks. Modifying the curriculum to include more community-integrated activities which students can design and control, by means of computer interaction, may provide the means for meeting such needs.

We raise these points to emphasise that certainty is hardly a distinguishing feature of the electronic, social and cultural habitat of today's educators. In learning to adapt creatively to the 'artificial' environments of the young, it may be more productive for educators to understand the content and pedagogy of advertising and commercial IT entertainment instead of educational theoretical dogma. As mass schooling loses its legitimacy, educational understanding seems less about grand theories of teaching and learning or indeed 'society' and more to do with how individual children create identities with a plethora of cultural materials and, indeed, with how 'we' come to know ourselves as constrained or liberated (Bauman 1992). The individual and social pluralism engendered by computing challenges education's traditional role of rationalising a particular kind of society by the cultural transmission of received wisdom. In reconsidering the three claims with which we began this chapter, the young children in our sample live in an all-encompassing electronic habitat and have developed ways of interpreting the world and performing in it that are at the cusp of the semiotic society. These children will help shape

230

and change the cultural habitat and in turn will be shaped by it. Inevitably, teaching and learning and the curriculum of schooling will respond to these challenges. The ultimate challenge, though, does not concern this particular teaching method or that curriculum content, but the institution of education itself.

References

Andrews, C. 1996 'Teachers' work: an analysis of teachers' work in a context of change', unpubl. PhD thesis, Faculty of Education and the Arts, Griffith University, Gold Coast

Basu, K. 1995 'Android epistemology: an essay on interpretation and intentionality', *Android Epistemology*, eds K. Ford, C. Glymour and P. Hayes, AAAI Press/The MIT Press, Menlo Park, CA, pp. 123–40

Bauman, Z. 1992 *Intimations of Postmodernity*, Routledge, London

Brandon, R. and Hornstein, N. 1986 'From icons to symbols: some speculations on the origins of language', *Biology and Philosophy*, vol. 1, pp. 169–89

Clark, D. 1992 'The future of interactivity—is it really a hardware issue?', *Proceedings of the International Multimedia Symposium*, Curtin University, Promaco Conventions, Perth, pp. 547–56

Cole, G. 1987 *The Learning Mystique: A Critical Look at Learning Disabilities*, Ballantine Books, New York

Cunningham, H. 1994 'Gender and computer games', *Media Education Journal*, vol. 17, Winter, pp. 13–15

Gergen, K. 1991 *Dilemmas of Identity in Contemporary Life*, Basic Books, New York

Gibson, W. 1984 *Neuromancer*, Ace, New York

Gomila, A. 1995 'From cognitive systems to persons', *Android Epistemology*, eds K. Ford, C. Glymour and P. Hayes, AAAI Press/The MIT Press, Menlo Park, CA, pp. 73–92

Green, B. 1996 'Literacy/technology/learning: notes and issues', unpubl. discussion paper, Deakin Centre for Education and Change, Faculty of Education, Deakin University, Geelong, Victoria

Green, B. and Bigum, C. 1993 'Aliens in the classroom', *Australian Journal of Education*, vol. 37, no. 2, pp. 119–41

Haraway, D. 1990 'A manifesto for cyborgs: science, technology, and

231

socialist feminism in the 1980s', *Feminism/Postmodernism*, ed. L. Nicholson, Routledge, New York

Kinsman, F. 1991 *Millennium: towards tomorrow's society*, Penguin, London

Lemke, J. 1993 'Education, cyberspace, and change', *The Arachnet Electronic Journal on Virtual Culture*, vol. 1 no. 1

——1997 'Metamedia literacy: transforming meanings and media', *Literacy For the 21st Century: Technological Transformation in a Post-typographic World*, eds D. Reinking, L. Labbo, M. McKenna and R. Kiefer, Erlbaum, Hillsdale, NJ

McCorduck, P. 1996 'Sex, lies and avatars', *Wired*, April, pp. 106–10, 158–65

Martinez, M. 1994 'Access to information technologies among school-age children: implications for a democratic society', *Journal of the American Society for Information Science*, vol. 45, no. 6, pp. 395–400

Negroponte, N. 1995 *Being Digital*, Alfred Knopf, New York

Olalquiaga, C. 1992 *Megalopolis: Contemporary Cultural Sensibilities*, University of Minnesota Press, Minneapolis, MN

Poster, M. 1990 *The Mode of Information: Poststructuralism and Social Context*, Polity Press, Cambridge, MA

Reinhardt, A. 1995 'New ways to learn', *Byte*, March, pp. 50–71

Richard, B. 1996 'Does culture industry take over? The sell-out of critical youth cultures in Germany', paper presented at the American Educational Research Association Annual Meeting 8–12 April, New York

Rothenberg, D. 1994 'Information technology in education', *Annual Review of Information Science and Technology*, vol. 29, pp. 277–302

Shimai, S., Masuda, K. and Kishimoto, Y. 1990 'Influences of TV games on physical and psychological development of Japanese kindergarten children', *Perceptual and Motor Skills*, vol. 70, pp. 771–6

Singh, P. 1995 'Discourses of computing competence evaluation and gender: the case of computer use in primary school classrooms', *Discourse: Studies in the Cultural Politics of Education*, vol. 16, no. 1, pp. 81–110

Smith, R., Curtin, P. and Newman, L. 1995 'Kids in the "kitchen": the social implications for schooling in the age of advanced computer technology', paper presented at Australian Association for Research in Education Annual Conference, Hobart, 27–30 Nov.

Smith, R., Sachs, J.M. and Chant, D. 1988 'Use of information technology by young people in Australia and Sweden', *Nordicom Review (of Nordic Mass Communication Research)*, vol. 2, pp. 37–9

Smith, R., and Wexler, P., eds 1995 *After Postmodernism: Politics, Identity and Education*, Falmer, London

Turkle, S. 1995 *Life on the Screen: Identity in the Age of the Internet*, Simon & Schuster, New York

Wark, K. 1992 'Mario's video world invited children to play with power', *The Australian*, 16 Sept. p. 19

Wexler, P. 1987 *Social Analysis of Education*, Routledge, New York

11

Computer games, culture and curriculum

CATHERINE BEAVIS

The computer screen glows gold, black and blue as the outline of a domed eastern palace fills out in a desert landscape. To the sound of swirling oriental music, the game's title, *Prince of Persia*, fills half the screen with dark and ornate Arabic lettering. 'By Jordan Mechner' appears underneath. In an instant the image is gone, but the music remains, its insistent downbeat promising more. As for a silent movie, a framed caption announces:

> In the Sultan's absence, the Grand Vizier JAFFAR rules with the iron fist of tyranny. Only one obstacle remains between Jaffar and the throne: the Sultan's beautiful young daughter.

The titles fade. Blackness. The screen now reveals a tower room in the palace—the Sultan's daughter's prison and refuge. Torches flicker on bare stone walls, Persian carpets and cushions are flung across the flagstone floor; the darkness outside the arched window is broken only by twinkling stars. The princess paces the room, wringing her hands. As the music rises to a sinister crescendo, Jaffar forces his way into the room, flings his arms into the air, and delivers his ultimatum. The princess gasps and falls back. The screen flashes. As if by magic, an hourglass appears before her, the sands already

234

running through it. Jaffar turns on his heel and strides off screen, leaving the princess bewildered and desolate. A second caption fills the screen:

> Marry Jaffar . . . or die within the hour. All the princess's hopes rest on the brave youth she loves. Little does she know he is already a prisoner in Jaffar's dungeons . . . (Mechner 1992)

In more ways than one, it is a familiar scene. Computer and Nintendo/Sega games now feature in the home life of many students, in Australia and in most other Western countries. By 1993, in the UK, over 70 per cent of homes were equipped to play computer games, with games representing more than 95 per cent of software sold for home computers (Buckingham 1993a). Australian figures are comparable. Computer games represent only one aspect of the technology that saturates the lives of young people today as they 'tune in' to electronic media of many kinds. Indeed, one study found that adolescents were engaged with media for 110 per cent of their day—a statistic that makes more sense once it is understood that young people are engaged with several forms at once—perhaps listening to the radio while playing a computer game, or glancing at the TV in another corner of the room (Bates 1994). This is an experience of the world very different from that offered by most schools; a culture and identity significantly at odds with many of the assumptions made about contemporary curriculum.

In this chapter I explore two broad issues: first, how new media forms, in this instance computer games, affect schools and curricula; and second, how such forms, and young people's engagement in them, challenge and redefine current notions of narrative, textuality and reading. As a teacher educator in the field of secondary English, I am particularly interested in how new technologies are redefining both the subject of and contemporary notions about narrative and generic forms, and I draw on the best-selling game *Prince of Persia* (Mechner 1992) to examine how computer/video games might be read and used in relation to questions such as these. Released in two

formats—for the personal computer and in Nintendo form—
Prince of Persia provides a useful example of what is
collectively known as 'video games', a technological genre that
includes personal computer and home-video games, Virtual
Reality games and others played in commercial games arcades
(Shuker 1996, p. 126).

Computer games are problematic texts in a number of
ways. In *Prince of Persia*'s narrative scenario 'only one obstacle
remains', between the villain Jaffar and his usurpation of the
throne. The phrase is familiar from cinema serials of old, and
reworked in this new genre in much the way computer games
function intertextually and through pastiche. In narrative
terms, the 'obstacle' is the princess, the motivating force for
the game—the invitation for the reader/player's identification
and participation, and the raison d'etre for the hero's progress.
He—you—must rescue the princess before she can be
removed—an indication also of the gender politics that typify
most games.

The 'obstacles' that persist between youth culture and the
school, between traditional views of text and culture and those
thrown up by the new technologies, are less easily resolved.
Nonetheless, the challenge is worth taking in pursuit of the
'meaning' of new electronic genres. Their prominent place in
young people's lives can provide us with an impetus to reconceive the school curriculum in ways more closely connected
with students' experience and the rapidly changing world in
which we all live.

The business of games

As one of the most visible and engaging of the new technologies' media/cultural forms, computer games have attracted
considerable attention from educational and cultural studies.
They stir moral panic, challenge conceptions of youth culture,
raise difficult questions about the relationship between popular
culture and school education, polarise issues of culture and
identity, and confront our concepts of texts and textuality.

They are almost emblematic of the bewildering pace of change associated with the new technologies, and their global, multi-media dimensions.

Playing computer and video games occupies a considerable proportion of young people's time, both at home, and in games arcades. Shuker (1996) notes:

> An early survey of readers of *Creative Computing Video and Arcade Games* (1983, cited in Price 1985) found that respondents reported an average of sixteen hours a week playing games. More recently, Funk (1993, pp. 86–90) found that of the 357 North American seventh and eighth graders she surveyed about video-game play and preference, approximately sixty-four per cent of boys and fifty-six per cent of girls played one to two hours (per week) of arcade video games. (p. 133)

The fascination of these games, however, is not limited to adolescents. Nintendo's surveys show that a little over one third (36 per cent) of their users are boys aged between eight and eleven, and another third (34.5 per cent) are adults eighteen and over. There also appears to be a difference in appeal between the two major games competitors; for example, Electronic Art identifies the average age of Sega players as twenty, and the average age of Nintendo players as thirteen (Shuker 1996). Most commentators and research studies identify a gender bias, with most games having considerably greater appeal to males.

Computer games are big business. Between 1985 and 1993, more than 65 million Nintendo or Sega video-game machines had been sold to American households, with market software netting more than $7 billion in 1993 (Gross 1993). In 1994 the video-game industry was estimated to be worth $15 billion worldwide (Ingram 1994). In a market of this size, advertising becomes almost a new art form, with huge budgets set aside for research and what Palmeri (1994, p. 102) describes as 'Hollywood-like marketing techniques'—for example, the software manufacturer Acclaim Entertainment spent $10 million on an advertising blitz for *Mortal Kombat* and $6 million on

NBA Jam (Shuker 1996, p. 132). At the same time, games magazines, another new genre, almost obviated the need for advertising for some products. For example, in 1992 there was little advertising in the US for the new console, Supernintendo, but it gained considerable interest due to magazines such as *Computer Gaming Monthly* whose editor, Semrad commented: 'Nintendo keeps very quiet about the new console . . . we've been talking about it for almost two years now . . . It's on readers' minds all the time and it's the only thing they want to know about' (Diamond 1992, p. 73). Any analysis of the games 'phenomenon' must acknowledge their sophisticated, transnational marketing context, as well as the implicit identity politics and cultural changes.

Games and cultural identity

Any evaluation of future directions for the curriculum takes place in the larger context of the relationships between schools and society, and the role that schools are called upon to play in the formation and reformation of the community. Central to such debates run two threads: the purposes of schooling; and the relationship between education and culture. 'Culture' itself is multiple and constantly subject to change. Much of the debate about how schools respond to technological change and the inroads of multinational and economic forces is about definitions of culture and its role in the formation of identity. In this chapter, 'culture' is understood both in its broad sense—as those practices, mores and behaviours by which a community is identified—and in the narrower sense of specific 'artistic' heritages, representations and pursuits.

The question of whether, where and how schools might buy into the world of multimedia and new technology is thus embedded in larger issues to do with the content and purpose of schooling, and with the social cultures that 'ought' to be supported and renewed through school curricula. In 1991 the Australian state of Victoria introduced the Victorian Certificate of Education, a new course for the final years of school,

238

causing a media furore over the content and organisation of curriculum for the post-compulsory years. Public debate arose over assessment practices and the nature and range of the curriculum—specifically, in the case of English, the texts set for study. That such a subject filled the pages of daily newspapers for months, becoming part of an election campaign that eventually unseated the government of the day, attests to the power of community expectations of schools. It highlighted the position that English, as a subject, occupies in the construction and renewal of society through the cultivation of (common) cultural values and knowledge.

Debates such as these demonstrate how much importance we give to texts, in and out of schools, when we define culture and cultural identity, and when it comes to deciding which cultures are to constitute the curriculum. Traditional high-culture positions, advocated perhaps most famously by Leavis, posit a profound gulf between high culture and popular texts, with the study of literature providing both a training in sensibility and some form of inoculation. In the words of Eagleton (1983), such an approach involves:

> . . . nurturing through the study of literature the kind of rich, complex, mature, discriminating, morally serious responses . . . which would equip individuals to survive in a mechanised society of trashy romances, alienated labour, banal advertisements and vulgarising mass media. (p. 33)

In Australia, advocates of this view regularly urge the restoration of the 'transmission of our cultural heritage to its proper place in the curriculum' (Kramer 1991, p. 46). This heritage is perceived as unitary and self-evident, the population as monocultural, and schools, particularly English curriculum, the appropriate vehicle by which the national and 'universal' values might be passed on and kept alive. It is a view that excludes any consideration of what contemporary and popular texts might contribute to the curriculum, beyond the rare few almost mystically identified as part of 'the living stream of culture' (p. 46). In this view, popular and contemporary texts, electronic texts amongst them, are conceived as 'inadequate and second rate substitutes . . . from which [young people] will learn nothing that matters' (Kramer 1991, pp. 44–5).

Kramer and others sharing her view do more than simply advocate maintaining an Anglocentric, transmission type of curriculum. They see popular culture as oppositional and antagonistic. They promote a 'limited' conception of what constitutes culture and what warrants the title 'literature'; for them, the spectrum of the population from which any 'heritage' might grow is extremely narrow. Such a view marginalises the cultural experience of much of the community, much of the time. It views young people as passive receptors of whatever confronts them, and assumes that 'high culture' has the enobling and inoculating role of which Leavis spoke. In its steadfast emphasis on 'high culture' and the past, this view regards society and its future as significantly at odds with the rapid technological, economic and political change transforming late twentieth-century existence. Something more flexible is required if schools are to help students mediate between past and present worlds, to reread the present in terms both of what has gone before and what is and might be possible.

It is clear that high culture is also minority culture, significantly at odds with the experiences and textual pleasures of the bulk of society. Willis's 1990 figures on participation in traditional and popular art forms reflect the pattern of contemporary cultural preference in the UK:

- Only 5 per cent of the UK population, and only 2 per cent of the British working class, attend the theatre, opera or ballet, or visit museums or art galleries.

- 2 per cent of all young people, excluding students, attend the theatre, the most popular traditional arts venue.

- 98 per cent of the population watch television for about 23 hours a week.

- About 90 per cent of young people listen to the radio, primarily for music, or to records or tapes.
  (Willis 1990, cited in Buckingham 1993a, pp. 3–4).

240

Since Willis's survey, even the apparent commonality of television viewing may well have become illusory. Buckingham (1993b) suggests that looking to television for common cultural experiences may be itself mere nostalgia since so many young people are turning away from television to the privacy of electronic games. The point remains, however, that participation in the 'popular' cultural forms of radio, television and video and computer games far outweighs attendance at the theatre and so on—an argument not for the abolition or exclusion of those forms from attention in school, but for the recognition of the wider bases of cultural participation and the need for school curricula to incorporate wider definitions of culture.

Willis's statistics attest also to how the high and popular forms of culture circulate in the community. Cultures are not fixed, nor accessed only at will; as Wark (1994) puts it, while 'we no longer have roots, we have aerials; we constantly download culture' (p. 55). In the contemporary world, different cultures are incessantly interacting, with 'high' culture just one of many that provide the stream of images, contexts and stories that contribute to the shaping of identity.

'Downloaded culture' undeniably poses challenges to old notions of culture and identity, yet new cultures and their trappings are not necessarily taken on uncritically. To quote Wark (1994) again:

> We filter it through our everyday experience, we use some of that language, we reinterpret some of that language and deliberately misunderstand some of it, and we go about our daily lives and we think we are Australian or we think we're from Melbourne or whatever when really we are using a whole bunch of codes that are pulled out of the ether. (Wark 1994, p. 55)

There are a number of arguments for including popular culture texts in the curriculum. One of the most persuasive is that of cultural inclusivity, coupled with the old pedagogical priority of 'starting from where the students are at'. What becomes critical in the context Wark describes is to learn how to 'read' such codes and cultures while also 'put[ting] some-thing back into the flow' (p. 55). Key issues here include which cultures schools should take on board, and what relationships exist or should be established between schools and society's cultural experiences. While few current policy documents oc-cupy exclusively high culture ground, the nature of the 'culture' represented in the curriculum, and suggestions about what is to be done with it, are often matters of some confusion.

If part of the role of schooling is to regenerate culture and community, the issue of which texts and cultures should be included is clearly more complex than a simple transmission of high culture texts and values, even if such transmission were possible. Blackburn (1985) and Batten (1989) recommend that the curriculum take account of young people's experiences and needs and the rapidly changing world in which they live. This would require looking at culture in a broad, multi-contextual way. As Buckingham (1993b) observes, 'If the curriculum is to equip young people to understand and participate in their society, it must invariably begin by acknowledging the cultural experiences of the majority' (p. 3). This argument makes pedagogical sense and has as the basis of its appeal both a sense of equity and the logic of cultural plurality. However, it does not deal with the relative status of texts, a difficult issue attested by the uncomfortable coexistence of such categories as 'everyday', 'classic', 'popular' and 'contemporary' in the 1993 national curriculum document, *A Statement on English for Australian Schools* (Curriculum Corporation 1993). And if such questions are left largely unexamined at the curriculum policy level, the way texts from different categories are 'treated' and read in schools will also remain problematic.

New texts, new literacies

It is not just a question of culture. The relationship between schools and the new technologies is also concerned with issues of power and access, and our recognition of how multimedia and digital technologies are changing what we understand as 'literacy' (see Lemke 1993, 1997; Luke 1996; Snyder 1996). As Lemke (1993) observes, 'The image of literacy that most of us now have will be obsolete before today's new readers and writers have finished primary school' (p. 13). As literacy is redefined by the protean capacities of electronic verbal and visual text generation, questions are raised about virtually all our current concepts of text: of authorship and authority; of ownership, intellectual property, creativity, originality and identity; of reading and writing, production and reception, making and consuming; of access and power.

One instance of how new technologies are redefining literacy is in the way that boundaries between reception and production, and between writing and reading are becoming blurred. We see these shifts in many products, whether games, hyperfiction or multimedia packages, instructional materials or even teacher resources like *The English Filing Cabinet* (Victorian Association for the Teaching of English 1994), which put a number of assignments and other teaching material on file for teachers to adapt as they choose. These products, effectively new kinds of texts, dramatically complicate what we understand of the intertextual nature of reading and writing.

Already in schools, word processing packages and spelling and grammar checkers have changed the nature of much student work, and of teachers' responses to it, and bear some troublesome implications for inflexible assessment practices. Many teachers find what they have thus far regarded as first principles for responding to student 'authorship' are seriously challenged when students employ computers as their writing technology. The language used in the management and supervision of the assessment of final year students' work in Victoria—'originality', 'authentication' and so on—reflects the disparities between the literacy concepts enshrined in policy documents and the new versions of literacy continually reconstructed in schools, in the face of computer-mediated technological change. Add to this complexity the fluid, multiple permutations of language, which appear constantly in media advertising and entertainment forms, and which reshape the lexicon at every cultural level. The changes wrought on textual cultures by new technologies have been so extensive that some researchers speculate whether the subjectivity of young people as readers/consumers has changed, so that teachers are faced with 'aliens in the classroom' (Green & Bigum 1993), and need to adapt the curriculum, and their expectations, accordingly.

Just what it is to be 'literate' in social terms is becoming increasingly complex and elusive. While multimedia and digital technologies are redefining literacy, issues of equity also become more pressing. The new literacies, with their heavy technological emphasis, could well exacerbate existing inequalities in access, currency and power. We know that the links between literacy and power are subtle; they are complicated further by new technologies involving economic and global interests and new technological 'literacy' skills.

The new literacies need to include the capacity to 'read' and 'write' the new technologies, and to understand what is entailed in the operation, reception and production of their texts. Lemke (1997) suggests at least four new literacies will be required in the age of the new information technologies: multimedia authoring skills, multimedia critical analysis, cyberspace exploration strategies and cyberspace navigation skills. I suggest adding to this list a set of literacies specific to reading beyond 'critical analysis': the capacity to negotiate and deconstruct visual and verbal images. The increasing importance of being able to read and work with images is highlighted by Luke (1996), who describes the future world as a 'media-, text- and symbol-saturated environment' in which 'for the unemployed, underemployed and employed alike, a great deal of service and information-based work, consumption and leisure [will] depend . . . on their capacities to construct, control and manipulate texts and symbols' (p. 3). It is through texts and images that much of the politics of representation and identity are being transacted; this tendency will accelerate, and the new technologies will require an expanded view of both literacy and textuality, which must in turn be taken up by schools.

244

Text and textuality in schools

If the sorts of texts students engage with in their out-of-school worlds are becoming more and more technology-based, the literacies needed to 'read' them are becoming more sophisticated. Changes such as those already mentioned raise questions not just about 'authorship' in writing, but also about what reading and writing in this technological context might entail, and about the nature of students' engagement with texts and technology. It seems to me this is central to the work of the language and literacy classroom. We urgently need to find ways to talk about and work with computer and other electronic texts alongside those which have traditionally been our concern. Subject English, concerned historically with 'communication', texts and textuality, literature and literacy, as well as student identity, is a prime site in which to explore young people's experience of mass-media texts and technological and cultural change, and for determining how such change affects them and their community.

It is not enough, however, simply to introduce such texts into the curriculum—the approaches used to study them are critical. Importing values, habits and assumptions about how 'non-literary' texts should be read, as distinct from how they are actually read in non-school contexts preempts rather than opens up exploration of what new and popular text types might entail. Far from driving out high culture texts, popular texts can help many students make a more coherent and pertinent study of the more traditional print texts. Yet care must be taken, since the inclusion of popular texts in the curriculum entails more than this. Popular and mass media texts must be read and explored in their own right, not merely as a means to something else, or as a sop to student interest, but as part of the lively, immediate and sophisticated reality of students' textual worlds (Beavis & Gough 1991; Beavis 1994). More than an expansion of the lexicon of texts, a reorientation towards reading and a text study that engages with issues of representation, context, framing and ideology is required.

There is a general recognition, in Australian national curriculum documents such as the *Statement on English for Australian Schools* (Curriculum Corporation 1993), of the need to include electronic games as part of the spectrum of school texts. What is less clear is where such games might fit within the categories on offer, how they might be characterised, and what teachers and students might do with them. The categorisation of texts into 'Literature', 'Everyday' and 'Mass Media' texts in the *National Statement on English for Australian Schools,* and in state documents like the Victorian *Curriculum and Standards Framework* (Victorian Board of Studies 1994) raises as many problems as it solves. There are complicated issues of definition and exclusion: most texts occupy at least two categories simultaneously, and there is an uncomfortable slippage between models of reading, views of readers and concepts of 'literature'. The classification of texts into categories of these kinds risks neglecting the reader's role in constructing the text—a key factor in defining it as literature. The role that cultural values, habits and assumptions play in designating or rejecting a piece of work as 'literature' must be continually revisited, particularly when dealing with new media/textual forms.

In many respects, debates about the study of electronic games in the curriculum replicate the debates about introducing texts from other non-print media—TV, film and so on. There, too, there is an element of moral panic about the prevalence and effect of electronic games, about what playing them might mean and about how they might displace other valued forms of activity, particularly the reading of books and socially interactive play.

Reading and teaching the computer game

The inclusion of computer games has much to offer to the study of text in the curriculum. Viewing electronic games as text raises questions of textuality and engagement, interestingly collapses reader/writer boundaries in the act of playing, teases out notions of readings as both multiple and constrained, reshapes and works within existing notions of narrative, and gives reading positions quite physical as well as prescriptive new dimensions. *Prince of Persia* (Mechner 1992) serves as a case in point.

Details from the game's handbook give some indication of the 'narrative', of the subject position required of players, and of the pot-pourri of genres and artefacts on which it draws. As the opening segments indicate, the game draws extensively on intertextual referencing from both literary and non-literary fields. The narrative relies on subtleties of meaning provided by the primarily literary texts it uses, and contributes to the story not verbal but visual and technological images for future retellings, rereadings and rewritings. These include the architectural configuration of the palace, the fluidity of the animation, the inversion of the world, the heart-stopping fall from one level to another and death. Readers are invited to view characters psychologically, to 'identify' with them, and to treat them as structural elements in the overall game plan. And in their constant revisiting (literally) of key sequences, such games play havoc with traditional narrative conventions of repetition, iteration and closure.

Besides using 'literary' intertextual referencing to folk tales in the style of *Aladdin* or *The Arabian Nights* and other narratives structured around princess-rescue, the game also draws on players' knowledge of texts and genres of quite different kinds, including the rules and patterns for progression in various computer and Nintendo games, entailing movement from one level to another by overcoming obstacles through feats of strength or by other means. The game also draws on classic film for visual aspects such as subtitles in the initial framing of the narrative and animation. With an eye to marketing (a feature of many texts, and one that students might usefully identify), the *User's Guide* represents the game as a virtual fusion of cultural forms—cinema and computer software. At the same time, it constructs Mechner ('Jordan'), to whom the game is credited, as not just author but auteur, stretching and further hybridising notions of both writing/generating and textual genre:

> Jordan Mechner, 27, is the author of the award-winning computer game *Karateka*. Hailed by *Games Magazine* as 'a software landmark', *Karateka* broke new ground in the use of cinematic techniques to tell a story within a computer game, and has sold over 400,000 copies worldwide.
>
> To achieve the extraordinary realism of the animation in *Prince of Persia*, Jordan studied hours of live-action footage, including swordfighting sequences from classic Hollywood swashbuckling films of the Thirties. Two years in the making, *Prince of Persia* is the culmination of a lifelong fascination with animation, and ten years of hacking on the Apple ll. (Mechner & Eheler 1992, p. 16)

The links with cinema and other media forms go further: the use of musical leitmotifs, and of sound effects; the way progress depends on visual as well as verbal narrative plot elements; the ways repetition and change are employed and the games are played with prediction; the means taken to compensate for the game's 'fixed frame' parameters by contrast with the variety of shot types available to the cinematographer, and so on. The game is an amalgam not just of intertextual literary references, but of 'intergeneric' or 'intercultural' ones as well—and as such, is typical of a great many of the contemporary texts that make up much of students' 'reading' out of school.

In many ways playing computer games resembles other forms of engagement with text. Playing the game parallels the reading of print materials, with some significant differences. To take one model of the reading process, players are engaged in strategies of predicting and checking but not sampling, unless a complete rereading is made. Revising is done mostly by living through the consequences of a wrong reading which is, of course, dying! Unlike the case with print texts, reading strategies and intertextual knowledge alone will not drive the story forward—that depends entirely on the player's manual agility. The player has to know not only narrative conventions and what has gone before, but also which keyboard controls perform which functions. In addition to the cognitive processing of image and narrative, perceptual motor skills are necessary for coordinating and activating information of this kind—the protagonist, the reader and the narrative are literally embodied, with all constructed and constrained by the player's dexterity.

In terms of the reader position offered, as well as the role and attitudes the player is invited to take up, there is the literal positioning of the player at the keyboard, and the second-person form of address which this game, like most others, shares with the 'Choose-Your-Own-Adventure' genre. This is probably the print form such games most closely resemble, but there are differences here too: most notably, the game has a more limited range of options for action and outcomes, yet offers the player greater control over events if not over directions. In this, perhaps, the closest parallel is not print text at all, but rather performance, where the play comes to life only by being acted/performed, and is subtly different every time. Viewed in this way, pleasures entailed in studying the game come not so much from playing it as from exploring how narrative is redefined, tracking down intertextual references, teasing out similarities and differences between other text types and puzzling out the nature and implications of this new form.

Discussion of the game in the senior English classroom could go many ways. If part of the teaching of any text involves also some reflexive exploration of reading and textuality, *Prince of Persia* lends itself readily to considerations of how it is read; what players have to know in order to make sense of it, how it positions them as readers, its ideology and the options for refusal, together with some analysis of apparent assumptions and implications for players/readers. The game invites the exploration of issues of framing (MacLachlan & Reid 1994): how this text is framed and how framing contributes to the construction of meaning more generally.

The place of intertextual and generic knowledge is an issue that might be raised by asking students what readers need to know in order to make sense of the game, and by asking them to identify the cultural and generic references and associations at play in the text, and what effects these create. Intratextual as well as extratextual elements to be considered include the verbal, visual and aural, leitmotifs, accoutrements, architecture and more. You might also ask students how progress is signalled, what constitutes winning, how 'winning' affects the characters, and so on.

For another related orientation your class might consider reader positioning, including the effect of the second-person address and the limitations and possibilities consequent upon being literally at the controls; how character is constructed and how players interpret that. Students might consider how playing the game is and is not like reading a book. From this you might ask questions about values and ideologies, scope for recognition and resistance, gender roles and the relative popularity of the game for girls and boys. Scope could be given here to issues of identity and the construction of subjectivity. The study might also invite some consideration of the basis of the appeal of texts such as these, in-school and out-of-school readings, and of what stance players/readers and other members of the community might want to take towards them.

A junior-secondary classroom perspective

So far, the interpretation of how *Prince of Persia* might be read and taught arises from a very literary, adult view. A contrasting perspective came from junior secondary students in a Melbourne state school, when I consulted them late in 1994 about their views of computer games. Using data-show technology, two Year 8 classes were shown the opening sequence of *Prince of Persia*, where players are inducted into the narrative and ambience of the game in a manner analogous to that of the opening pages of a novel, and taught how to play. After the demonstration, we discussed some of the issues raised above, to do with students' reading of the game, then turned to their own interests regarding computer games—their tastes and preferences and their observations on what computer games had to offer in the classroom.

The students' observations bore out Sheff's (1993) view that the appeal of video/computer games is related to their content: 'homogenisation of folklore, literature and popular culture, plus their exceptional interactive nature and the young players' exertion of control' (cited in Shuker 1996, p. 135). Like me, the students read the game intertextually, and were conscious of a number of elements familiar from other genres. However, although our frames of reference overlapped, they were different. Where I took *The Arabian Nights* as my major literary referent, for them it was the Disney film *Aladdin*. This was the text through which they met the narratives and iconography I associated with childhood stories of Sinbad and Aladdin, with Persian miniatures and Moorish architecture. As far as the music, we were equally hazy as to where it was first encountered; for all of us it signified the exoticism of the Middle East. Whereas I read the splitting of the hero into two figures, the 'prince' and his shadow, in Jungian terms, delighting that the shadow had to be embraced before resolution could be achieved, for the students this was part of a repertoire of computer tricks, so they read it in magical rather than psychological terms.

The conceptions of narrative, and the degree to which the computer text might be read in ways analogous to those of traditional story reading were significant points of difference. For me, the advancement of the action was dictated primarily by narrative logic, but their expectations were coloured by the patterns of obstacles and advancement encountered in other games. In such a context, 'cheats' that would short-circuit elements of the game were discussed avidly—a phenomenon rather like jumping to the end of a print text narrative instead of letting it 'unfold'. One student, Michael, wrote an extra level for the game, much as students might write an extension or missing chapter in the style of the author. His contribution took the form of an outline, on arithmetic paper, of what was effectively a maze: the text elements Michael incorporated were the architecture of the 'palace', the traps and hazards, and a linear graphic form of the hero as an icon or token to negotiate traps and spaces. His 'response' resembled the conceptual maps

251

often included in hyperfiction, so that his text, more visual than verbal, represented an appropriately hybrid version of an analytic assessment piece.

What the students' responses and game preferences suggest is that the phenomenon of computer games and their meanings is by no means stable. Nor have we yet identified ways in which teachers and students might work together on such texts without falling into the traps of appropriation and approval/disapproval which bedevil classroom studies of popular culture. What it also demonstrates, however, is the appeal and multiple layers of such games, and the importance of finding ways to think and talk about them as new cultural forms.

Future directions

The point of including games in the spectrum of curriculum texts is not to displace one form with another, but to enrich and diversify the students' range of narratives and textual experience, to create continuities between school and out-of-school reading, pleasure, analysis and critique. Electronic and other texts from students' worlds provide a basis for much useful work in extending definitions and understandings of literacy and textuality, in relation to the specific media text under study and in relation to reading and making texts of more traditional kinds. The study of electronic games helps us to identify the shifting forms of contemporary narrative, to see how textual forms emerge in the orbit of rapidly evolving technology, and to determine what engagement with texts might mean in a multimedia, multiliterate environment.

The challenges offered by social, cultural, economic and technological change require a complex reconceptualisation of education and literacy that takes account of the present context of schools and young people's lives. Embracing contemporary culture, and exploring it in its own terms, has a great deal more to offer young people and society than a curriculum based on narrow perceptions of (whose?) cultural heritage.

Whatever future it is that we are schooling young people for, it is clear that the curriculum must be responsive to the rapidly changing world we and they already inhabit, and must nurture and challenge young people so that they can contribute actively to shaping the future as it evolves.

Acknowledgements

Thanks to Terry Hayes and his students for their most productive discussion of computer games, and to Bill Green for reading and commenting on earlier drafts.

References

Bates, R. 1994 'Introduction', *Schooling What Future? Balancing the Educational Agenda*, Deakin Centre for Education and Change, Geelong, Victoria, pp. 1–5

Batten, M. 1989 *Year 12 Students' Expectations and Experiences*, ACER Research Monograph no. 33, Australian Council for Educational Research, Melbourne

Beavis C. 1994 'On not being Homer: popular culture in lower secondary English', *Interpretations*, vol. 27, no. 1, pp. 58–77

Beavis, C. and Gough, N. 1991 'Worldviews and popular culture: what do they mean for how we teach?', *Literacy: Making it Explicit, Making It Possible*, Selected Papers from the 16th Australian Reading Conference, ed. P. Cormack, Australian Reading Association, Carlton South, pp. 122–32

Blackburn, J. 1985 *Ministerial Review of Postcompulsory Schooling*, Ministry of Education, Melbourne

Buckingham, D. 1993a *Changing Literacies: Media Education and Modern Culture*, Tufnell Press, Institute of Education, London

——1993b 'Just playing games', *The English and Media Magazine*, vol. 28. pp. 21–5

Curriculum Corporation 1993 *A Statement on English for Australian Schools*, Curriculum Corporation, Carlton, Victoria

Diamond, J. 1992 'Games to die for', *Australian Women's Weekly*, May, pp. 71–3

Eagleton, T. 1983 *Literary Theory: An Introduction*, Blackwell, Oxford

Funk, J. 1993 'Reevaluating the impact of video games', *Clinical Paediatrics*, vol. 32, no. 2, pp. 86–90, cited in Shuker 1996

Green, B. and Bigum, C. 1993 'Aliens in the classroom', *Australian Journal of Education*, vol. 37, no. 2, pp. 119–41

Gross, N. 1993 'Watch out—those Game Boys are growing up', *Business Week*, 22 Nov., p. 106, cited in Shuker 1996

Ingram, M. 1994 'Cashing in on the video game wars', *Financial Times of Canada*, 11 June, pp. 6–7, cited in Shuker 1996

Kramer, L. 1991 'A heritage for our children', *Our Heritage and Australia's Future: A Selection of Insights and Concerns of Some Prominent Australians*, ed. J. Ramsey, Schwartz and Wilkinson, Melbourne, pp. 40–7

Lemke, J. 1993 'Critical social literacy for the new century', *English in Australia*, Sept., no. 105, pp. 9–15

——1997 'Metamedia literacy: transforming meanings and media', *Literacy For the 21st Century: Technological Transformation in a Post-typographic World,* eds D. Reinking, L. Labbo, M. McKenna and R. Kiefer, Erlbaum, Hillsdale, NJ

Luke, A. 1996 'Text and discourse in education: an introduction to critical discourse analysis', *Review of Research in Education 1995–6*, ed. M. Apple, American Educational Research Association, Washington DC, pp. 3–48

MacLachlan, G. and Reid, I. 1994 *Framing and Interpretation*, Melbourne University Press, Carlton

Mechner, J. 1992 *Prince of Persia*, Brøderbund Software, Novato

Mechner J. and Eleher, B. 1992 *Prince of Persia: User's Guide*, Brøderbund Software, Novato

Palmeri, C. 1994 'Kombat marketing', *Forbes*, 28 Feb., p. 102, cited in Shuker, 1996

Price, J. 1985 'Social science research on video games', *Journal of Popular Culture*, vol. 18, pp. 111–25, cited in Shuker 1996

Sheff, D. 1993 *Game Over: Nintendo's Battle to Dominate an Industry*, Hodder and Stoughton, London, cited in Shuker 1996

Shuker, R. 1996 'Video Games: Serious Fun', *Continuum*, vol. 9, no. 2, pp. 125–45

Snyder, I. 1996 *Hypertext: The Electronic Labyrinth*, Melbourne University Press, Carlton

Victorian Association for the Teaching of English 1994 *The English Filing Cabinet*, Victorian Association for the Teaching of English, Carlton

Victorian Board of Studies 1994 *Curriculum and Standards Framework*, Victorian Board of Studies, Carlton

Wark, M. 1994 'Understanding media culture, student identities and learning', *Schooling What Future? Balancing the Educational Agenda*, Deakin Centre for Education and Change, Geelong

Willis, P. 1990 *Common Culture: Symbolic Work at Play in the Everyday Cultures of the Young*, Open University Press, Milton Keynes, cited in Buckingham 1993

Index